Cosmopolitan Patriots

Jeffersonian America

Jan Ellen Lewis, Peter S. Onuf, and
Andrew O'Shaughnessy, *Editors*

Being a cosmopolite is an accident, but one must make the best of it. If you have lived about, as the phrase is, you have lost the sense of the absoluteness and the sanctity of the habits of your fellow-patriots which once made you so happy in the midst of them. You have seen that there are a great many *patriæ* in the world, and that each of these is filled with excellent people for whom the local idiosyncrasies are the only thing that is not rather barbarous. There comes a time when one set of customs, wherever it may be found, grows to seem to you about as provincial as another; and then I suppose it may be said of you that you have become a cosmopolite. You have formed the habit of comparing, of looking for points of difference and of resemblance, for present and absent advantages, for the virtues that go with certain defects, and the defects that go with certain virtues.

HENRY JAMES, *Occasional Paris*

Contents

Note on Translation and Dates

Unless otherwise noted, all translations from the French and German are the author's.

In 1793 the French Revolutionary Government introduced a new Republican calendar, designed to symbolize and embed in everyday life the idea of a new age. The calendar began at Year I in September 1792, with the proclamation of the French Republic, and each new calendar year also began in September. The twelve thirty-day months all received newly created and untranslatable names that were meant to evoke the seasons. The calendar remained in official use until Napoleon Bonaparte abolished it in 1806. For events in France and French documents that fall within the period covered by the Republican calendar, I have used its dating system, while providing the equivalents in the Gregorian calendar in parentheses.

Acknowledgments

The acknowledgments of first-time authors are often distinguished by their interminable length and naked emotionalism, which has earned them the apt, if unflattering, comparison with Academy Award acceptance speeches. However, given that authors tend to spend more time on their first books than on any other (if indeed there are any others) and need more help to write them, perhaps these faults can be excused.

I am indebted to the editors of the published papers of many individuals in this book, as well as to the librarians and archivists at the repositories I visited during my research. Some of these travels were made possible by financial support from International Security Studies at Yale University and the Yale Center for International and Area Studies. The Mellon Foundation's seminar at Caltech and the Huntington Library in the summer of 2004 provided a wonderful setting to write and try out ideas. My most important sponsor has been the Robert H. Smith International Center for Jefferson Studies. It was at the Center's beautiful Jefferson Library that I began my research in the fall of 2002 as a Batten Fellow. Three years later, I was delighted to return to Charlottesville, this time as the Gilder Lehrman Junior Research Fellow. I am deeply grateful to the Center's fabulous staff and its director, Andrew Jackson O'Shaughnessy.

An earlier version of chapter 1 was published as "Exporting American Revolutions: Gouverneur Morris, Thomas Jefferson, and the National Struggle for Universal Rights in Revolutionary France," in the *Journal of the Early Republic,* vol. 26 (Fall 2006): 419–47 (© 2006 Society for Historians of the Early American Republic). It is reprinted here by permission of the University of Pennsylvania Press. A shorter version of chapter 5 was published as "The End of a Beautiful Friendship: Americans in Paris and Public Diplomacy during the War Scare of 1798-1799," in *Old World, New World: America and Europe in the Age of Jefferson,* edited by Peter Nicolaisen, Peter

S. Onuf, Andrew O'Shaughnessy, and Leonard J. Sadosky (Charlottesville, 2009).

I would not have been able to write this book without the guidance and support of my teachers. At the John F. Kennedy Institute of the Freie Universität Berlin, Michaela Hönicke-Moore and Anneke de Rudder inspired me to study American history. As an exchange student at Yale University, I had the good fortune to chance upon Joanne B. Freeman's seminar on early American politics. Without her, I would never have considered pursuing a Ph.D., let alone in eighteenth-century history. Joanne also introduced me to her own mentor, Peter S. Onuf, whose ideas, enthusiasm, and legendary ability to help his students think about the big picture profoundly shaped this book.

I also have learned a great deal from David Brion Davis, with whom I have worked for many years as a research assistant, and whose extended essay, *Revolutions,* was one of the inspirations for this project. Not only was Ellen R. Cohn extremely generous in allowing me to take time off from my work at the Papers of Benjamin Franklin to complete this book, but her own writing is a model of clarity, elegance, and precision.

Many friends and colleagues read various parts of this book and provided invaluable criticism and suggestions. My deep thanks to Richard Buel, Rachel Chrastil, Christa Dierksheide, Joseph J. Ellis, Julie Flavell, Frank Kelleter, Lloyd Kramer, Jan Lewis, Serena Mayeri, Brian Murphy, Rebecca Rix, Leonard J. Sadosky, J. C. A. Stagg, Eric Stoykovich, and George Van Cleve. I am particularly grateful to Seth Cotlar, who encouraged me both at the very beginning and at the very end of this project, and for the extensive, detailed comments I received from Sophia Rosenfeld. I have benefited greatly from the advice and assistance of Richard Holway, Raennah Mitchell, and Ruth Steinberg of the University of Virginia Press, and from the careful copy editing by Carol Sickman-Garner. Many thanks also to Lien-Hang T. Nguyen for putting me in touch with the Taylor family, who allowed me to stay in their cozy Paris apartment. Americans in Paris Charly J. Coleman and Nathan Pearl-Rosenthal offered hospitality and emergency assistance.

My greatest debt is to my partner, wife, fellow historian and troublemaker, and co-parent, Anita Seth. She read more drafts than anyone else, and her invariably incisive comments enormously improved them. But more importantly, her generosity, courage, and integrity have shaped my understanding of both the past and the present. While our daughter, Hannah,

Acknowledgments

would surely object to the absence of talking animals in this book, her love of German books, Indian food, and American cartoons embodies the cosmopolitan spirit that is one of its subjects.

This book could only be dedicated to my parents, Ingeborg and Peter Schöberl, whose unfailing patience, support, and love made everything possible.

Introduction

When Thomas Paine entered his prison cell in the basement of the Palais de Luxembourg in the afternoon of 8 Nivôse II (28 December 1793), he was confident that his detention would be brief. After all, he was a hero of the American Revolution and the most widely read and celebrated author of the Atlantic world. Only the year before, the French Legislative Assembly had declared Paine an honorary French citizen and he had been elected as a deputy to the National Convention. Surely, the Committee of General Security had made a mistake in ordering his arrest as a British citizen and enemy alien.[1]

A month later, a delegation of Americans in Paris, led by Paine's friend, the author Joel Barlow, appeared before the Convention to appeal for Paine's freedom. The president of the Convention, Marc Vadier, who as chair of the Committee of General Security had signed the order for Paine's arrest, cordially affirmed the bond between the American and French republics and acknowledged Paine's achievements. Still, he insisted that Paine was a native Briton who had aligned himself with "the false friends of our revolution." Meanwhile, the American minister to France, Gouverneur Morris, declined to press for Paine's release. Regardless of Paine's citizenship, Morris argued, as an elected official in France, he was subject to French law. All

1

that Morris had to offer Paine was the advice that if he lay "quiet in prison" he might have "the good luck to be forgotten."[2]

By sheer luck, the executioner did indeed forget Paine. On 6 Thermidor II (24 July 1794), at the height of the Great Terror, Paine's name appeared on the list of prisoners to be brought before the Revolutionary Tribunal. As Paine later remembered, "the door of our room was marked, unobserved by us, with that number in chalk [indicating which cells were to be emptied that night]; but it happened, if happening is a proper word, that the mark was put on when the door was open and flat against the wall, and thereby came on the inside when we shut it at night, and the destroying angel passed by it. A few days after this Robespierre fell."[3] When Paine was released from the Luxembourg in November 1794, after ten months and nine days, he was completely broke, in poor health, and full of bitterness toward the American government that had abandoned him.

Thomas Paine's fall from quintessential citizen of the world to stateless outcast fits neatly into the conventional narrative about the fate of cosmopolitan universalism in the age of revolution. According to this view, American and French revolutionaries initially appealed to the universal principles of natural rights and the "science of government," and identified their cause as that of all mankind. But in the midst of the French revolutionary wars, this rhetoric gave way to a fiery and exclusionary nationalism. Americans turned away in disgust from the European conflagration and began to appreciate their nation's exceptional destiny.[4]

In a similar vein, the cruel French treatment of the American icon Paine seems to confirm the oft-proclaimed divergence between the American Revolution–characterized by moderation, pragmatism, and consensus– and the French Revolution, marked by radicalism, ideological abstractions, and violent conflict.[5] However, if we do not take the dissimilarity of the two revolutions and the existence of fully formed nation-states as given, Paine's fate allows us to see a different relationship between cosmopolitanism and nationalism.

Paine's fame in America and France rested on his reputation as a nation-builder. The revolutions in both countries were linked by the idea that nations were not facts of nature but could and needed to be actively built. This sense of nationalism as a political program of nation-building differed from earlier expressions of patriotic allegiance to countries and dynasties regarded as timeless and unchanging. In the last two decades of the eighteenth century, the newly empowered political elites on both sides of the Atlantic self-consciously set out to build nations through declarations, constitutions, laws, education, festivals, and other forms of political culture.[6] The popularity of Paine's writings and his naturalization in America and France reflected how central cosmopolitan universalism was to the construction of these new national communities.

Cosmopolitanism and nationalism were not at odds with each other, but complementary, in two ways. The main challenge facing the Atlantic nation-builders was the unification of populations that were highly diverse in terms of ethnicity, gender, social rank, religion, and language. Only through appeals to universal principles and an inclusive definition of citizenship could all these different groups be assimilated to the nation. Paine succinctly expressed this political program in *Rights of Man, Part II* (1792) and presented the United States to his European audience as a ready-made model for nation-building: "Made up, as it is, of people from different nations, accustomed to different forms and habits of government, speaking different languages, and more different in their modes of worship, it would appear that the union of such a people was impracticable; but by the simple operation of constructing government on the principles of society and the rights of man, every difficulty retires, and all the parts are brought into cordial unison."[7]

Just as cosmopolitan universalism served the purpose of nation-building, so nation-building served cosmopolitan ends. For the newly independent United States and revolutionary France, domestic and foreign policies were inseparably intertwined. Nationhood could only be ratified on an international stage if other states accepted the new nations as equals. Thus, the ultimate aim of nation-building was recognition by other nations. For Americans, this meant in particular transforming the Atlantic world from an arena of imperial competition into a system of sovereign and independent states. Paine sought to contribute to this transformation by popularizing American and French ideas about the importance of free trade in creating a more peaceful and prosperous global order. However, acrimonious debates about how the new regimes in America and France would fit into the existing international system fueled the formation of partisan factions in both countries.[8]

Paine's incarceration, instead of reflecting the demise of revolutionary cosmopolitanism, was a direct result of this symbiotic relationship between cosmopolitanism and nationalism. The native Briton Paine had become an American citizen under a liberal naturalization law designed to attract immigrants and based on an inclusive notion of consensual membership in the American polity. His honorary citizenship in France reflected a similar political conception of nationality. According to this new model of citizenship, the author of *Common Sense* and *Rights of Man* was more of an American or a French citizen than a Loyalist born in the British colonies or an aristocratic émigré born in France.

Yet with the nation under construction, the meaning of concepts like "citizen" and "foreigner" remained unstable. The republican definition of citizenship, based on universal political principles like natural rights and civic virtue, was seemingly more inclusive than the earlier classification, based on birth and being a royal subject. However, it also proved to be more restrictive, by including only those who conformed to highly contested and still-evolving political standards. Paine liked to believe that he had been imprisoned for being a citizen of the world. In fact, he was arrested for aligning himself with a losing political faction in the National Convention. Once his allies, the Girondins, had been defined as "false friends" of the revolution, and thereby as "foreigners" to the nation, Paine's days as a French citizen were numbered. In revolutionary Philadelphia, Paine already had experienced a similarly dramatic, if less life-threatening, decline from celebrity to pariah. Shortly after the sensational success of *Common Sense,* Paine's intervention in the Silas Deane controversy in 1778 caused him to lose his position as secretary to Congress's Committee on Foreign Affairs and be condemned in the press as a "stranger without either connections or apparent property in this country."[9]

Gouverneur Morris's refusal to claim Paine as an American citizen shows that demarcating the boundaries of the national community was as much a problem for the conservative American minister as for the French Jacobins. Like his superiors in the Washington administration, Morris was concerned about the growing number of Americans who took on multiple citizenships or claimed to have expatriated themselves from the United States. For example, a sailor who had been arrested on a British ship by the French authorities and demanded release as an American contacted Morris in July 1793. Morris responded that the seaman should first explain how he came to be

4

on board a ship of the Southern Whale Fishery in London: "The Benefits secur'd to you by the British Laws must in such Case compensate for the Inconveniences to which you are now exposed for I cannot in good faith ask for you the Protection of that Flag which you had abandon'd to promote a rival Interest."[10]

As partisan political conflict divided their national communities, the French and American governments became convinced either that their opponents would use recent immigrants to seize power or, more ominously, that their opponents were themselves "foreigners," out to subvert the nation from within. It was a pressing issue for political elites in the United States and France to define more clearly who their nations' citizens were and what distinguished them from the citizens of other nations, and to increase the attachment of citizens to their own nation. In the late 1790s, both governments adopted more exclusive concepts of national citizenship, which were based as much on birth, heritage, natural allegiance, and political loyalty as on choice.[11] But like the earlier expansion of the boundaries of the national community, their contraction in response to political divisions occurred not despite the revolutionaries' adherence to universal principles but because of it.

Seen from this perspective, the paths of the republics in America and France never diverged. Instead, the story of American and French nation-building is one of similarity in difference. Both nations underwent analogous processes of self-definition in order to accentuate what made them unique and distinct from each other. Each nation created its own distinctive set of institutions, symbols, and loyalties, and suppressed or expelled minorities unwilling to assimilate. Thus, they established a model of nation-building that became paradigmatic for other nations throughout the world.

In order to examine these intersecting developments, this book adopts an unusual vantage point on the two republics. It looks at the nation-building projects in the United States and France through the eyes of Americans in Paris. This perspective might seem overly narrow. After all, Americans in Paris were far away from events at home, at a time when the average letter from Paris to New York traveled for thirty-five days, and to Virginia for as long as two months. Moreover, even at the height of the Franco-American friendship, the role of Americans in French politics remained largely symbolic, and their impact on the course of the French Revolution minimal. However, I argue that it is precisely their doubly marginal position—at a remove from the American political scene and on the fringes of the French Revolution–that caused Americans in Paris to reflect on the similarities and differences between nation-building in the United States and France. In particular, their situation as foreigners confronted them with the paradoxes and ambiguities inherent in the relationship between cosmopolitan universalism and national particularity.[12]

Eighteenth-century cosmopolitanism denoted the idea that all human beings shared essential moral characteristics that transcended boundaries of nationality, language, religion, and custom. It entailed a moral obligation and emotional attachment to all other human beings, who should be regarded as fellow citizens of the world. At the same time, cosmopolitans in this period were fascinated with the question of diversity between nations, within nations, and among individuals, and tried to explain this heterogeneity through history, geography, climate, politics, and other influences. Even among cosmopolitans committed to the idea of human uniformity and moral equality, universalism could take a variety of forms, depending on how each negotiated the tension between the belief in human unity and the recognition of cultural, social, and political difference.[13]

Before the American and French revolutions, advocates of cosmopolitanism could be found mainly among men of letters, scientists, and merchants, who saw themselves as members of a universal society, bound together through the ideal and practice of sociability. For much of the eighteenth century, authors considered cosmopolitan love of humanity and patriotic love of country as related expressions of concern for the common good.[14] Only in the second half of the century, in the context of an unprecedented debate all over Europe about the boundaries and meanings of citizenship, and as the terms "nation," "patriot," and "citizen" acquired new political connotations, did the compatibility of cosmopolitanism and patriotism become questionable.[15]

For Americans, their revolution reinforced the connection between patriotism and cosmopolitanism. Loyalty to the United States coexisted and competed with other allegiances, at both the local and the transnational levels. Just as many Americans continued to think of their home state as their "country" well into the nineteenth century, many felt deeply attached to the universal principles of republicanism, popular sovereignty, and cosmopolitanism.[16]

As they tried to define who they were as a nation, Americans looked toward their mother country Britain, and increasingly to their new ally France, as role models. On a trip to France in 1779, the merchant Elkanah Watson expressed the hope that "our alliance and intercourse with France may enable us, as a nation, to shake off the leading-strings of Britain–the English sternness and formality of manner, retaining, however, sufficient of their gravity, to produce, with French ease and elegance, a happy compound of national character and manners, yet to be modeled." Both the British and the French models of patriotism contained strong universalist strains. American colonists found it easy to adapt the Protestant Providentialism of the British Empire for their own national purposes. French patriotism was infused with a similar sense of divine mission and favor. The universalism and unifying ambitions of the Catholic faith continued to exert a significant influence on revolutionary French nationalism, which claimed to further the progress and regeneration of all mankind.[17]

French support of the War of Independence did much to counteract British Francophobia in America. By 1789, Americans of all social ranks and political stripes enthusiastically welcomed the French Revolution. Just at the moment when their new federal constitution went into effect, events in France helped to legitimize the American Revolution and ended American republicans' sense of isolation in a world of kings. Moreover, the French Revolution fundamentally changed how Americans understood their own revolution. It was no longer a provincial conflict on the edges of the British Empire, but the starting signal of an age of global revolution. Only the French Revolution realized the more radical implications of its American predecessor: political doctrines could spread across frontiers; nations existed independent of states, and peoples independent of their rulers. American newspaper readers obsessively scrutinized reports from France for potential lessons for their own republic. In the eyes of many, to be an American patriot meant being a cosmopolitan, as the promise of America was realized abroad as much as at home.[18]

Like their compatriots at home, Americans in Paris were convinced that the American Revolution offered a universal model for other nations to emulate. But they also subscribed to the widely held belief that each nation had to develop according to its own particular manners and customs. Throughout the 1790s, Americans grappled with this inherent tension in cosmopolitanism between unity and difference. In order to explain how something could be universal and particular at the same time, they found a perfect metaphor in a phenomenon that, like political constitutions, easily crossed borders yet assumed distinct shapes in each nation: fashion. In a 1799 letter to Lafayette, Alexander Hamilton, citing Montesquieu, declared his belief that "a government must be fitted to a nation as much as a Coat to the Individual, and consequently that what may be good at Philadelphia may be bad at Paris and ridiculous at Petersburgh."[19]

The British caricaturist James Gillray expressed the same idea in "Fashion before Ease; or, A good Constitution sacrificed for a Fantastick Form" (1793), which ridiculed Paine's holding up France as model for political change in Britain in *Rights of Man, Part II.* The cartoon (see fig. 1) depicts Paine, who used to work as a stay-maker, violently squeezing Britannia's natural form into an ill-fitting corset made according to current "Paris Modes," as advertised outside his store, and the measure of the "Rights of Man," dangling from his coat pocket. Paine's tricolor cockade and grotesque face, turned blotchy red by drink and revolutionary fanaticism, conformed to the common image of French sans-culottes in British satires. The caption is a play on the word "constitution," which could denote physical constitution, impaired by fashionably tight corsets, as well as political constitution, whose organic fit to the British body politic was endangered by French radical chic.

Each of the following chapters explores aspects of the relationship between universalism and particularism in the process of revolutionary nation-building, moving chronologically through the decade of the French Revolution and focusing on one or several individuals. Chapter 1 elaborates on the problem of constitutions as an expression of both universal principles and national character through Thomas Jefferson's and Gouverneur Morris's contributions to the debate about a new French constitution in the summer of 1789. Chapter 2 examines different assessments of the role of revolutionary violence in forging or dividing the nation by looking at the divergence in William Short's and Thomas Jefferson's understandings of the unfolding French Revolution and its transatlantic implications between 1790 and 1793. Chapter 3 focuses on the work of Joel Barlow to investigate the contradictions inherent in two key concepts of nation-building–regeneration and sensibility–that both created cosmopolitan bonds and accentuated national distinctions. Chapter 4 investigates the problem of universalism

FIGURE 1. James Gillray, "Fashion before Ease; or, A good Constitution sacrificed for a Fantastick Form." (Courtesy of The Lewis Walpole Library, Yale University)

and particularism in the debates about popular sovereignty and organized opposition in the United States and France, with James Monroe's tenure as American minister to France between 1794 and 1796 as the case study. Chapter 5 analyzes the transatlantic controversy over cosmopolitan universalism during the crisis in Franco-American relations following the XYZ Affair in 1798–99. Finally, chapter 6 traces the Jefferson administration's attempts to dissociate itself from the French Revolution after the election of 1800, while redirecting the universalist ambitions that American Republicans had projected onto France to the uncharted territory of the Louisiana Purchase.

It should be clear that this book is neither a social history of the American community in Paris nor a series of biographical sketches.[20] Instead, the writings of a small number of Americans with political experience and connections in both the United States and France serve as focal points for a discussion of ideas that circulated widely on both sides of the Atlantic. Considering how the ideological conundrums of the transatlantic revolutionary moment became embodied in the lives of individual Americans allows us to keep in view the human reality of these abstract ideas. It also serves to highlight gaps between ideology and practice and enables us to explore the resulting tensions, uncertainties, and struggles.

The book aims to identify elements that the two republics had in common, while also recognizing local variations. It is less a *Transfergeschichte* (a history of the transfer of ideas and culture between nations) than a *histoire croisée,* an intersecting or entangled history. *Histoire croisée* distinguishes itself from comparative history and transfer history by not proceeding from predetermined entities or terms and instead emphasizing process, mutual influences, and the relativity and plurality of perspectives (of both historical actors and historians) in drawing connections and comparisons. This approach seems particularly appropriate for a historical moment when the meanings of terms such as "nation" and "world," "citizen" and "foreigner," were still in flux, and for a group of historical actors self-consciously positioned between two ongoing revolutions.[21]

Nation-building is itself a political program based on comparisons and distinctions. Scholars have long debated whether the origins of what Etienne Balibar has called "the nation-form" (that is, the standard model of what constitutes a nation) can be found in the European center or with the anti-colonial "Creole pioneers" on the American periphery. But if we shift attention from the locus of innovation to the process of imitation, we find that nationalists have always constructed their national communities by implicit and explicit comparison with other nations.[22]

Previous studies of the relationship between the American and French republics have either contrasted their ideologies in the abstract or focused on the images and stereotypes that one nation projected on the other. Two major exceptions to this rule are the works of Robert R. Palmer and Jacques Godechot. Yet when they began in the mid-1950s to write the history of an age of Atlantic revolutions, both historians encountered strong resistance from historians in the United States and France who insisted on the uniqueness of their respective revolutions. The two nations' divergent global fortunes over the next half century–America's rise to superpower status and France's increasingly diminished role in world affairs–served to reinforce the nationalist, insular, and exceptionalist tendencies of their historiographies.[23] While Atlantic history has become a respectable and fashionable field, it generally operates within an imperial framework, either through inter-imperial comparisons or intra-imperial studies of centers and peripheries. As David Armitage notes, "The potential for comparative trans-Atlantic histories along an east-west axis remains largely unexplored."[24]

Arguments over whether the American Revolution or the French Revolution should be considered more significant or inspiring have obscured parallels in the two republics' nation-building projects. Many French historians still do not regard the American Revolution as a genuine revolution, due to its supposed conservatism and lack of class conflict. In the United States, negative images of the French Revolution have long held sway among the public and historians alike (with the exception of French specialists). When scholars have found the American Revolution and the French Revolution to be at all comparable, it was usually to demonstrate the superiority of the American. In 1991, Gordon Wood published an influential synthesis of the American Revolution, arguing that it was in fact the only successful and truly "radical" revolution in history. More recently, negative depictions of the French Revolution have become central to a slew of French-bashing books that bear an uncanny resemblance to Federalist propaganda of the 1790s.[25]

Much of the comparative evaluation of the two revolutions depends on the adopted timeframe. The "moderate" American Revolution preserved a brutal slave system that eighty years later became the object of a civil war whose level of upheaval and violence easily rivaled that endured by France

11

in the 1790s. By contrast, the "extremist" French Revolution established a national entity whose integrity remained unchallenged even during times of violent internal conflict. Taking an even longer view, histories of globalization have put both revolutions' singularity and claims to world-changing significance in perspective.[26]

There are, of course, undeniable differences between the revolutions in the United States and France. A number of factors can help explain why the political transformation in America was less convulsive than its French counterpart. Compared to France, the United States had more experienced legislators who could draw on a longer tradition of self-government. American revolutionaries did not have to confront entrenched legal orders that made social distinctions, law, politics, and religion all closely related. Unlike the French, Americans did not have to tackle widespread poverty, or fight a war with several neighboring monarchies, or deal with religious divisions, or figure out how to integrate a resident monarch into their new political order.[27]

We do not have to equate George Washington and Robespierre, the Terror and the Alien and Sedition Acts, or Thomas Jefferson and Napoleon, to see that what Anne Sa'adah calls "the politics of exclusion" was practiced in both republics throughout the 1790s.[28] Over the course of that decade, political divisions in both republics intensified, the basic rules of politics and the boundaries of the polity remained contested, organized opposition to government continued to be viewed as illegitimate, and therefore inclusion in and exclusion from the national community remained a potent weapon of political combat.

Rather than playing the two revolutions off against each other by taking the achievements of one as a measure of the other's failure, this book examines their contributions to an ideology and practice, nation-building, whose challenges remain an urgent concern today. The questions discussed here have over the last two centuries confronted the countless other Americans who tried to promote supposedly universal American political principles in other cultures (more often than not in the form of what Robespierre famously called "armed missionaries"): How do cultural differences affect a nation's capacity for political change? Can a nation overcome its historical particularities, and if so, should it? Does each society have to find its own path of development?

Since long before the United States wielded any power on the world stage, Americans have assumed that their political system was singularly relevant for other peoples all over the globe. At the same time, they have never quite known how to translate it to other national contexts. Much like their modern-day descendants, Americans in revolutionary Paris saw themselves as benevolent tutors of republicanism. But in the end the Americans and their nation emerged as much transformed by the encounter with the French Revolution as those they had sought to teach.

1

Exporting American Revolutions

GOUVERNEUR MORRIS, THOMAS JEFFERSON, AND THE
DEBATE ABOUT THE FRENCH CONSTITUTION, 1789

On 7 December 1791, Gouverneur Morris sat down at his desk at the Hô-tel Richelieu in Paris to spend some time on a personal project. As he later noted in his diary, "This Morning employ myself in preparing a Form of Government for this Country." The following day, Morris received a visit from a French gentleman who informed him that he knew America "per-fectly well tho he has never seen it," and was convinced that the "American Constitution is good for Nothing." The visitor, who had studied the subject of constitutions for fifty years, had been kind enough to write a letter to President Washington, enclosing a new constitution. As a central figure in both the Continental Congress and the Constitutional Convention, Morris was himself an old hand at constitution-making, and the encounter left him with the disconcerting feeling of having met his French double. "I get Rid of him as soon as I can," Morris wrote, "but yet I cannot help being struck with the Similitude of a Frenchman who makes Constitutions for America and an American who performs the same good Office for France. Self Love tells me that there is a great Difference of Persons and Circumstances but Self Love is a dangerous Counsellor."[1]

In this moment of uncharacteristic humility, Morris encapsulated the predicament of Americans in revolutionary Paris. Like many of his compatriots, Morris assumed that the American experience of revolution and nation-building was universally relevant and that he had some important lessons to teach to the French. He was therefore disconcerted to find that while the French revolutionaries did take great interest in the American precedent, they were apt to use it in their own particular ways, and, in this instance, even turn the tables on their would-be teachers.

The French Revolution forced Americans abroad to wrestle with ambiguities within their own revolutionary tradition that most of their compatriots at home had not yet carefully examined. Although there was no consensus in the United States about the meaning of the American Revolution, Americans in Paris generally agreed that its lessons were universally applicable. However, at the same time that they extolled the universalism of American ideas and accomplishments, they also believed that these accomplishments reflected particular qualities of the American people, and that the successful application of these ideas elsewhere would require the same qualities in other nations.

This chapter examines the ambiguity in the American revolutionary tradition of universalism and particularism by using as an example the activities of Gouverneur Morris and Thomas Jefferson in Paris in 1789. During the first crucial phase of the French Revolution, from the convening of the Estates-General in May 1789 to the October Days, Morris and Jefferson, the American minister to France, were the most prominent representatives of the new American nation in Paris. Their reputations as political theorists and revolutionaries caused both liberal and conservative French reformers to seek out their advice in the heated debates about the new French constitution.

Morris's biographers like to emphasize the contrast between the boisterous New Yorker and the soft-spoken Virginian, using Jefferson's idealistic naïveté as a foil for Morris's worldly pragmatism. Although Jefferson and Morris brought to Europe two fundamentally different interpretations of the meaning of the American Revolution, they were equally enthusiastic about providing guidance to their French hosts based on their respective interpretations. Yet at the same time, both men worried that the national character of the French would impede their ability to follow in American footsteps.[2]

American nation-builders had learned from Montesquieu that to be sustainable any government had to correspond to the spirit of the people under its rule. Morris never questioned the right of the French to reshape their political system, but he concluded from the violence he witnessed in the streets of Paris that the French needed the guidance of a strong, centralized government even more than the American people. Jefferson came to believe in the mutability of the French national character, whose deformed state he attributed to the oppressive power of a despotic state, and he accepted revolutionary violence as the first articulation of a popular political consciousness. Still, Jefferson also questioned whether it was truly possible for any people to break completely with their past.

Since he understood the French national character to be unchangeable for the foreseeable future, Morris chiefly concerned himself with devising a constitutional division and balance of powers that would most likely ensure the stability of the French state. Jefferson's belief in the malleability of national character was closer to the view that came to dominate the French National Assembly, according to which the new constitution was a tool of nation-building. Drafting a new national constitution entailed not only an institutional rearrangement but also a profound recasting of the French nation's social and political life. This meant, however, that the ambiguity of the term "constitution" as both a fundamental state of being (reflecting a particular national character) and as the act of establishing a new government (based on universal principles) was compounded by the nationalist paradox of creating a new constitution in the name of the very same nation that the new constitution would bring into existence.[3]

Jefferson's and Morris's adherence in their constitutional recommendations to Montesquieu's doctrines of national character and moderation proved to be a major point of contention in their interactions with the French revolutionaries. The denizens of Parisian salon society, as well as members of the National Assembly, initially welcomed the Americans' presence and regarded their expertise as highly relevant to the French nation-building process. The political factionalism that increasingly divided the Assembly in the summer of 1789 at first elevated the position of the Americans as allies who could lend international cachet to a political program. But as the dialectic of action and reaction between the *monarchien* and Patriot factions continued, the mediating position that both Jefferson and Morris had sought to occupy was progressively marginalized, and most of their advice on the constitution was ultimately ignored.

Unfortunately, while Jefferson and Morris left rich accounts of their discussions with political figures in Paris, French commentary on the two

Americans is much harder to find. French revolutionaries regularly made reference to the United States in public debates, but seldom recorded private encounters with the Americans in their midst. This imbalance is not surprising. The Americans had ample opportunity to muse about the French Revolution's implications for their infant nation. Meanwhile, the French were struggling daily to keep pace with the revolution's rapid changes and myriad problems. In the case of post-revolutionary memoirs, this neglect might also reflect French disenchantment with the American revolutionary model that developed over the course of the 1790s.

Nonetheless, the two Americans, with their very different concepts of the meaning of the American Revolution, served the French revolutionaries as catalysts for formulating and justifying their own political principles and choices. In turn, their reception in Paris reinforced Jefferson's and Morris's belief in the vanguard role that the American republic was destined to assume in the world, yet also confronted them with the limits of American influence abroad.

When Gouverneur Morris reached Paris in late January 1789, the city was in the grip of a particularly long and cold winter. "And this is the smiling European Spring of which so much is said and sung," he noted with characteristic sarcasm in the diary he began to keep shortly after his arrival in France.[4] Morris took up lodgings at the Hôtel Richelieu on one of Paris's most elegant streets, near the Palais Royal, and within a week presented himself at the Hôtel de Langeac, the residence of the American minister plenipotentiary, Thomas Jefferson. The two men had "only a slight Acquaintance," as Morris put it, but Jefferson had already been informed of Morris's mission to salvage his friend Robert Morris's tobacco business, help him sell western land tracts to French speculators, and find private investors to purchase the American war debt from the insolvent French government.[5]

Remembering the "severe seasoning" of his own first months in Paris five years earlier, Jefferson tried to help Morris through the culture shock caused by the scale, noise, and incessant activity of the most populous city in Europe. Morris was grateful to have found a guide to the city's social and political networks, just as Jefferson had earlier depended on Benjamin Franklin's contacts and advice. By the early summer, the two Americans had formed high opinions of each other's abilities.[6]

Unlike Jefferson, who preferred to receive small groups of visitors at his home, Morris threw himself with abandon into the social circles of the Parisian nobility. As he made the rounds of his new acquaintances, Morris was naturally drawn into the political conversations that dominated all social gatherings. The announcement of the summoning of the Estates-General in July 1788, coupled with the end of centuries of prepublication censorship, had turned Paris into what Jefferson described as a world gone "politically mad," where "men, women, and children" talked about nothing but politics.[7] How were the deputies to the Estates-General to be chosen? And how was the assembly to be organized when it met? Would the three estates comprising it–the clergy, the nobility, and the commoners–meet and vote separately, which would allow the two privileged estates to dominate the proceedings? Or would they form one common body in which votes would be counted by head?

Morris's opinions were much in demand, as he already enjoyed a reputation as an expert on politics and international finance, due to letters that his late friend the marquis de Chastellux had circulated among French officials. Chastellux had also praised both Morris and Jefferson in his *Voyages de M. le marquis de Chastellux dans l'Amérique septentrionale* (1786).[8] Morris benefited from the French nobility's fascination with all things American, and both relished and resented the stereotypical expectations of his hosts. But Morris was also extremely sensitive to real and imagined slights by French aristocrats, and suspected that the flattering attention he received from noblewomen like the duchesse d'Orléans amounted to nothing more than a faddish exoticism.[9]

Initially, Morris was reluctant to express political beliefs openly, lest he encroach on the American minister's territory. He also found that his ideas were "too moderate" for Jefferson's liberal friends, like Madame de Tessé and Madame de Lafayette, who were quick to label him an "Aristocrat." But eventually Morris was overcome by what James Madison called his notorious "fondness for saying things and advancing doctrines that no one else would." Moreover, in July he began an affair with a noblewoman, Adélaïde de Flahaut, called Adèle, who repeatedly used Morris as an intermediary between her friends at court and deputies in the National Assembly.[10]

Adèle also served as the hostess of a small but select salon at the Louvre, which for Morris became an invaluable source of information, gossip, and contacts. Its guests ranged from high-ranking officials like the foreign minister the comte de Montmorin, and diplomats like the comte de Ségur, to writers, scientists, and *philosophes* including the comte de Buffon, the marquis de Condorcet, Antoine-Laurent Lavoisier, and Madame de Staël. Like other *salonnières* (salon hostesses), Adèle created a space of cosmopolitan sociability where she facilitated dialogue between men of different nationalities and political persuasions. Americans in Paris had long expressed their suspicion of the ease with which the French, and especially French women, mixed liaisons and friendships with politics and patronage, and Morris and Jefferson were no exception.[11] Still, they depended on these half-public, half-private channels as the primary means through which they as foreigners could hope to influence French politics. And yet even a salon like Adèle's, for all its freedom of debate and variety of opinions, also served as a filter, limiting the Americans' understanding of events on the streets beyond its beautifully decorated walls.[12]

Due to his official position as U.S. minister, Jefferson in particular walked a fine line between conversing with friends about current events and intervening in the affairs of a foreign state. The day after the opening of the Estates-General in Versailles on 5 May, Jefferson wrote to Lafayette to express his concern about Lafayette's divided loyalties between the instructions of his noble constituents and his support for the demands of the Third Estate. In clear violation of diplomatic protocol, Jefferson urged Lafayette to disregard the directives of his constituents and propose a compromise in the form of a bicameral legislature. At the end of these detailed recommendations, however, Jefferson reminded his French apprentice that he "must not consider this as advice," but merely as "the effusion of . . . sincere friendship." Morris likewise justified his interventions as the result of his emotional attachment to Lafayette and the French people: "I took the liberty in some late conversations to give you my sentiments on public affairs. I know the folly of offering opinions, which bear the appearance of advice, but a regard for you and the sincerest wishes for the prosperity of this kingdom pushed me beyond the line, which caution would have drawn for one of less ardent temper."[13]

Even though Morris was among those who thought that the social and political change following the American Revolution had gone too far, he was profoundly inspired by the political fervor he encountered in Paris. In a letter to his friend the comte de Moustier, the French minister in New York, shortly after his arrival, Morris expressed his delight to find "on this Side of the Atlantic a strong resemblance to what I left on the other—a Nation which exists in Hopes, Prospects, and Expectations. The reverence for ancient Establishments gone, existing Forms shaken to the very Foundation, and a new Order of Things about to take Place in which even to the very names, all former Institutions will be disregarded." The "strong resemblance" that Morris perceived between the prospects for reform in France and the challenges that American revolutionaries had confronted only a few years earlier bolstered his confidence that he had something valuable to contribute to the debates raging all over Paris. In fact, these debates could easily be interpreted as a flattering acknowledgment of America's own political achievements. Jefferson had a few weeks earlier excitedly reported to Madison that American state and federal constitutions, and especially their bills of rights, were widely read and imitated in the French capital: "Every body here is trying their hands at forming declarations of rights. You will see that [Lafayette's draft] contains the essential principles of ours accommodated as much as could be to the actual state of things here."[14]

In addition to the validation that French imitation bestowed on American accomplishments, Morris and Jefferson had more pragmatic reasons for wanting to point the French reform movement in the right direction. A regenerated French nation would be a strong ally against America's former colonial masters, while the collapse of French power might embolden Britain to wreak revenge on the new republic. Combining self-interest and altruism, Morris explained to George Washington: "We have I think every Reason to wish that the Patriots may be successful. The generous Wish which a free People must form to disseminate Freedom, the grateful Emotion which rejoices in the Happiness of a Benefactor, and a strong personal Interest as well in the Liberty as in the Power of this Country all conspire to make us far from indifferent Spectators. I say we have an *Interest* in the *Liberty* of France." Eager to win the respect of their Parisian hosts, convinced of the relevance of the American precedent, and concerned about the possible disintegration of the French state, Jefferson and Morris regarded it as their cosmopolitan *and* patriotic duty to take an active role in the French Revolution.[15]

While their motives were similar, Jefferson's and Morris's understanding of the nature of the American constitutional model, as well as their ideas about its implications for France, were strikingly different. Morris arrived in Paris fresh from the Constitutional Convention, where he had argued for a strong central government capable of containing the hostility between the rich and the poor intrinsic to a market economy. The antagonism between a popular lower house and a patrician upper house would secure a voice for freeholders while limiting popular "excesses," and control the usurpations of the wealthy while tying their interests to the welfare of the government. The executive needed to be as independent as possible and endowed with an absolute veto on legislation to be able to fulfill its role as the guardian of the people against "legislative tyranny." Although in the end the powers of the president did not fully live up to Morris's expectations, and despite his strong reservations about the compromise with state interests over slavery, he considered "the present plan as the best that was to be attained." These concessions never caused Morris to question the validity of his constitutional principles, which he saw as equally applicable to Philadelphia and Paris.[16]

Commenting on the deliberations in Philadelphia from Paris, Jefferson worried that men like Morris–those "gentry" who would like to turn the American president into "a bad copy of the Polish king"–needed to shed their colonial mentality by coming to Europe, "to see something of the trappings of monarchy." This would make them realize that, "with all the defects of our constitutions, whether general or particular, the comparison of our governments with those of Europe are like a comparison of heaven and hell." The centralized government that Morris tirelessly championed on the floor of the convention would not only pose a threat to civil liberties and states' rights but also tarnish America's progressive image among reformers in France. Since Jefferson had observed the troubles of the Confederation period from afar through letters and European newspapers, his defining experience of the American Revolution remained the Continental Congress and its rejection of monarchical and any other strong executive power.[17]

Moreover, conversations with the "most enlightened and disinterested characters" in Paris had convinced Jefferson that "a bill of rights is what the people are entitled to against every government on earth, general or particular, and what no just government should refuse or rest on inference." Although Madison had tried to persuade Jefferson of the disadvantages of attaching such a list of rights to the constitution, Jefferson remained deeply concerned about his country's and his own reputation among "the enlightened part of Europe" who "have given us the greatest credit for inventing this instrument of security for the rights of the people, and have been not a little surprised to see us so soon give it up." For Jefferson, the American constitution was both too European in its centralization of state power and not European enough by falling short of the expectations of the Old World's enlightened elite.[18]

Jefferson and Morris represented two fundamentally different but equally plausible versions of what the American Revolution had come to mean to Americans and Europeans by 1789. Jefferson saw himself as an author and representative of the revolution of 1776, which stood for the popular repudiation of all forms of coercive governmental power. Morris came to Paris as one of the architects of the revolution of 1787, which symbolized the peaceful redistribution and centralization of state power under the guidance of a national elite.

Despite their different conceptions of the American example, both Jefferson and Morris were convinced of its universal validity and, initially, optimistic about the positive influence of their respective interpretations on French efforts to reform one of the most entrenched European monarchies. In a letter to the British nonconformist minister and philosopher Richard Price in January 1789, Jefferson proudly affirmed the model character of the American Revolution, which seemed "to have awakened the thinking part of this nation [France] in general from the sleep of despotism in which they were sunk." In March, he predicted to poet and diplomat David Humphreys that "this nation will in the course of the present year have as full a portion of liberty dealt out to them as the nation can bear at present, considering how uninformed the mass of their people is." A week earlier, Morris had similarly refuted the skepticism of his half brother, Staats Long Morris, a major-general in the British army and a member of Parliament, about the ability of the French to follow in American footsteps: "You are right in your Idea that our Contest has given a *confused* Notion of Liberty to this Country. But there are many Persons here whose Views are very clear and distinct. It is highly probable that a Constitution will be established as free as is consistent with their Manners and Situation."[19]

Still, it was precisely the "manners and situation" of the French people that presented the most serious obstacle to political progress. The transatlantic debates over the American constitution had already hinted at the tension between the supposedly universal nature of certain political principles and the different needs and capabilities of various peoples at particular historical moments. Since both Jefferson and Morris had hardly any contact with French people outside the nobility or beyond the capital, their assessments of the French national character tended to be highly abstract. Sweeping disparagements alternated with idealizations of the French as "a people of the very best character it is possible for one to have," which were accompanied by fervent declarations of love and gratitude.[20]

For Morris, the crudity of the poor, the indolence of the rich, the naïveté of the political class, and the congenital fickleness of all Frenchmen meant that it was not in the French peoples' own best interest to take the American republic as their model. The fundamental problem was the French national character, the "one fatal Principle which pervades all Ranks": "It is a perfect Indifference to the Violation of Engagements. Inconstancy is so mingled in the Blood, Marrow, and very Essence of this People, that when a Man of high Rank and Importance laughs to Day at what he seriously asserted Yesterday, it is considered as in the natural order of things." Consequently, Morris believed that the French should first try to emulate the British monarchy, with its bicameral legislature and powerful sovereign.[21]

Unfortunately, the National Assembly was imbued with "all that romantic Spirit, & all those romantic Ideas of Government, which happily for America, we were cured of before it was too late," as Morris quipped to Washington in late July 1789. The potential harm that these "romantic ideas," such as a unicameral legislature or a weak executive, could cause in France heightened Morris's responsibility to correct false impressions. He was acutely aware of the paradox of American republicans advocating to the French the adoption of a system that they themselves had only recently rejected: "I have here the strangest Employment imaginable. A Republican and just as it were emerged from that Assembly which has formed one of the most republican of all republican Constitutions I preach incessantly Respect for the Prince[,] Attention to the Rights of the Nobility, and Moderation not only in the Object but also in the Pursuit of it. All this you will say is none of my Business, but I consider France as the natural Ally of my Country and of Course that we are interested in her Prosperity–besides (to say the Truth) I love France."[22]

Jefferson had entertained similar ideas two years earlier, in early 1787, when he counseled Lafayette that "Keeping the good model of your neighboring country before your eyes, you may get on step by step toward a good constitution." But even then Jefferson was clearly uncomfortable with this endorsement of the British monarchy and added sheepishly, "You see how we republicans are apt to preach when we get on politics." By the summer of 1788, conversations with the "most enlightened and disinterested characters" of Paris, including Condorcet and the duc de La Rochefoucauld, had changed his mind. While still remaining within Montesquieu's framework of the interactive relationship between *mœurs* and laws, Jefferson had become convinced that public opinion, molded through unfettered political debate and under the influence of enlightened men, could improve the nation's mores and overcome its deep-seated prejudices and ingrained bad habits. Before his own eyes and within only two years, Jefferson proclaimed in March 1789, a "complete revolution in this government" had taken place, "effected merely by public opinion."[23]

Whereas Morris was convinced that due to their flawed national character the French needed the guidance of a strong, centralized government even more than the American people, Jefferson was optimistic that the same poor state of the French national character was remediable in the immediate future. Still, both conclusions were based on the same interpretative framework, the comparative study of national characters that Americans had adopted from Montesquieu's *De l'esprit des lois* (1748). What made the dialogue between American and French revolutionaries so difficult at times was not the Americans' parochial insistence on the superiority of their own system, but rather their faithful adherence to this traditional precept of European political science.

In early June 1789, the breakdown in negotiations among the three estates about the questions of separate verification and vote by order or by head led to the first open disagreement between Jefferson and Morris. Both regarded the current situation as "very critical," but the American minister announced to Morris that "he, with all the Leaders of Liberty here, are desirous of annihilating Distinctions of Order [in the Estates-General]. How far such Views may be right respecting Mankind in general is I think extremely problematic, but with Respect to this Nation I am sure it is wrong and cannot eventuate well."[24]

From this point onward, Jefferson's and Morris's roadmaps for the French nation increasingly diverged, even though their relationship remained cordial until Jefferson's departure in late September. Morris continued to regard the clergy and the nobility as a necessary balance to the volatile Third Estate, while Jefferson believed that they had become a mere impediment to the negotiations between the king and the people. Still, Jefferson remained concerned that the deputies would demand too much at once and thereby precipitate a royal backlash. Jefferson's concern reflected the lessons he had drawn from the failed Dutch Revolution in 1787. In his view, the Dutch Patriots had tried to implement too many reforms too quickly, and had thereby driven "moderate Aristocrats" back into the fold of the reigning Stadtholder and brought about "a schism" in their movement.[25]

Such a "schism" was about to take place among the French Patriots who were committed to moderate social and constitutional reform of the monarchy. Given the intimate scale of the Parisian beau monde, it is not surprising that Jefferson and Morris shared many acquaintances among the Patriots and depended on them to obtain even a superficial understanding of the power struggles in the Estates-General and later in the National Assembly. Jefferson's contacts in Paris included veterans from the War of Independence like Lafayette and Charles and Alexandre Lameth; intellectuals like Condorcet, La Rochefoucauld, and Pierre-Samuel Du Pont de Nemours; and young liberal courtiers like the duc de Liancourt. In addition to benefiting from Adèle's salon, Morris learned much political news from his conversations at the Club Valois, which in mid-1789 was still frequented by both liberals and conservatives, including Lafayette, Condorcet, La Rochefoucauld, the abbé Emmanuel-Joseph Sieyès, the duc de Montmorency, and its chairman, the duc d'Orléans.[26]

Among the French Patriots, many of those who had befriended Jefferson saw themselves as followers of the American model, which earned them the name Américanistes. They were, however, constitutional monarchists, rather than republicans, and in their understanding the American model prescribed a powerful, unicameral legislature, which was actually quite rare in the United States. The popularity of a unicameral legislature among the Américanistes stemmed from the example of Pennsylvania's first state constitution, which they (erroneously) ascribed to Benjamin Franklin, who had collaborated with La Rochefoucauld on translating and publishing all American state constitutions in France. For the Américanistes, the most important lessons of the American precedent were the need for a declaration of rights, as universal as possible, and the prospect of a fresh start and liberation from the dead hand of the past. "Far from us those detestable principles that the representatives of the nation must fear to enlighten it," proclaimed the duc de Montmorency, who had fought for American independence. "Let us follow the example of the United States. They have given a great example to the new hemisphere; let us give it to the universe."[27]

Jefferson's association with these prominent liberals has often been taken as evidence that he was part of the mainstream of the early French Revolution. In his 1821 memoirs Jefferson himself encouraged this interpretation by boasting of his insider status: "I was much acquainted with the leading patriots of the assembly. Being from a country which had successfully passed thro' a similar reformation, they were disposed to my acquaintance, and had some confidence in me." What Jefferson failed to mention here was that during the summer of 1789 deep divisions had opened within the ranks of the "leading patriots."[28]

In response to the reforms of July and August, especially the abolition of feudal privileges on the night of 4 August and the *Déclaration des droits de l'homme et du citoyen,* the moderate conservatives in the Assembly–led by Jean-Joseph Mounier, Pierre-Victor Malouet, the marquis de Lally-Tollendal, and the comte de Clermont-Tonnerre–formed a coalition, dubbed *monarchiens* by their opponents. Even though the *monarchiens* had no desire to return to the Old Regime, they were extremely wary of moving too far and too fast. Terrified by recent popular uprisings in the provinces, they advocated a strong central authority and sought to maintain ultimate sovereignty in the hands of the king. The discussions of France's future surrounding the convening of the Estates-General had inspired a renewed craze for all things English among parts of the French nobility. For the many Anglomanes among the *monarchiens,* the English monarchy, with its strong independent executive and bicameral legislature, proved that stability and civil liberties did not have to be mutually exclusive.[29]

Morris was taken aback by this reemergence of French Anglomania, as he reported to George Washington: "This Country presents an astonishing Spectacle to one who has collected his Ideas from Books and Information half a dozen years old. Every Thing is *à l'Anglois* and a Desire to imitate the English prevails alike in the Cut of a Coat and the Form of a Constitution." But given his belief in centralized government and the necessity "to preserve if possible some constitutional Authority to the Body of Nobles as the only Means of preserving any Liberty for the People," as he told Lafayette, it was not surprising that he found himself in agreement with the constitutional vision of the *monarchiens* and associated with key figures like Lally-Tollendal and Malouet.[30]

Like their former Patriot allies, the *monarchiens* welcomed the presence of the Americans both as a source of guidance and as a political resource that could bestow international prestige on their own domestic agenda. Even as they declared the American example to be largely irrelevant, due to the differences, as Lally-Tollendal noted, between "an infant people announcing its birth to the universe," and "an ancient and immense people, one of the world's first, which gave itself a form of government for the past fourteen centuries and obeyed the same dynasty for the past eight," other *monarchiens* like Mounier repeatedly cited the new U.S. constitution and the state constitutions to justify an executive veto, bicameralism, and property qualifications for elected representatives.[31]

In late July, Morris received two requests, one through Adèle de Flahaut, for advice on the constitution from unidentified members of the Assembly's Constitutional Committee, which was dominated by the *monarchiens.* Since he considered it "a Duty to render every Service I can to this Country," Morris immediately set to work on an essay titled "Observations on Government, Applicable to the Political State of France." He began by reiterating his belief that "the French have not those manners, which are suited to a free constitution," although this fact was "by no means dishonorable to that nation," since it was merely the result of living under a despotic government. He openly acknowledged as the source of this idea the "important maxim, which Montesquieu has advanced; *That laws and manners have a mutual influence on each other.*"[32]

While Morris's plan for a new French government was ostensibly tailored to the French people's particular needs and capabilities, its basic principles bore a striking resemblance to those he had formulated in Philadelphia two years earlier. Again he argued that the natural hostility between the rich and the poor had to be contained by installing the nobility, "a body constantly opposed to the popular wish, nay, constantly laboring to oppress," in their own legislative chamber. This would serve to unite the people against a common foe and thereby "save them from their most dangerous enemy. It will save them from themselves." As a result, in "the legislative struggle, where each having a veto neither can prevail, the good of all must be consulted, to obtain the consent of each." Abolishing the traditional orders of the realm would not alter "the natural inequality of man," and weakening the power of the king would only give the wealthy a freer hand in exploiting the people.

Finally, again echoing Montesquieu, Morris insisted that despite the defects and injustices of the current regime and despite the abstract right of the people to choose their own form of government, "to exercise such right is madness in the extreme," because "frequent variations in the law are a serious evil, and . . . frequent changes in the form of government are the most afflicting misfortune." The substance of these recommendations was in perfect agreement with the positions that the *monarchiens* were defending on the floor of the National Assembly. But in his advocacy of the same constitutional principles on both sides of the Atlantic, Morris showed himself to be as much of a universalist as Jefferson. For Morris, class conflict posed a fundamental challenge to constitution-makers anywhere, and the need to contain it was the common denominator between the United States in 1787 and France in 1789.[33]

The harsh and pessimistic tone of Morris's warnings against popular sovereignty reflected his recent experience of mob violence in the streets of Paris. On 22 July, while strolling under the arcades of the Palais Royal, Morris had witnessed how the severed head and naked body of the royal official Joseph-François Foulon de Doué were dragged through the streets to the house of his son-in-law, Louis Bertier de Sauvigny, the intendant of Paris, who was then also "put to Death and cut to Pieces, the Populace carrying about the mangled Fragments with a Savage Joy." This event deeply traumatized Morris and inspired in him an "ardent Desire . . . to return to my native Country." As a student of Montesquieu, he could not help but interpret the atrocities as a mark of the French national character, whose "tyrannical" disposition he compared to the "mildness of American character."[34]

The day after the killings, Morris told Jefferson about his experience, which caused Jefferson to comment in a letter to John Jay on the people's "bloodthirsty spirit." Still, Jefferson never witnessed any violence firsthand and remained convinced that the situation would calm down if the "obnoxious" objects of the people's righteous anger had the good sense "to keep out of the way." Jefferson generally approved of spontaneous revolts, like Shays's Rebellion, as an expression of a popular political consciousness and a necessary check on government power. He found his views on the salutary effect of popular uprisings confirmed when the National Assembly reacted to reports of riots and general resistance to authority in the countryside by abolishing the feudal regime and its privileges on the night of 4 August. For Jefferson, the popular uprisings validated the French Revolution as the direct continuation of its American predecessor, understood as the radical affirmation of the people's right to rid themselves of rulers who violated their natural rights. In the letter to Maria Cosway in which Jefferson famously quipped, "The cutting off heads is become so much á la mode, that one is apt to feel of a morning whether their own is on their shoulders," he also expressed his "singular" fortune "to see in the course of fourteen years two such revolutions as were never before seen." [35]

Reactions to this latest outburst of revolutionary violence were similarly divided among the deputies in the National Assembly. For the comte de Clermont-Tonnerre, as for Morris, popular violence cast a shadow over the entire reform project: "I fear we might all become barbarous; I thought of the Saint-Bartholomew's Day Massacre . . . and I asked myself, painfully, if we were even worthy of being free." Although the majority of deputies strongly condemned vigilantism, a small group defended the murders as popular justice against two "scoundrels." Like Jefferson, they regarded violence as a necessary evil to protect the revolution from its enemies. As Antoine-Pierre Barnave put it in an often-cited phrase: "This blood that was shed, was it then so pure?"[36] (As the revolutionary crisis intensified over the following years, the latter attitude toward political violence would become an important point of commonality between the more radical American and French revolutionaries, which I will discuss in the next chapter.)

In this explosive climate, the *monarchiens* were delighted that a prominent American revolutionary like Morris would inveigh against radical social reforms, which could be read to imply that the social and political situation in France did not lend itself to an American-style solution. Conversely, Morris's conservatism increasingly became an embarrassment to the liberal admirers of the American republic. At a dinner party, Lafayette directly challenged Morris to be more sensitive to his responsibilities as an American and told him that "I injure the Cause, for that my Sentiments are continually quoted against the good Party. I seize this Opportunity to tell him that I am opposed to the Democracy from Regard to Liberty."[37]

Perhaps also in order to offset Morris's influence, Lafayette tried to enlist Jefferson's support in the debates over the number of houses in the legislature and the veto power of the king. In July, Jefferson had politely declined a request to meet with the Constitutional Committee, arguing that it would be inappropriate for the official representative of a foreign nation to become involved in domestic politics. At the same time, however, he secretly worked with Lafayette on a declaration of rights, which Lafayette submitted to the Assembly on 11 July. On 25 August, Jefferson received an urgent message from his French collaborator, imploring him "for Liberty's sake" to host a dinner the following evening for Lafayette and seven other deputies of the National Assembly.[38]

The reason for this hastily arranged meeting was a stalemate within the Constitutional Committee. The *monarchien* majority had found it impossible to reach a consensus with the radicals Sieyès and Isaac-René-Guy Le Chapelier on the issue of royal veto power over legislation. The *monarchiens* demanded an absolute veto, like that of the English monarch, while Sieyès and Le Chapelier rejected any kind of veto. Disturbed by the split among former Patriot allies, Lafayette hoped that the neutral ground of Jefferson's apartment and the American minister's prestige would help facilitate a compromise.

The dinner on 26 August began at four and continued until ten at night, bringing together the leading *monarchiens* Jean-Joseph Mounier, the comte d'Agoult, and the marquis de Blacons, and the liberal Patriots who favored a suspensive veto–Adrien-Jean Du Port, Antoine-Pierre Barnave, Alexandre de Lameth, and the comte de Latour-Maubourg. In addition to discussing the veto and the number of legislative chambers, the French deputies at the Hôtel de Langeac also debated the issue of whether the new French constitution should provide for its own revision and, if so, whether at stated, regular intervals or as circumstances required.[39]

Although the meeting failed to bring about reconciliation between the two sides and the committee was forced to pass on the veto question to the full Assembly, it marked for Jefferson the highpoint of his involvement in the French Revolution. In his memoirs, Jefferson fondly remembered being "a silent witness to a coolness and candor of argument unusual in the conflicts of political opinion; to a logical reasoning, and chaste eloquence, disfigured by no gaudy tinsel of rhetoric or declamation, and truly worthy of being placed in parallel with the finest dialogue of antiquity." This was the pristine image of the French Revolution that Jefferson would carry back with him to the United States, glossing over the deep rifts in the French political elite and unsullied by any firsthand experience with the riots and popular violence that so disturbed Morris and the French deputies.[40]

Whether or not we believe Jefferson's claim that he remained "a silent witness" during the six-hour meeting, it was in any case not his constitutional expertise that Lafayette had been counting on to inspire a compromise. Even more than other public actors in the French Revolution, Lafayette was highly conscious of the power of political symbolism. By enlisting an American Founding Father to preside over the meeting of the divided French Patriots, Lafayette was in fact not providing a neutral space for debate, but likely intended to impress upon his colleagues the gravity of the revolutionary moment, when the world was looking to France to open a new chapter in human history.[41]

Participants on both sides went home in the belief that their own positions had carried the day. Jefferson was so impressed with the high-minded debate that he failed to notice that the meeting had fallen short of its purpose, and reported to John Jay that unanimity had been achieved in favor of a suspensive veto and a unicameral legislature. Mounier claimed in a pamphlet that Jefferson had agreed with his opposition to constitutional revisions at fixed intervals, and to legitimize his own position invoked Jefferson's prestige as "an American, renowned for his wisdom and virtues, who knows both from experience and in theory the institutions suited to preserve liberty." However, the reception of Mounier's pamphlet, described by Jefferson's secretary William Short, demonstrated how deep the rift between the two sides had in fact become: "One proof of the progress of opinion here is that the work of Mounier is considered at present by the noblesse and clergy as a chef d'oeuvre in government, and supporting true principles, whilst it is execrated by the majority of the national assembly. The opinion of both parties is certainly outrée."[42]

The work on a declaration of rights, the formal abolition of feudal privileges on 11 August, and now the conversation with the French deputies, all focused Jefferson's mind on the question of whether the past could legitimately bind the present by law or debts, or whether "the earth belongs in usufruct to the living." The debate over the royal veto was essentially a debate over the traditional rights of the French king and, as Lally-Tollendal put it, whether "a contract that has been sacred for so many generations can bind the present generation." In his famous letter to James Madison of

6 September 1789, Jefferson argued that the only legacy each generation was allowed to leave to its successor was the absence of constraining legacies and the freedom to make its own choices. The letter combined Jefferson's experiences as a debt-ridden planter in Virginia and as a cosmopolitan constitution-maker in France. However, as Herbert Sloan has pointed out, there was an ambiguity hidden in Jefferson's brief for the rights of successive generations. In proclaiming the freedom of every generation from the debts of its forebears, Jefferson at the same time placed severe limits on the autonomy of each generation to break with the past, as it remained duty-bound to preserve, and pass on unimpaired to the next generation, the heritage entrusted by the past. Just as Morris's conservatism was cosmopolitan in its universal applicability, so Jefferson's radical cosmopolitanism contained a conservative core.[43]

Jefferson's and Morris's ambivalence about whether the French nation should constitute itself anew based on universal principles or reform in accord with particular traditions and circumstances stemmed from two sources: first, the lessons they had imbibed from Montesquieu's *De l'esprit des lois;* and second, the failure of their own revolution to provide a clear answer to this dilemma.

Not only had Montesquieu introduced his American readers to mechanisms like the separation and balance of governmental functions; he had also imparted an understanding of the need for moderate government in accord with the material circumstances and spirit of the people under its rule. Jefferson's *Notes on the State of Virginia* was clearly modeled on *De l'esprit des lois* in its analysis of environmental influences on the evolution of national character.[44] If, as Montesquieu maintained, each government was a particular configuration of equalities and inequalities, there was only one political evil–despotism–but several political goods, including moderate monarchy, republican government, and the mixed English regime. The task of the legislator was therefore to pursue a universal end–opposing despotism–by relative means, namely, by carefully choosing which among a variety of relatively good regimes or "constitutions" was the most appropriate to the specific circumstances at hand. Morris explained: "Different Constitutions of Government are necessary to the different Societies on the Face of this Planet. Their Difference of Position is in itself a powerful Cause, their

Manners, their Habits. The scientific Taylor who should cut after Grecian or Chinese Models would not have many Customers either in London or Paris: and those who look to America for their political Forms are not unlike those Taylors in the Island of Laputa who, as Gulliver tells us, always take Measure with a Quadrant."[45]

However, there was an ambiguity in Montesquieu's use of the term "constitution" that would have serious implications for the efforts of American and French "scientific tailors" to fashion a new French regime. "Constitution" could refer to a people's fundamental mode of political existence and the configuration of the powers composing a form of government. It could also denominate the act of establishing a new government and creating a new nation. For Montesquieu, the unwritten English constitution was the classic example of an enduring structure in which the forms and functions of the constituent parts were clearly delimited for the preservation of liberty. But if the constitution of the English body politic was as unique and as suited to the English people as the constitution of a particular human body, could such an example be imitated? In fact, could one nation ever adopt a version of another's constitution? Finally, how could the constitution be an expression of national sovereignty and, at the same time, reconstitute the nation?[46]

For American revolutionaries, who had used both natural rights and the traditional rights of Englishmen to justify independence, as well as for the French National Assembly, which had to decide whether they were called upon to reform an already existing constitution or institute a radically new one, this conceptual ambiguity persisted. During his tenure in Paris, Jefferson had begun to question Montesquieu's relativism and suspect that the emphasis on variations among peoples and diverse interests within society were in fact mere rationalizations of aristocratic and clerical privileges. For the rest of his life, Jefferson would continue to wrestle with Montesquieu's "paradoxes" and "heresies." Morris's suggestion to the French that they follow the English example but adapt it as much as possible to French conditions assumed that the French deputies had the right to break with absolutist traditions, but left unresolved exactly how much innovation the French people could handle before disintegrating into anarchy.[47]

The precedent of the American Revolution offered precious little guidance on this question. The Declaration of Independence had established the principle of national sovereignty, but to apply this principle indiscriminately elsewhere, and especially in France, might be "madness in the extreme." Moreover, American revolutionaries had been unable to resolve the Montesquieuian paradox that a constitution was said to both reflect and shape the political habits of the nation at the same time. On the one hand, the "reflection and choice" of political action rather than ancestry were supposed to create a nation and form its spirit, meaning that reasoned debate based on common sense and first principles would bring about very similar results in Philadelphia and Paris. On the other hand, national character was widely regarded as an immutable constraint on political action. Amazed by the heated debates in Paris, the English traveler Arthur Young scoffed at the very idea of "making a constitution, which is a new term they have adopted and which they use as if a constitution was a pudding to be made by a receipt [i.e., a recipe]."[48]

The ambiguous legacy of the American Revolution meant that Thomas Jefferson and Gouverneur Morris would never be entirely comfortable either as chefs offering a universal constitutional recipe or as tailors fashioning a custom-made legal coat. Morris tried to convince the French that they needed to uphold their traditional social order, but he had prescribed the same program to ostensibly a very different society at home. His conservatism was therefore no less cosmopolitan and universalistic than Jefferson's belief in the possibility of radically new departures in organizing the nation. And in Jefferson's case, this belief was limited by the awareness, painfully gained through personal debts, that no individual or society would ever be able to escape completely from the burden of the past.

Despite the Americans' temporary usefulness, French revolutionaries grew increasingly impatient with the mixed signals they received from Morris and Jefferson. The Americans were much too respectful of the status quo—just like Montesquieu, who, as Mounier acknowledged, "in seeking the spirit of institutions, always attempted to justify whatever he found established." Even Jefferson's vision for France in September 1789 amounted to nothing more daring than "a good constitution, which will in it's principles and merit be about a middle term between that of England and the United States." *Monarchiens* therefore found it easy to dismiss the American model as either irrelevant to an ancient kingdom like France or a pale imitation of the English system.[49]

Meanwhile, the more radical Patriots continued to adhere to the American model in theory. An account of the first year of the revolution extolled the example of Benjamin Franklin and declared that before him, "the majority of publicists had reasoned like educated slaves of their masters; like Montesquieu they had used all their wit to justify the status quo and coat our institutions with a deceptive poison."[50] In practice, however, they came to regard the American panacea of moderation as completely inadequate for overcoming the obstacles to reform in French society and the divisions within the French nation. For example, American bills of rights still distinguished between the people and their government and were designed to protect the former against the latter. Yet, in order to contribute to the building of a nation, a declaration of rights had to abolish all such divisions and strive for the universal. As Sieyès put it: "It cannot say: man, the citizen, will not bear such and such a chain. It must break them all. . . . It ceases to be a settlement, transaction, a condition of a treaty, a contract, etc., between one authority and another. There is *only one* power, *only one* authority."[51]

On 9 and 11 September, the National Assembly voted overwhelmingly in favor of a unicameral legislature and a suspensive royal veto. The arguments of the *monarchiens* had been no match against popular pressure, the seeming irrationality of redividing a legislature so recently unified after a long struggle, patriotic disdain for following English models, and deepening mistrust of the king. But above all, the deputies were asserting their right to create a radically new constitution from scratch, based on the principle of national sovereignty. Any remaining doubt about the fundamental change in the French regime was dispelled on 5 October, when, under the threat of popular violence, the king was compelled to accept the Declaration of Rights and the incomplete constitution. The king's forced return to Paris increased the already intense polarization of the Assembly, first by fortifying the opposition of the *monarchiens*. At the same time, a more coherent radical coalition, soon known as the Jacobins, began to match the organization of the *monarchiens,* on which it was in many ways modeled.

Not surprisingly, Morris felt deeply frustrated that the deputies had completely ignored his advice. Resenting what he regarded as Lafayette's entirely undeserved popularity after the October Days, he resolved "not again [to] trouble him with Advice unless he asks it, and perhaps not then." After yet another unsuccessful attempt to explain to bishop and future foreign minister Charles-Maurice de Talleyrand-Périgord the "general Principles tending to the Wealth and Happiness of a Nation and founded on the Sentiments of the human Heart," Morris vented his exasperation in his diary: "Oh! It is dreadfully tiresome to explain down to the first Principles for one of those Half Way Minds which see just far enough to bewilder themselves." In his view, the murder of the two officials at the Palais Royal and the siege of the royal quarters at Versailles during the October Days were portents of the chaos that was bound to ensue under a weak constitutional monarchy subverted by radical populists from the left and reactionary aristocrats from the right.[52]

Jefferson left Paris in late September 1789, fully confident that the revolution had been brought to a successful conclusion: "I will agree to be stoned as a false prophet if all does not end well in this country. Nor will it end with this country. Here is but the first chapter of the history of European liberty." For Jefferson, the emblematic event of the early French Revolution was the calm and constructive debate at his residence on 26 August, which confirmed both his faith in the abilities of the French political elite and his belief that in France there was "but one opinion, . . . the general one of the nation." In his final letter to John Jay as minister to France, Jefferson acknowledged the split in the Assembly between "the moderate royalists" and those he called the "Republicans," even though no one in the Assembly advocated the establishment of a republic in France. However, he predicted, citing the conference at his house as evidence, that because they all held "the same honest views" and due to Lafayette's influence, the two parties would continue to work together.[53] In the following years, Jefferson's monolithic perception of French politics and national opinion would lead him to become one of the most vocal apologists for the Terror and French expansionist warfare, thereby ironically supporting a regime characterized by the very same centralizing ambitions that he abhorred in his Federalist opponents.

Initially, Jefferson and Morris saw their Parisian sojourn as an opportunity to educate the French intelligentsia about the New World and its republican principles. The similar challenges of dismantling the old order and legitimizing a new regime linked the American and French revolutions and reinforced the idea that the two nations could inspire and instruct each other. Jefferson's and Morris's writings clearly convey the excitement that they felt when French intellectuals and statesmen solicited their opinions and advice. The cosmopolitan society of political debate and intellectual exchange that they had imagined themselves a part of at home had now materialized in the salons of Paris.

The events of 1789 confronted the two Americans with unexamined ambiguities in their own revolutionary tradition. Their cosmopolitanism and the novelty of their role as exporters of revolutionary ideology clashed with their assumptions about national characters and anxieties about radical change. While the failure of Jefferson and Morris to shape the first French constitution seems to highlight the persistence of local differences in the age of revolution, their main obstacle was that their ideas were too traditionally French, rather than too innovatively American. Morris's and Jefferson's horizons of change remained bounded by pieties of French political science, which were increasingly rejected by the French deputies and rendered irrelevant on the streets of Paris. The vision of a new beginning based on equality, popular sovereignty, and national regeneration replaced the pre-revolutionary ideal, to which the Americans and many of their friends among the French nobility had subscribed, of enlightened elites guiding the people on the road to progress.

2

"Was ever such a prize won with so little innocent blood?"

POLITICAL VIOLENCE AND THE GLOBAL STAKES OF THE FRENCH REVOLUTION, 1790-1792

On 26 April 1791, William Short, the American chargé d'affaires in Paris, shared with Thomas Jefferson his reaction to Thomas Paine's *Rights of Man, Part I,* published in London the previous February. Short professed his surprise that Paine had not already been indicted in England, for his book was "libelous in many parts and treasonable in still more." Overall, Short found the work to be "much in Paine's style, that is to say incorrect–with strong expressions and bold ideas." On the very same day in Philadelphia, Jefferson sent a note to Jonathan B. Smith, the father of Paine's American publisher, expressing his approbation of *Rights of Man* and his hope that its publication in America would counteract "the political heresies which have sprung up among us." The inclusion of Jefferson's endorsement in the American edition of *Rights of Man* caused a political scandal and a lasting estrangement between Jefferson and John Adams, the "heretic" in question.[1]

Jefferson's and Short's dramatically different reactions to Paine's work reflected the increasing polarization of politics in the United States, no less than in France. Since Jefferson's departure from France in September 1789, Short, who hoped to become his successor as minister, had witnessed with growing alarm the rise of a popular political movement challenging

39

the Patriot leadership in the National Assembly. The day before Short commented on *Rights of Man,* he reported to Jefferson: "The current of public opinion with respect to the King, and with respect to Royalty in general seemed to be taking a direction that threatened a new revolution, or at least indicated that the present would be carried still further." Meanwhile, Jefferson had become concerned about a creeping counterrevolution in America, engineered by John Adams, Alexander Hamilton, and other "Tories" in Washington's cabinet and in the Senate. The publication of *Rights of Man* promised to serve as an ideological litmus test, separating the true believers from the "heretics," and the republican wheat from the aristocratic chaff. Just as Jefferson celebrated *Rights of Man*'s galvanizing effect on the morale of American republicans, his protégé Short feared the same effect on their French counterparts.[2]

As Jefferson had anticipated, the impact in the United States of *Rights of Man,* the most popular among the many responses to Edmund Burke's *Reflections on the Revolution in France* (1790), proved to be particularly powerful. Whereas in Britain the book represented a contribution to an ongoing debate about domestic politics, for American readers Paine's authorship created a tangible link between the revolution in France and their own revolutionary past. Moreover, at a moment when the American political system was still in the process of formation, *Rights of Man* served as a catalyst for a distinctly cosmopolitan brand of dissent, which criticized American elites and their policies within the context of political developments in Europe. This reception of *Rights of Man* in America was reinforced by events in France. In July 1791 the French royal family unsuccessfully tried to escape from Paris, plunging the nation into political turmoil that culminated in the creation of the French Republic in September 1792. With the rise of a popular republican movement in France, doubts about the universality of the American republican model, such as those discussed in the previous chapter, disappeared among American supporters of the French Revolution. From now on, the fates of the American and the French republics were inseparably linked. At the moment of its founding, the French Republic already appeared on the verge of destruction at the hands of a powerful coalition of European monarchies. As Jefferson explained to Short in January 1793, the "liberty of the whole earth" was at stake in France.

Adopting the conservatism of his aristocratic social circle in Paris, Short strongly opposed the establishment of the French Republic. Ironically, it was Short's disapproving accounts of events in France that provided the basis for Jefferson's hopeful vision of the French Revolution as a regenerative force for both Europe and America. Due to the partiality of Short's reports, Jefferson had only a vague understanding of the political divisions within France. But the arguments he used in his famous "Adam and Eve" letter to convince Short of the inevitability and even necessity of revolutionary violence bore a remarkable resemblance to those used by French revolutionaries at the time. Both American and French revolutionaries (including some constitutional monarchists) defined the nation as a community constituted through shared political principles. This definition could create solidarity, even across national boundaries, among those who subscribed to the same universal principles. But the definition also intensified conflict with domestic political antagonists whose opposition to the principles that defined the nation exposed them as "heretics" or "foreigners." The denationalization of political opponents made it easier to justify the exercise of political violence. However, given the rapid pace of events and constantly shifting political landscape in France, defining membership in the national community in terms of political beliefs could also rebound on the true believers themselves. By the time Paine's *Rights of Man* appeared in French translation, even Paine's political allies in Paris regarded it as outmoded and therefore suspect.

In late January 1790 William Short proudly informed Jefferson that the marquis de Lafayette and the duc de La Rochefoucauld had nominated George Washington, Benjamin Franklin, Jefferson, and himself as honorary members of the Société de 1789. The group aimed at stabilizing the constitutional monarchy and bringing the French Revolution to an end. Its members condemned popular violence, advocated the protection of property rights, and sought to develop a working relationship with the king. Short agreed with all of these objectives and assumed that his mentor Jefferson would too. But he also shared Jefferson's earlier concern about divisions among the French Patriots and predicted that the society would "produce parties and discontent among those who were of the same principles and good friends." A few weeks later, Short noted to John Jay that, after depriving the king of most of his powers, the deputies in the National Assembly were now turning against each other: "As frequently happens when there is no common enemy, parties have arisen among those who were formerly united, and who are more inveterate and more dangerous to each other than any enemy could be."[3]

The abbé Emmanuel-Joseph Sieyès and the marquis de Condorcet had first conceived the Société de 1789 in the fall of 1789 as an intellectual salon without a specific political agenda. However, it quickly turned into a meeting place for self-declared moderate supporters of the constitutional monarchy. The revolutionary crisis had politically polarized the salons and made conversations there more impassioned and confrontational. Salons had always had particular orientations and clienteles, but the *salonnières* had prided themselves on keeping their societies diverse and broadminded. With the emergence of political factions like the *monarchiens,* this balance became ever more difficult. Irreconcilable differences between opponents and supporters of the constitution eventually broke up Adèle de Flahaut's salon. Aristocratic political clubs like the Société de 1789 grew out of the connections formed in salons, lodges, and academies, but tended to have more homogeneous memberships and narrower ideological parameters.[4]

By April 1790 the Société had developed into a veritable party, with dues, membership rolls, committees, its own journal, and sumptuous quarters in the Palais Royal. Its members included leading deputies of the National Assembly like Isaac Le Chapelier, the comte de Mirabeau, Jean-Paul Rabaut Saint-Etienne, and Bertrand Barère; the mayor of Paris, Jean-Sylvain Bailly; prominent intellectuals and journalists like Jacques-Pierre Brissot de Warville, Antoine-Claude Destutt de Tracy, and Du Pont de Nemours; as well as financiers and Old Regime jurists and bureaucrats. As the invitation to the American revolutionaries suggests, the society sought to continue the salon tradition of cosmopolitan sociability. In a draft of the society's constitution, Sieyès emphasized the discussion and promotion of *l'art social,* universal principles of good social order. Human progress, Sieyès argued, required a global exchange of ideas akin to the global commerce in goods. At the same time, the society would not admit anyone whose patriotic sentiments were not beyond reproach.[5]

Several members of the society regarded the United States as France's most important trading partner, both intellectually and commercially. Lafayette, Condorcet, and La Rochefoucauld were all prominent Américanistes and close friends of Jefferson. Lafayette continued to seek American advice, asking Short and Gouverneur Morris for suggestions on reforming the French judiciary in January 1790.[6] Brissot, who had traveled through the United States in 1788, had collaborated with the financier Etienne Clavière on a book entitled *De la France et des États-Unis ou de l'importance de la Révolution de l'Amérique pour le bonheur de la France* (1787), which highlighted the potential of transatlantic commerce, due to the ideal compatibility of American agriculture and French manufactures. The book also served as the founding document of the Société Gallo-Américaine, which was dedicated to promoting commercial relations between the two countries and fostering mutual understanding and friendship.[7] In June 1790 La Rochefoucauld delivered a eulogy for his friend Benjamin Franklin before the society. He cited the American as a formative influence on the new French constitution, in particular its unicameral legislature. At a moment when the French constitution remained controversial even among the members of the Société, La Rochefoucauld pointedly reminded his audience that Franklin had put aside his reservations about the U.S. Constitution and signed the document to ensure unanimous approval.[8]

The Société's illustrious ranks and its moderate, cosmopolitan, and pro-American program all made William Short eager to accept the honorary membership. The twenty-five-year-old Short had come to Paris in 1784 as Jefferson's secretary. Along with James Madison and James Monroe, he was part of a circle of promising younger men whom Jefferson had taken under his wing in the early 1780s. Remotely connected by family ties–Short's uncle, Henry Skipwith, was married to the half sister of Jefferson's wife, Martha–Jefferson and Short had formed a closer relationship when Short's father died, shortly after Martha's fatal illness in late 1782. Jefferson once referred to Short as his "adoptive son," and had helped him obtain his first legal business in Richmond, and in his election to the Virginia Executive Council. For a young provincial like Short, the position as Jefferson's secretary opened up a whole new world. Short gained entrance to the salons of Jefferson's noble friends, like the duchesse La Rochefoucauld d'Enville (La Rochefoucauld's mother), Madame de Tessé, and the comtesse d'Houdetot, and their polite conversations about literature, science, and politics. Moreover, the handsome young American fell in love with two young married Frenchwomen. Between 1786 and 1790, he courted Anne-Hipolyte-Louise Royer, the teenage daughter of the family with whom Short was boarding to improve his French.[9] Later, he began a long-term affair with Alexandrine-Charlotte-Sophie, duchesse de La Rochefoucauld, known as Rosalie, the wife of the much older La Rochefoucauld. Entranced by the political ferment and romantic promise of Paris, Short had little inclination to return to Virginia, and counted on Jefferson's patronage to obtain the position of U.S. minister to France. Gouverneur Morris, upon meeting Short in the summer of 1789, noted that the young Virginian spoke of "the Paris Societies in the Tone of an older Man than he is, and therefore I think after Mr. Jefferson's departure he will run into them, peut-être à l'abandon."[10]

Short's reports to Jefferson inevitably reflected the views of his aristocratic social circle, which he presented as the mainstream of French political opinion. Moreover, Short's conservatism was reinforced by his correspondence with Gouverneur Morris. The two Americans frequently exchanged news and opinions about the situation in France while Morris served as Washington's personal emissary to London from January to September 1790. Short generally deferred to the views of more experienced correspondents, and he had great respect for Morris's detailed knowledge of French politics and prescience at a time of rapid change. Morris responded to Short's letters quickly and at length, while Short often had to wait months for a letter from Jefferson, who became secretary of state in March 1790.

Short and Morris agreed that the French seemed determined to repeat many American mistakes, such as decentralizing the national government in the reorganization of provinces into *départements* and introducing paper money. The most serious threat to the stability of the French state, however, came from its own people. Short predicted that the Société de 1789 and the radical elements in the Jacobin Club would "in order to strengthen themselves [be] obliged to vie with each other in courting the people, the source of all strength." Morris likewise regarded this as a cause for great concern: "Those who court the People have a very capricious Mistress. A Mistress which may be gained by Sacrifices, but she cannot be so held for she is insatiable. The People will never continue attached to any Man who will sacrifice his Duty to their Caprice." Morris had always distrusted the ability of the populace to govern itself. In this feminized image, the French people took on characteristics commonly associated with the Court as the source of corrupted and capricious power. As the two Americans saw it, the National Assembly was undermining the king's authority and opening the floodgates of popular discontent without establishing a new authority to secure law and order, thereby inviting ambitious demagogues to fill the power vacuum. Short and Morris believed that if the French nation were to survive the revolution, it would have to be in spite of the French people, through the adoption of necessary but unpopular policies, like raising taxes, and the strengthening of existing institutions.[11]

Many members of the Société de 1789 agreed that until the people were able to understand the true principles of the revolution, a small group of rational men had to make the laws, advise the monarch, and operate the state. At the same time, the Société made little effort to educate the people or cultivate public opinion. Its select membership and its ties to the Old Regime establishment initially made the Société an effective counterweight to the more radical voices in the Amis de la Constitution, also known as the Jacobin Club, after its meeting place in a Dominican convent near the National Assembly. But given the intense competition for members and influence between growing numbers of political clubs, the same characteristics opened the society to charges of elitism, corruption, and even counterrevolution. From its inception, the Société condemned social unrest and called for the preservation of the existing social and economic order. In an essay entitled "Warning to the French People of its True Enemies," published in August 1790 in the society's journal and as a pamphlet, the poet André Chenier drew a sharp distinction between patriotic demonstrations in support of the common good and illegitimate riots that weakened the nation. The following month, the society enthusiastically welcomed the violent repression of a rebellion led by National Guard regiments in Nancy, which had been supported by the local Jacobin clubs. The society went so far as to declare that the mutineers could not be considered true Frenchmen, since they had broken the social contract that bound the nation together.[12]

In his influential pamphlet *Qu'est-ce que le Tiers État?* (1789), Sieyès, co-founder of the Société de 1789, had already demonstrated the effectiveness of defining political opponents as alien to the nation. Sieyès's answer to the rhetorical question "What is the Third Estate?" was "Everything."[13] In alerting the Third Estate to its unique role as the complete embodiment of the nation, Sieyès was simultaneously urging it to dissociate itself from those sections of the population, particularly the nobility, that were "nothing," that is, not a genuine part of the nation. The desire to replace a society divided by rank and estates with one unified nation was clearly evident in the National Assembly's abolition of feudal privileges and in its decision in favor of a unicameral legislature. But in the context of the political struggles within the Assembly and particularly between the Assembly and its critics on the outside, each competing group began to present its own position as the exclusive manifestation of the will of the nation, which in turn was defined as always unanimous and infallible.

Short likewise applauded the "vigorous measures" adopted in Nancy, "which fortunately met with success." He noted, however, that "its success made a very different impression here [in Paris], in and out of the assembly." Outside the legislature, "the mob of Paris" and "many journalists" accused the Assembly, the royal ministers, and Lafayette as head of the National Guard, of counterrevolution. In fact, radical journalists were turning Sieyès's dictum that the Third Estate was "everything" against its author. In a characteristically hyperbolic pamphlet published on the first anniversary of the fall of the Bastille, Jean-Paul Marat exposed the Société de 1789 as the center of a vast conspiracy to deliver France to the enemies of the nation. Camille Desmoulins denounced the society's stand on the Nancy rebellion, suggesting that its members had reveled in the news of "this Saint-Bartholomew of patriots." Louis-Marie Prudhomme charged that the club was a cabal of aristocrats, royal ministers, and wealthy speculators, and declared "eternal war on the vile slaves of the Court, on ambitious and false patriots!"[14]

The ubiquitous rumors of conspiracy and counterconspiracy found spectacular confirmation when the French royal family attempted to escape from Paris on 20 June 1791. The king left behind a declaration condemning the entire revolution as anarchical, illegitimate, and irreligious. The so-called flight to Varennes, where the royal family was captured and returned to the capital, was a watershed in the revolution. Due to the king's central role in unifying the French nation, his breach of trust was a devastating blow to the majority of French citizens. All political and social traditions were now open to question, and political alliances and associations thrown into disarray.[15]

The Société de 1789 effectively dissolved. It had already begun to wither away in the spring of 1791, after both of its founders, Sieyès and Condorcet, defected back to the Jacobins. But the real causes of the society's demise were internal divisions, its inability to attract a popular following, and the relentless attacks of its radical competitors. Yet the debate over whether France could and should become a republic also split the society's archrival, the Jacobin Club. Traditional supporters of the constitutional monarchy and those who had concluded that without the king the social order would fall apart took the opportunity to distance themselves from their more radical colleagues, led by provincial lawyer Maximilien Robespierre. Together with Lafayette, the former Jacobins set up a rival club, the Feuillants. At the same time, the king's flight united various popular societies in a republican movement that openly called for the abolition of the monarchy. Short described to Jefferson the tone of the numerous addresses to the Assembly from Jacobin clubs all over the country as "alarmingly republican." He warned that "a great opposition is forming in the spirit of the people without, to that of the members within, the assembly. The latter . . . wish to support the form of a monarchy. The former are becoming every day under the influence of their clubs, leaders and journals, more and more averse both to the substance and form."[16]

Prior to the summer of 1791 there were virtually no Americans on either side of the Atlantic who expected or advocated a French republic. Even Paine's *Rights of Man, Part I* had adhered to the common distinction between Louis XVI, the benevolent king who had helped the thirteen colonies gain their independence, and the institution of monarchy. All authorities on political science, most famously Montesquieu, maintained that republicanism was viable only in small states, because larger states lacked the homogeneous society considered necessary to sustain popular institutions. It still remained to be seen whether the American republic, as a federation of small states, would turn out to be the exception that proved the rule.

However, the debates in Paris following the king's flight quickly convinced Thomas Paine that a French republic was possible. He joined Condorcet's newly founded Société des Républicains, along with Brissot, Clavière, and radical journalist Nicolas de Bonneville, and engaged in a newspaper debate with Sieyès about what constituted a truly representative government for France. It was to Short's great relief that Paine left Paris for London in mid-July: "He was here the avowed apostle of republicanism and begun to alarm all moderate people by his counsel for the abolition of monarchy." Short hoped that "he will not return here for some time," as he was convinced Paine "would have done harm here if he had remained."[17]

Paine's sudden radicalization was so alarming to Short because Paine previously had been closely associated with Jefferson, Lafayette, and the French Patriot Party. *Rights of Man* had not been intended as a reply to Burke's

47

Reflections, but its initial purpose was to champion the achievements of the Patriot Party, and particularly Lafayette. Paine's defense of the legal distinction between active and passive citizens, his censure of the killing of Bertier and Foulon, and his account of the October Days all celebrated Lafayette's enlightened leadership in saving the revolution from anarchy.

It was only in the context of Paine's joining the republican movement in France that the American republic, largely irrelevant to the vindication of a constitutional monarchy, assumed a central place in his writings on Europe. Although *Common Sense* had asserted that the cause of America was "in great measure the cause of all mankind" and had praised "the Republican materials" of the English constitution, it nowhere had sought to foment revolution in Britain, France, or other established European monarchies. The dedication of *Rights of Man, Part I* to George Washington had anticipated "the happiness of seeing the New World regenerate the Old," but this regeneration had clear limits. Direct reference to the American Revolution in the first part mainly had served to highlight the role of Lafayette and other French officers in carrying its spirit of reform back to France. Only after Paine made the republican turn in France did America become an immediate model for Europe, and the French Revolution an extension of the principles that Paine himself had set out in 1776. In a letter to Washington of July 1791 while working on the second part of *Rights of Man,* Paine expressed his surprise that "principle is not confined to Time or place, and that the ardor of Seventy six is capable of renewing itself."[18]

Across the Atlantic, Jefferson and many others drew the same conclusion: that the fates of the revolutions in America and France were now more closely connected than ever before. The crisis created by the flight to Varennes was the result "of that form of government which heaps importance on Ideots, and which the tories of the present day are trying to preach into our favour. I still hope the French revolution will issue happily. I feel that the permanence of our own leans in some degree on that; and that a failure there would be a powerful argument to prove there must be a failure here."[19]

For the moment, however, the constitutional monarchists in the National Assembly managed to force the French republican movement underground through mass arrests, the closing down of clubs, and censorship of radical newspapers. Again, Short heartily approved these "rigorous" measures, as, in his view, the republican agitators were likely to be "emissaries of foreign powers." He assured Jefferson that although Condorcet supported "the

Republican side with his pen," fortunately there was "no member of the assembly of your acquaintance on that side." In fact, Condorcet's conversion to republicanism led to a bitter falling-out with his old friend La Rochefoucauld. The triumph of the constitutional monarchists was short-lived. The Legislative Assembly, elected in late September 1791, contained almost no clerics or nobles. Its deputies, as Morris noted, were "deeply imbued with republican or rather democratical principles."[20] The most powerful faction to emerge from the Assembly was the Girondins (also known as Brissotins or Rolandins at the time), a coalition of deputies from the Gironde region, like Jean-Marie Roland, and Paris journalists and intellectuals, like Brissot and Condorcet.

In March 1792 the king was forced to dismiss the Feuillant ministry and appoint the Girondin leadership, including Clavière, Roland, and army general Charles-François Dumouriez, in their place. A horrified Short reported to Jefferson: "The *club des Jacobins* have at length obtained the triumph they have been long aiming at by all sorts of means. They have forced the King to take the members of his council from their body, so that all the present ministers except that of the war department, are the most violent, popular and leading members of the club des Jacobins whose exaggerated and dangerous principles have been long known wherever the French revolution has been heard of."

This condemnation of the Girondins suggests the strength of Short's attachment to the conservative constitutional monarchists, because it contradicted his primary official duty, the promotion of American trade interests, which were bound to benefit from the ascendancy of the pro-American Girondins. Short grudgingly acknowledged that the change in the ministry "exhibits a favorable prospect for changing the decrees of the former assembly relative to the articles of our commerce," that is, the repeal of high import duties on American salted provisions and tobacco. Short promised Jefferson, "We may count on an alteration in the decrees relative to our commerce being proposed by that minister [Clavière] and supported in the assembly, by Warville and the popular party who form a decided and large majority."[21]

Jefferson approved of this latest change in the French government not only because of the improved chances for a new commercial treaty. Anticipating his "Adam and Eve" letter, he wrote to James Madison: "Notwithstanding the very general abuse of the Jacobins, I begin to consider them as representing the true revolution-spirit of the whole nation, and as carrying the nation with them. The only things wanting with them is more experience in business, and a little more conformity to the established style of communication with foreign powers."[22] Ironically, despite Short's denunciation of the Girondins' "exaggerated and dangerous principles," it was his anxious dispatches on "public opinion" and "the spirit of the people" that had furnished Jefferson with the materials for his optimistic assessment of "the true revolution-spirit of the whole nation." Jefferson concluded that French public opinion had matured much faster than he had anticipated in 1789 and was ready to embrace republicanism.

On 16 August 1792, three years after their last meeting in Paris, Gouverneur Morris, the new American minister to France, wrote to Jefferson: "Another Revolution has been effected in this City. It was bloody." Morris's appointment had passed in the U.S. Senate only by a narrow margin and created much resentment in Paris, where his close ties to the royal ministers and the king were well known. Short, who had pinned his hopes on obtaining the position, had tried everything to discredit his rival in America, even sending Jefferson a hostile French newspaper article on Morris. Although Short was named minister resident to the Batavian Republic, he took Jefferson's failure to support his promotion in Paris as a personal betrayal.[23]

Over the summer of 1792 Morris had conspired with Minister of the Interior Terrier de Monciel, Minister of the Navy Bertrand de Moleville, former Foreign Minister Montmorin, and *monarchiens* Malouet, Lally-Tollendal, and Clermont-Tonnerre to smuggle the royal family out of France. But it was too late. On 10 August 1792 the National Guard and sans-culottes crowds stormed the Tuileries palace on the orders of the Paris sections (electoral districts). The Legislative Assembly declared the monarchy suspended and put the king under house arrest. Although Morris's predictions had been vindicated, he found that it was "nevertheless a painful reflection that one of the first countries in the world should be so cruelly torn to pieces."[24]

Still, Morris was convinced that he needed to remain at his post in Paris. First, he felt obliged to give whatever protection he could to his aristocratic friends and associates. Some of Morris's co-conspirators managed to escape, but others, like Clermont-Tonnerre, were murdered in the street or, like

Montmorin, imprisoned. Morris was besieged with requests for passports, from Americans and non-Americans. When Baltimore merchant Thomas Griffith visited the American minister's residence on 13 August, he "found at his house a number of gentlemen and ladies, who from former intercourse with America, and in many cases services rendered to the United States considered themselves entitled to protection in the hotel of the minister." These included Morris's lover, Adèle de Flahaut, and her son, his friend the Countess of Albany, Foreign Minister Claude Bigot de Sainte-Croix, and Monciel. Morris asked Griffith to witness, "if my protection of these persons should become a matter of reproach to me, here or at home (and I have reason to expect it will, from what I have already experienced), that I did not invite them to come, but that I will not put them out now that they are here, let the consequences be what they may."[25]

Second, although the "different Embassadors and Ministers are all taking their Flight and if I stay I shall be alone," Morris argued that his departure would call into question the republican principle of popular sovereignty: "Going hence [to England] however would look like taking Part against the late Revolution and I am not only unauthoriz'd in this Respect but I am bound to suppose that if the great Majority of the Nation adhere to the new Form the United States will approve thereof because in the first Place we have no Right to prescribe to this Country the Government they shall adopt and next because the Basis of our own Constitution is the indefeasible Right of the People to establish it." Despite Morris's sympathy for the victims of the Second Revolution, he regarded the universal principle of popular sovereignty as more important than the particular character of the new regime. As we have seen in the previous chapter, Morris's universalist relativism had not deterred him from trying "to prescribe to this Country the Government they shall adopt." But withholding recognition from the French Republic, regardless of how wrongheaded or criminal it appeared to him, would have allowed other nations to challenge the legitimacy of the American republic. Even before he received Morris's letter, Jefferson expressed the view that the United States should recognize any foreign government that was "formed by the will of the nation substantially declared." While Jefferson was predisposed to detect in a republican revolution the "will of the nation," which he like the French revolutionaries understood as necessarily unanimous, it seems likely that he would have denied that the same will was at work in a restoration of the monarchy. Still, despite their diametrically opposed views on the French Republic, Morris's and Jefferson's different universalisms again led them to similar conclusions.[26]

Conversely, William Short, who had moved to The Hague in May, immediately rejected the new regime as illegitimate. Identifying completely with the perspective of his aristocratic circle in Paris, he declared to Jefferson that his thoughts during the events of "that execrable day and night" of 10 August were with the royal family, who suffered "a thousand deaths daily." Short even refused to transmit a previously agreed-upon installment of the still-outstanding American debt to France to the Amsterdam banking house of what he called, in a letter to Secretary of the Treasury Alexander Hamilton, "the usurpers in France." Morris had to remind his young colleague that the "Corner Stone of our own Constitution is the Right of the People to establish such Government as they think proper."[27]

Although they disagreed about the legitimacy of the French interim government, Short and Morris were both horrified by the extreme violence in Paris during the so-called September Massacres. In the first two weeks of September, crowds and makeshift tribunals killed about half the prison population of Paris, between 1,100 and 1,400 men and women. The central committee of the Paris sections was the driving force behind the massacres, which shocked even the radical Jacobin deputies, known as the Montagnard, or the Mountain, led by Robespierre, George-Jacques Danton, and Marat. But neither they nor the Girondins dared to condemn the carnage. Some Girondins concluded that, innocent victims notwithstanding, the people had been right to act quickly and indiscriminately before prison inmates with ties to local traitors and émigrés had the chance to overrun the capital. Condorcet blamed the legacy of absolutism, and deplored the "unhappy and terrible situation, in which the character of a naturally good and generous people is forced to wreak such vengeance."[28]

On 4 September La Rochefoucauld was arrested near his estate and, on the way to Paris, killed in front of Rosalie and his mother.[29] Short hoped that the murder of a close friend would make Jefferson realize how far the French Revolution had deviated from its original aims and from the American model: "The names of the unfortunate victims who were known to you will shew you that the constant practise of public and private virtues–continued sacrifices of rank and fortune and whatever most men value highest, to the desire of public good–constant and disinterested efforts in favor of public liberty, so far from securing respect and protection have become motives for proscription, imprisonment and massacre in the eyes of those monsters who then directed the blind multitude."[30]

Morris's reports of the September Massacres to Jefferson contained unusually graphic descriptions of crowd violence. He focused on the killing of the Princess de Lamballe, a close friend of the queen and superintendent of the royal household:

> Madame de Lamballe was (I believe) the only Woman kill'd, and she was beheaded and emboweled, the Head and the Entrails were paraded on Pikes thro the Street and the body dragged after them. They continued I am told at the Temple [where the royal family was detained] till the Queen look'd out at this horrid Spectacle. . . . A Guard had been sent a few Days since to make the Duke de la Rochefoucauld Prisoner. He was on his way to Paris, under their Escort, with his Wife and Mother when he was taken out of his Carriage and killed. The Ladies were taken back to la roche guyonne [the family's country estate] where they are now in a State of Arrestation. Monsieur de Montmorin was among those slain at the Abbaye.[31]

It is notable that Morris emphasized the violation of a female body and a female sensibility in this letter, while he reported the death of two close male associates in a matter-of-fact style. This emphasis is reminiscent of Burke's famous account of the invasion of Marie Antoinette's chambers during the October Days, which heralded the end of the "age of chivalry." Both texts sought to demonstrate the revolution's monstrosity by juxtaposing the primitive violence of the mob and the delicacy and refinement of a noblewoman. If a nation's state of civilization could be gauged by its treatment of women, as many authors in Europe and America believed, then the degradation and abuse of women (as well as their political activism) in France was a clear sign that the revolution threatened to undermine the most basic social values.

Morris was not the only one captivated by the princess's violent death, which in retellings took on ever more barbaric forms (including rape, dismemberment, genital mutilation, and evisceration) and made her a special object of fascination well into the nineteenth century. In the republican press, her body became a metaphor for the aristocratic conspiracies that only brute force could avert, expose, and destroy. For royalists and conservatives, the princess embodied the process of decivilization and degeneration inherent in the dismemberment of the monarchy.[32]

Perhaps Morris remembered from the murder of Foulon and Bertier in July 1789 that Jefferson tended to think about political violence in abstractions. Perhaps he was trying to compel the secretary of state to grapple with the reality of what he saw as the uncontrollable forces that the Jacobins had unleashed. In any case, Morris realized how easy it would be for American sympathizers with the revolution to dismiss his and others' accounts of atrocities as mere propaganda: "What will be your Feelings at the Scenes which have lately passed," he asked Robert Morris. "I will not pretend to describe what I wish to forget, and I fear also that a just Picture would be attributed rather to the Glow of Imagination than the lively coloring of Nature."[33]

In fact, Jefferson was not alone in putting a favorable spin on even the most disturbing news from France. American newspapers regularly blamed unwelcome information on the messenger, the British press, or found other ways to rationalize the revolutionary violence in France. The Republican *National Gazette,* whose creation Jefferson had encouraged, reported that the September Massacres had "made an example of two or three thousand scoundrels." The paper considered the mass executions well justified, as they served "to rescue the liberties of millions of honest men," and paled in comparison with the "vain wars" instigated by the French king, which had "covered the earth with the blood of individuals from one end of Europe to the other."[34]

On 22 September 1792, the newly elected National Convention declared France a republic. The same day, the French army stopped the advance of Prussian forces at Valmy, thereby saving the new republic from immediate destruction. This turn of events struck Short as "extraordinary, astonishing, and unaccountable." He considered the French victory a misfortune for the French people, as it strengthened the Jacobin regime: "The spirit which they [the Jacobins] will propagate is so destructive of all order and tranquility—and so subversive of all ideas of justice—the system they aim at so absolutely visionary and impracticable—that their efforts can end in nothing but despotism after having bewildered the unfortunate people, whom they render free in their way, in violence and crimes, and wearied them with sacrifices of blood, which alone they consider worthy of the furies whom they worship under the names *Liberté* and *Egalité.*"[35]

Unlike Short's earlier dispatches, his letters following 10 August prompted a substantial response from Jefferson, which has become famous as the "Adam and Eve" letter. On 3 January 1793, Jefferson felt it was time to deliver a stern lecture to his protégé about the stakes involved in the revolutions in America and France. "The liberty of the whole earth was depending on the issue of the contest," he reminded Short, "and was ever such a prize won with so little innocent blood? My own affections have been deeply wounded by some of the martyrs to this cause, but rather than it should have failed, I would have seen half the earth desolated. Were there but an Adam and an Eve left in every country, and left free, it would be better than as it now is."[36]

Until the mid-1990s, most studies of Jefferson did not pay much attention to this letter, and some ignored it entirely. It only became controversial when Conor Cruise O'Brien's *The Long Affair* (1996) used it as evidence of Jefferson's genocidal mindset, which supposedly made him a forerunner of Pol Pot. Since then, it has become obligatory for Jefferson biographers to dismiss this claim and ascribe the passage quoted above to Jefferson's "penchant for rhetorical bravado."[37] However, this reading merely begs the question why Jefferson felt that this occasion called for such undeniably extreme "rhetorical flourishes." The answer lies in Jefferson's decade-long relationship with Short, whose role as addressee has been completely ignored.

Since 1788, the two major themes of their correspondence had been Short's persistent appeals to Jefferson to help him get a diplomatic appointment and Jefferson's continual concern that Short might become estranged from his native country. After his rapid advancement in Virginia, Short had good reason to count on Jefferson's patronage. He repeatedly pointed to his popularity among the diplomatic corps and important figures from Jefferson's circle. Perhaps at Short's suggestion, Lafayette and the duchesse La Rochefoucauld d'Enville sent flattering evaluations of Short's character to Washington and Jefferson.[38]

However, Jefferson considered Short's deep immersion in French polite society not an asset but a liability for a republican representative. He disapproved of Short's infatuation with French women, which he suspected contributed to Short's desire to remain in France. Therefore, to prove his point that the "only resource then for a durable happiness is to return to

America," Jefferson linked the choice between France and America to the choice between a fleeting affair and the blessings of a stable marriage. Any romantic attachment other than marriage, no matter how alluring in the short term, could only lead to loneliness later in life. The foundation for a long and happy marriage needed to be laid now, in Short's youth, and, most importantly, in America. (In a sense, this is the choice Jefferson himself had made in Paris. Instead of pursuing the married English artist Maria Cosway, Jefferson had begun a relationship with his adolescent slave, the Virginia-born Sally Hemings—a relationship that conveniently for Jefferson could be as stable and marriage-like as he wished without ever forcing him to break the promise he had made to his dying wife not to remarry.) The longer Short stayed in Europe, the less likely he was to succeed in the United States, until he would become a stranger in his native country, at home nowhere.[39]

This advice seems at odds with Jefferson's cosmopolitanism and love of France. However, he believed that Americans could only benefit from the sophistication of French culture after their moral character had been fully developed at home and they had learned to appreciate their own simpler society. Otherwise, the unfortunate traveler would long to be part of a foreign nation that would never completely accept him, and become estranged from his own country, which would inevitably fail to live up to his inflated expectations.[40]

In response to Short's numerous self-promoting letters, Jefferson sent a stern reminder that to gain an important diplomatic position, Short would have to become "known to the public" in America and gain "their confidence which is as necessary as that of the person appointing in a government like ours." When Short nonetheless persisted in his appeals, Jefferson became even more offended by the suggestion that it was in his power to procure his protégé a public office. Short's sense of entitlement was a disturbing sign that he had "forgotten [his] countrymen altogether, as well as the nature of our government." He once again assured Short that "it is for your happiness and success to return. Every day increases your attachment to Europe and renders your future reconcilement to your own country more desperate."[41]

Appealing to Jefferson's cosmopolitanism, Short denied that he had to choose between loyalty to his native home and attachment to his adopted country. In fact, his long residence in Europe had given him a broader perspective on American national interests and "a more perfect acquaintance with such circumstances of the U.S. as are necessary for advancing their interests here, because from hence the U.S. are generalized and always examined under the idea of their relations with foreign countries." With his ideas "unfettered by those of detail and locality" and constantly required to think of the United States as one nation, an American in Paris or London had a different but equally valuable viewpoint on American affairs as a resident of Philadelphia. Yet, for Jefferson, the American nation was more than the sum of its interests. For an American representative to be able to speak on behalf of the nation, he had to be intimately familiar with the national character of the people, which was still in an ongoing process of evolution. This is why Jefferson believed it necessary to recall "foreign servants after a certain time of absence from their own country, because they lose in time that sufficient degree of intimacy with it's circumstances which alone can enable them to know and pursue it's interests."[42]

Likewise, "the extreme warmth" with which Short had "censured the proceedings of the Jacobins of France" in his reports caused Jefferson personal "pain," because it proved how alienated Short had become from his compatriots. "I have expressed to you my sentiments, because they are really those of 99 in a hundred of our citizens," Jefferson explained. "The universal feasts, and rejoicings which have lately been had on account of the successes of the French shewed the genuine effusions of their hearts. You have been wounded by the sufferings of your friends, and have by this circumstance been hurried into a temper of mind which would be extremely disrelished if known to your countrymen." Just as Short was wrong to count on personal favors to achieve public recognition, so it was entirely inappropriate for him to put his own moral judgment, clouded by personal attachments, over that of both the American and the French peoples. Jefferson did not deny that the revolution had claimed innocent victims. In fact, he avowed that his "own affections have been deeply wounded by some of the martyrs to this cause," like La Rochefoucauld. Still, this did not give Jefferson or Short the right to presume that they knew better than the people or to put private feeling before public duty.[43]

The shared fundamental premise of the republican revolutions in America and France was that the people were the source of all legitimate authority. Over the course of his tenure in Paris, Jefferson had become convinced that, despite the important role of enlightened elites in educating and shaping public opinion, it was the people's moral development, not that of a few individuals, that determined the course of public policy. When Brissot had asked Jefferson in February 1788 to join the Société des Amis des Noirs, which was dedicated to the abolition of the Atlantic slave trade and gradual emancipation in the French colonies, the American responded that although he supported the society's program, taking a public stand would be inappropriate for the official representative of a nation where slavery was still widely accepted. Moreover, joining an antislavery organization abroad, Jefferson claimed, would hurt his efforts to work for emancipation at home. This answer might appear to be a feeble excuse, as Jefferson did nothing to advance the cause of antislavery after his return to America. However, it accurately predicted the nationalist attacks in France against the Amis des Noirs, which was accused of conspiring to subvert national interests and destroy colonial trade. It also reflected Jefferson's belief that it was both unethical and counterproductive to advance too far ahead of public opinion, even for the best of causes.[44]

As he had done in the summer of 1789, Jefferson still regarded revolutionary violence as a necessary, if regrettably imprecise, articulation of a popular political consciousness. Like Condorcet, Jefferson argued that the French people, whose moral development had been retarded by centuries of oppression, were bound to overshoot the mark: "It was necessary to use the arm of the people, a machine not quite so blind as balls and bombs, but blind to a certain degree." Rather than proclaiming moral absolutism, as O'Brien read Jefferson's letter, it expressed a profound moral relativism.[45]

Jefferson's moral relativism did not diminish his political universalism. He had long regarded the successful creation of a national community based on common principles to be "worth a great deal of blood." In 1786, before the Dutch Revolution, he wrote to Charles Dumas that struggles for national self-determination were "a great sacrifice to the present race of men but valuable to their posterity." Now it was the turn of the United States and France to undergo this process of nation-building, with all its unfortunate, but unavoidable, costs. Despite its former attachment to the king, the French "Nation" was "now generally Jacobin." Likewise, except a few individuals "high in office" or "possessing great wealth," the United States was "entirely republican." According to Jefferson, even President Washington "considered France as the sheet anchor of this country," and had asked him to remind Short that "you should consider yourself as the representative of your country and that what you say might be imputed to your constituents."[46]

Although Jefferson claimed that Washington had read Short's dispatches and disapproved of their critical tone, Jefferson's own notes of the conversation in question indicate that Washington made no such criticism. In fact, Jefferson had earlier that year expressed his concern about Washington's "want of confidence in the event of the French revolution," for which he blamed Morris: "The fact is that Gouverneur Morris, a high flying Monarchy-man, shutting his eyes and his faith to every fact against his wishes, and believing every thing he desires to be true, has kept the President's mind constantly poisoned with his forebodings."[47]

Ironically, Jefferson's own view of the French Revolution was shaped by the "forebodings" in Morris's and Short's letters. Jefferson was rather hazy about the French political landscape, and especially about the divisions within the Jacobins between the Girondins and the more radical Montagnards. This lack of differentiation reflected the conservative leanings of Short and Morris, who pejoratively referred to both the Girondins and their opponents as "Jacobins." For Jefferson, the difference between the "Jacobins," whom he equated with the Girondins, and the Feuillants, was the same as that between the Patriot Party and the *monarchiens* at the time of his tenure in Paris, "both having in object the establishment of a free constitution, and differing only on the question whether their chief Executive should be hereditary or not." During Jefferson's time in Paris, both Patriots and *monarchiens* had been constitutional monarchists. In contrast, after the flight of the king, several leading Girondins had become republicans, and the Montagnards advocated a popular democracy. Moreover, Jefferson's analysis completely ignored the schisms caused by such measures as the abolition of nobility and the Civil Constitution of the Clergy, as well as the growing activism of formerly "passive citizens" from the lower classes.

It was precisely this elision of deep divisions within the French nation, as well as his own, that allowed Jefferson to portray the enemies of the revolution as outside the body politic. French revolutionaries, from Sieyès to Louis de Saint-Just, made the same rhetorical move during the trial of the king. Because the American and French nations embodied universal principles, those who claimed to speak for the nation came to regard their opponents as "foreigners," estranged from the regenerated community of citizens. This sharp distinction between insiders and outsiders temporarily reinforced the ties of solidarity between republicans in America and France. "The successes of republicanism in France have given the coup de grace to [the Federalists'] prospects," Jefferson enthused to Short. The outcome of the struggle in the beleaguered French republic was critical for the future of the American republic and thus for the "liberty of the whole earth."[48]

The exclusion of whole groups from the republican community allowed Jefferson and the more radical French revolutionaries to imagine the elimination of their opponents as a ritual of purification and regeneration. Jefferson's vision of "half the world desolate," with "but an Adam and an Eve left in every country," used the same apocalyptic "language of purgation" with which Marat and Saint-Just justified the bloody vengeance of the people against their enemies. In a message from the National Convention to President Washington that linked French triumphs over "the coalition of Kings" at Jemappes, Savoy, and Flanders to American victories at Saratoga, Trenton, and Yorktown, the French republicans vowed that "not a frenchman shall remain, or they shall be free. Liberty shall become extinct in Europe, or our principles shall triumph every where over the league of despots."[49]

Irrespective of his own religious beliefs, Jefferson used language redolent of Scripture (heretics, martyrs, Adam and Eve) for its emotional impact, particularly in this case, as he was trying to bring a prodigal son back to the fold. Despite his Manichean worldview, Jefferson did not belong to the growing number of American millennialists who believed that the French Revolution portended the imminence of the Last Days. Jefferson's use of religious metaphors had more in common with those French revolutionaries who sought to substitute what David Bell termed "the cult of the nation" for religious dogma as the unifying force of post-revolutionary society, but whose vision of the nation as a universal human community retained a distinctly religious quality.[50] (The next chapter examines more closely the idea of national regeneration, a concept that even after having been secularized remained quasi-miraculous.)

However, the message of the National Convention and Jefferson's letter also betrayed a tension between an inclusive vision of transatlantic republican solidarity and an exclusive idea of national destiny. For Jefferson, the "liberty of the whole earth" really meant the liberty of the national community "in every country." Likewise, the National Convention equated "Liberty" and "our principles," that is, French principles, which were both universal and national. The phrase "an Adam and an Eve left in every country," which designated conjugal consent as the foundation of national unity and self-determination, echoed Jefferson's admonitions to Short from March 1789 to end his French affair in favor of an American marriage. For all the affinities between American and French republicans, each country had its own "Adam and Eve," its own particular form of gender relations, and therefore its own national character. As Jefferson had reminded Short, once he returned to America, he would realize that "the happiness of your own country is more tranquil, more unmixed, more permanent."[51]

This kind of fatherly advice came to an end with the 3 January letter: "I have written to you in the stile to which I have been always accustomed with you, and which perhaps it is time I should lay aside. But while old men feel sensibly enough their own advance in years, they do not sufficiently recollect it in those whom they have seen young." Despite Jefferson's effort to close the letter on a cordial note, there was an undertone of disappointment. By refusing to return to the United States, Short had squandered his talents, failed to be most useful to his country, and ignored Jefferson's repeated counsel. At the same time, the demands and complaints that filled Short's frequent letters to Jefferson revealed an unhealthy dependency on his mentor. It was time for Jefferson to grant Short his independence from an unequal relationship that had become painful to both parties.[52]

In his response to Jefferson's letter, Short assured him, "No body on earth can wish better to France than I do whatever form of government its inhabitants may give themselves—their happiness and prosperity I desire most sincerely both as a friend to humanity and citizen of America." Short hoped that his assessment of the Jacobins would be proven wrong, but insisted that Jefferson would have come to the same conclusions "if you had been in the way of seeing and examining them with your own eyes."[53] Would Jefferson's views on the French Revolution have been different had he stayed in Paris? The aristocratic manners and pro-British attitudes he found upon his return to America certainly shaped his understanding of the French Revolution's significance for the future of the United States. Still, it seems likely that had he remained in Paris, Jefferson would have followed a similar path of political radicalization as his friend Thomas Paine. The two men had conversed and corresponded regularly in 1789, and both supported the French constitutional monarchy until the flight of the king. Moreover, the conversion to republicanism of his closest French ally, Condorcet, would have exerted a strong influence on Jefferson.

While the flight of the king, the Second Revolution, and the creation of the French Republic clarified the ideological front lines for Jefferson, the same events left a conservative revolutionary like Short lost and confused. Short could not help but note the irony that while Jefferson reproached him for his lack of republican fervor, as an American, he was considered at The Hague, "by all the people with whom I kept company, as a violent Jacobin." It was even more galling that Short's condemnation of the Jacobins should attract the attention of the president, "whilst he remained ignorant of Mr. Morris's words at Paris not only against the Jacobins but against the principles of the revolution—and his deeds against the constitution itself." Understandably, Short felt that Morris was being rewarded for holding the exact same opinions for which he was being censured.

As the French Revolution emerged as one of the central issues in American politics, Short's conduct as chargé d'affaires in Paris came under close scrutiny. In a report to the Senate on foreign loans, Hamilton blamed Short for having failed to make any payments on the American debt to France between December 1791 and August 1792. The report was designed to refute charges that it was Hamilton who had unduly delayed payment of the debt out of hostility to the French Revolution. It included copies of letters on this subject by Short and Morris, and thus made public both Short's denouncements of the Second Revolution and Morris's insistence that the interim government had to be treated as the French people's legitimate representative. Jefferson noted that Short's diatribes against French republicans were "extremely grating here, tho they are those of Hamilton himself and the monocrats of his cabal." Ironically, the letters made Morris appear as a "democrat," compared to Short.[54]

If it might seem predictable that an inexperienced American with aristocratic sympathies would get caught in the crossfire, in fact, the shifting political landscapes in France proved treacherous for even the most celebrated revolutionaries. The second part of Paine's *Rights of Man*, published in February 1792, created an even bigger sensation than the first, earning its author honorary French citizenship and a conviction for treason in England. Paine declared his break with the constitutional monarchists by dedicating the book to Lafayette. Although he claimed that he and Lafayette differed, "not as to principles of government, but as to time" which would be necessary to realize them, Paine clearly suggested that Lafayette had fallen behind the times: "I wish you to hasten your principles, and overtake me."[55]

However, despite the perfect fit of *Rights of Man, Part II* with Girondin ideology, the French reception of the translation of both parts by François Lanthenas, published in April 1792, was markedly reserved, especially in comparison with the overwhelming response in Britain. Eliminating the dedication to Lafayette, Lanthenas noted: "Paine, that uncorrupted friend of freedom, believed too in the sincerity of Lafayette. . . . Bred at a distance from courts, the austere American does not seem any more on his guard against the artful ways and speech of courtiers than some Frenchmen who resemble him."[56]

Paine's transatlantic celebrity as a best-selling author made him a useful ally in the struggle between the Girondins and their opponents among the Jacobins, the Montagnards. But there remained some lingering resentment even among his allies that Paine had left France for England on 13 July 1791, four days before the National Guard had shot republican petitioners in the so-called Massacre of the Champ de Mars, and had forced the republican movement underground. Having shared none of the sacrifices, Paine now seemed to reap all the rewards. Girondin leader Marie-Jeanne Roland noted dismissively that she considered Paine "better fitted to sow the seeds of popular commotion, than to lay the foundations or prepare the form of government."[57] Even at the moment of his greatest triumph, soon crowned by his election to the National Convention in September 1792, Paine remained an outsider. The sharp distinction between those on the inside of the national community and those on the outside had made all enemies into foreigners. From there, it was only a small step to turning all foreigners into enemies.

3

Cosmopolitan Sensibilities and National Regeneration

THE WORK OF JOEL BARLOW, 1792–1794

On 28 November 1792 sobs resounded in the Salle de Manège near the Tuileries Palace, the former royal riding school that had served as the meeting place of French parliamentarians since the October Days. In an emotional address to the National Convention, the American poet Joel Barlow, appearing as a representative of the British Society for Constitutional Information, invoked the bonds of sentiment that naturally linked all nations.[1] The common people of Europe were tired of war and oppression, Barlow declared, and had begun to understand that "both the one and the other are the offspring of unnatural combinations in society as relative to systems of government, not the result of the natural temper of nations as relative to each others' happiness." France's neighbors were only waiting "to be delivered by your arms from the dreaded necessity of fighting against them." Waging war to end all wars, the French would replace monarchical patriarchy with "the bond of fraternal union to the human race, in which union our own nation [England] will surely be one of the first to concur."[2]

According to Barlow, the response from the French legislators was overwhelming: "The scene was truly interesting to every feeling of humanity, and drew tears from a crowded assembly. It gave rise to reflexions, which can scarcely be conceived." The event marked "the reconciliation of brothers,

64

who had long been excited to a mortal enmity by misunderstanding and mutual imposition." The president of the National Convention, Barlow's friend abbé Henri Grégoire, ordered the address to be printed, distributed to all French départements, and translated into other European languages.

No doubt the deputies of the National Convention found it reassuring to hear from an American representing a British organization that other nations would welcome the French as liberators. Only nine days earlier, in a dramatic gesture, the Convention had promised aid and fraternity to all European peoples who wished to recover their liberty. Barlow offered a beguilingly simple solution to the Convention's daunting task of simultaneously transforming France into a republic and defeating the republic's enemies abroad. The American posited that the kind of political, social, and moral regeneration that the French revolutionaries were trying to accomplish would not require force but would occur naturally through persuasion and emotion. As people everywhere became aware of the self-evident truths that the old regimes had suppressed, they inevitably would come to see the world and their place in it through more rational eyes. Fortunately for the French, Barlow claimed, people throughout Europe had already begun to understand that "unnatural combinations in society" were responsible for their problems and that they had more in common with the French people than with their own oppressive governments.

Barlow here addressed one of the central questions of the age: how to transform, or regenerate, former royal subjects into republican citizens. On the one hand, people were the product of their particular circumstances, which was why monarchical societies had been able to replicate themselves for so long. On the other hand, republicans had to believe that if they only created the right conditions, then the mentality that had sustained inequality could be eradicated and replaced by one more suited to a republic. This problem had already been at the heart of the debate about the new French constitution in 1789, before anyone had dreamed of a French republic. What both debates had in common was a fundamental ambiguity about the agent of social and political transformation: who was in charge of regeneration, and who was in need of being regenerated? Just as the constitution was said to both reflect and shape the political habits of the nation, republicans described the process of regeneration sometimes as occurring naturally and already in motion and sometimes as requiring sustained and substantial efforts on the part of the revolutionary state. The failure of the constitution to create a national consensus and the growing hostility between France and other European powers lent even greater urgency to these questions.

The concept of sensibility proved extremely useful in eliding such issues of agency and power. The reaction of the French delegates to Barlow's speech demonstrated in miniature how sensibility and regeneration would work in tandem. A foreigner speaking on behalf of another nation, Britain, from which his own country had recently separated and which was traditionally hostile to France, managed to move his audience to tears. The shedding of tears made tangible the power of sensibility, which would form the bridge between what people in France and elsewhere had been and what they could become. In addition to changing peoples' minds to counteract monarchical "impositions," it was necessary to purify their hearts to allow the "natural temper of nations" to emerge, which desired peace, reconciliation, and universal happiness. Sensibility regenerated individuals and entire nations from within through shared emotions rather than through the exercise of external power. It was testimony to the public significance accorded emotions at the time that Grégoire ordered accounts of this display of the affective ties between America, Britain, and France to be printed, translated, and distributed as widely as possible, with the intention of reaching the hearts and minds of a national and international audience. But ascribing so much power to sensibility, which appeared both as a part of human nature and as a faculty that could be molded and directed by the state, left unresolved who would be the agent and who would be the object of regeneration.

This ambiguity was reflected in the double image of the French Revolution in Barlow's writings. Barlow elaborated on the benign vision of the workings of regeneration in his *Advice to the Privileged Orders* and *Letter to the National Convention,* which earned him French citizenship in early 1793. At the same time, he understood that regeneration in France and Europe also depended on the power of "French arms" and in his poem *The Conspiracy of Kings* and his *Letter to the People of Piedmont* celebrated a much more martial image of the revolution, obliterating all resistance in its path.

Barlow entered the French debate about regeneration at a critical moment. The war in Europe and the deepening divisions within French society raised the question of how to deal with those who refused to submit to the demands of regeneration. Even more dangerous than the conspiracy of kings encircling France were the enemies within, from refractory priests and provincial rebels to "foreigners" and "false patriots." Barlow endorsed harsh measures against all enemies of national regeneration, or as he put it, using the "rod of correction." Sensibility served not only to forge bonds between revolutionaries across national boundaries, it also promised to expose hidden enemies through their lack of genuine fervor. But as the frequent political turnabouts made sensibility an increasingly unreliable guide, and France began to suffer a string of defeats on the battlefield, literal foreigners like Barlow came under suspicion of trying to sabotage national regeneration. In particular, the discrepancy between the cosmopolitan rhetoric of Americans in Paris and the strained relations between the American and French republics sowed seeds of doubt among French revolutionaries that would continue to grow over the course of the decade.

Barlow's position at the intersection between the American and French revolutions granted him unique insights into commonalties between the two revolutions but also blinded him to some of the particular challenges facing French revolutionaries. Barlow recognized that French and American republicans shared the same longing for spontaneous order in society, for the disappearance of conflict and power, and for the complete transparency of emotions and motives. The notion of war as a unifying act of national renewal and redemption, which Barlow's friends among the Girondins championed, was quite familiar to Americans from their own War of Independence. Barlow became convinced that because French revolutionaries faced greater obstacles than their American predecessors, the example of regeneration in France was crucial to completing the same process in the United States. However, Barlow displayed little appreciation of the nature of these obstacles, most notably the issue of religion and its relationship to the revolution. This lack of understanding left Barlow and other Americans unprepared for the intensity of the civil war and the Terror that convulsed the French Republic in 1793-94.

Before he traveled to France in 1788, Barlow adhered to the federalist ideology that prevailed throughout New England at the time.[3] He praised John Adams's *Defence of the Constitutions of the United States* (1787) and collaborated with John Trumbull, David Humphreys, and Lemuel Shaw on a series of poems entitled *The Anarchiad* (1786-87), which satirized the agrarian insurrection led by Daniel Shays. After achieving renown as a poet with *The Vision of Columbus* (1787), Barlow went to France as the agent of Scioto Associates and tried to sell land holdings in the Ohio Country to French investors and émigrés. Upon his arrival in Paris, Barlow was taken aback to hear French aristocrats criticize the American constitution as reactionary and agreed with Jefferson and Morris that the French were "as intemperate in their view of liberty as we were in the year seventy-five."[4]

When the fraudulent business practices of Scioto Associates caused a scandal in France, Barlow decided to pursue a new career as a political pamphleteer. In 1792, now a member of a close-knit circle of radical British writers that included Paine, Mary Wollstonecraft, William Godwin, and Joseph Priestley, Barlow authored *Advice to the Privileged Orders*, a response to Burke's *Reflections* and a clarion call to the monarchs of Europe to reform peacefully from above or be toppled violently from below. He predicted that the future of Europe would not depend on writers like him or Burke, but rather on "a much more important class of men, the class that cannot write; and in a great measure, on those who cannot read. It is to be decided by men who reason better without books, than we do with all the books in the world."[5]

Barlow's transformation from a defender of American class privilege to the spokesman of the illiterate European masses has aroused much suspicion among both contemporaries and historians.[6] Yet Barlow was hardly the only ambitious provincial whom the French Revolution offered a new beginning; both Barlow's friend Jacques-Pierre Brissot and his future nemesis Maximilien Robespierre were among those seizing the chance for a new identity. Barlow's enthusiasm for the French Revolution endured through the Terror, the Quasi-War, and the first years of Napoleon's reign because it was based on more than opportunism. The experience of the French Revolution transformed his understanding of human nature and of the possibilities for social and political reformation. "It must be confessed," Barlow argued in *Advice to the Privileged Orders*, "that the opinions we have formed of the human heart stand a chance of being erroneous; as they have been formed under the disguise of impressions which do not belong to its nature. The picture of man could not have been fairly drawn while he sat with a veil upon his face." The rejection of Old Regime ideas and institutions had removed this veil and cleared the path for man's complete regeneration. The new man "rises into the light, astonished at what he is, ashamed of what he has been, and unable to conjecture at what he may arrive."[7]

The regeneration that Barlow celebrated in this passage was one of the key concepts of the French Revolution. From its original religious connotations of baptism and resurrection, *régénération* acquired new secular meanings in the second half of the eighteenth century, most notably in Diderot and d'Alembert's *Encyclopédie* and in the marquis de Mirabeau's *L'ami des hommes* (1756–60). In the years leading up to the summoning of the Estates-General in 1789, more and more writers began to use it to describe the societal renewal that they felt needed to occur in France. They believed that regeneration was no longer only in God's hands but that concerted human action could change the course of history. According to Alyssa Sepinwall, the centrality of the concept of regeneration distinguished French revolutionary discourse from its American counterpart. But even though American revolutionaries did not use the same term, they shared the concerns that helped make the concept so popular in France. How could a former colony or a former monarchy produce a citizenry capable of sustaining a republican form of government? How could newly minted republics create unified nations out of extremely diverse populations?[8]

As defined by Barlow's close friend Henri Grégoire, regeneration meant that all citizens had to be "melted into the national mass," making one out of many. Religious denominations, ethnic minorities, and regional interests all would have to give up their differences and assimilate to the national union, based on the principles enshrined in the Declaration of the Rights of Man. American republicans placed less emphasis on homogeneity but faced the related quandary of being committed simultaneously to the ideal of equality, based on universally shared political beliefs, and to notions of inherent difference (including regional, religious, social, sexual, and racial differences). How much would such differences have to be muted in order to ensure national unity? Were there differences that remained completely beyond the power of regeneration? The last question was particularly pertinent with regard to sexual differences and caused much debate in the American and French republics about whether women could ever be transformed into fully regenerated citizens.[9]

Moreover, like the concept of "constitution," discussed in chapter 1, which could refer to both an already existing condition and a newly established set of principles, the idea of national regeneration contained a more fundamental ambiguity. Was it something that happened naturally and needed no more encouragement than the reforms already established in

1787 or 1789? Or did successful regeneration require an explicit and complete renunciation of the past and an elaborate, continuous program of re-education for all citizens? Like most French revolutionaries Barlow argued that regeneration was both a natural process and a political project. In *Letter to the National Convention* (1792), Barlow criticized those who could conceive of government only as "the most complicated systems . . . without which it has been supposed impossible for men to be governed." Instead, he asked his readers to "conceive of the simplicity to which the business of government may be reduced, and to which it must be reduced, if we would have it answer the purpose of promoting happiness." The political organizations of the Old Regimes of Europe were artificial, ornate, and wasteful, whereas nature's operations were simple, efficient, and transparent. In the same text, however, Barlow called upon the French deputies to develop a plan for the socialization of the new man. "In raising a people from slavery to freedom, you have called them to act on a new theatre," Barlow reminded the conventioneers, "and it is a necessary part of your business, to teach them how to perform their parts."[10] The challenge was not just to make new and better laws; the state also needed to create new and better citizens capable of understanding and internalizing the law. Since unlike the monarchy the new order was not founded in external coercion, the republic had to inculcate a new ethic of self-control. Therefore, in *Advice to the Privileged Orders,* Barlow laid out a detailed program of public instruction and social welfare to reform republican citizens from the inside and ensure their happiness and voluntary acquiescence with the government.

The ambiguity of regeneration stemmed in part from a paradoxical understanding of human nature. Barlow subscribed to the materialist position that man is by nature neither good nor bad but that society, experience, and education form his character and his ideas. Barlow likely had encountered various materialist conceptions of human nature in the works of his friends Joseph Priestley and William Godwin in Britain and Volney (Constantin-François de Chasseboeuf) in France, as well as in the widely reprinted and translated *Le système de la nature* (1770), by Paul-Henri Thiry d'Holbach.[11] The main purpose of *Advice to the Privileged Orders* was to expose the many forms of false consciousness, or "habits of thinking," through which the church, the military, and the courts had propped up the "feudal system" of Europe. Centuries of monarchical and ecclesiastical rule had conditioned the peoples of Europe to accept the present social arrangements as the natural, inevitable conditions of human existence rather than as an artificial, unreasonable, and exploitative system designed for the benefit of the few.

However, Barlow could not entirely accept the atheistic materialism of d'Holbach, who denied any distinction between trained habits and human nature. Instead he equivocated that it was "almost impossible to decide, among moral propensities, which of them belong to our nature, and which are the offspring of habit; how many of our vices are chargeable on the permanent qualities of man, and how many result from the mutable energies of state."[12] Barlow located the source of war, crime, and other evils sometimes in human nature as formed by society and sometimes in society itself. He professed that the abstract distinction between men's first and second natures did not matter, leaving unresolved whether the revolutionary state was meant to liberate a benevolent human nature from artificial social shackles or whether it needed to reshape an indifferent human nature according to the new dictates of reason. It remained equally ambiguous whether Barlow believed that human nature was everywhere the same or whether it was a product of particular circumstances. This vexed question had already divided Jefferson and Morris. After his arrival in Paris, Barlow had shared the other Americans' relativist views on the political situation in France. In his diary, he had expressed the hope that the Estates-General would only grant the French people "that portion of liberty which they can bear," since there were not five men in Europe who understood "the nature of liberty and the theory of government so well as they are understood by five hundred men in America."[13]

Four years later, in *Letter to the National Convention,* Barlow proclaimed a universal doctrine of popular sovereignty, free of considerations of political experience, national character, and moral development: "I am confident that any people, whether virtuous or vicious, wise or ignorant, numerous or few, rich or poor, are the best judges of their own wants relative to the restraints of law, and would always supply those wants better than they could be supplied by others."[14] Still, the full title of Barlow's *Letter* announced that it dealt with "the Defects in the Constitution of 1791," suggesting that the French people had in fact not been able to give themselves the best possible form of government. Barlow presumed to give advice to the French while claiming that they did not really need any guidance.

Moreover, Barlow wrote about national regeneration as a foreigner.

American and French revolutionaries, Barlow insisted, could learn from each other. The Americans had demonstrated that learning to *think* of liberty and equality as the natural, rational conditions of social life could make them a reality. But it would be the French Revolution that completed the process of national regeneration in America: "The Americans cannot be said as yet to have formed a national character. The political part of their revolution, aside from the military, was not of that violent and convulsive nature that shakes the whole fabric of human opinions, and enables men to decide which are to be retained as congenial to their situation, and which should be rejected as the offspring of unnatural connections." The unformed state of their national character made Americans look to France for guidance: "The public mind being open to receive impressions from abroad, they will be able to profit by the practical lessons which will now be afforded them from the change of system in this quarter of the world."[15]

It was precisely the "violent and convulsive nature" of the French Revolution that made it such a valuable example to the more sheltered Americans, even though Barlow was vague about how his characterization of the French Revolution could be reconciled with the peaceful process of regeneration he had described earlier. And why would these practical lessons from France have any relevance to the Americans if their nature had been formed under a completely different society? Likewise, what good would it do for the French to learn that the Americans had been able to overcome their particular, socially conditioned "habits of thinking"? At times Barlow seemed to hope that his good intentions alone would overcome such difficulties: "I love to indulge the belief, that it is true [that men are everywhere the same] so far as to ensure permanency to institutions that are good; but not so far as to discourage us from attempting to reform those that are bad."[16] But the real connection between the regeneration of the American and the French nations, according to Barlow, consisted in the power of sensibility.

A familiar concept throughout the Atlantic world since the mid-eighteenth century, sensibility had become an important subject in literature, aesthetics, philosophy, social commentary, and medicine.[17] While each field defined sensibility in a variety of ways, from the basic physiological capacity to react to stimuli to the source of sympathy, virtue, and compassion, they all endowed it with great power over the physical and moral natures of mankind. Sensibility provided a causal connection between the human body and its psychological, intellectual, and moral faculties, which helps to explain its attraction to a halfway materialist like Barlow. In a definition closely related to moral sense philosophy, sensibility denoted the capacity for intense moral feeling, particularly the ability to feel compassion for the suffering of others. Like the moral sense, sensibility became a surrogate for the classical republican virtue that political theorists for centuries had thought necessary for sustaining republican government. Natural sentiments like sociability, pity, benevolence, love, and gratitude took the place of virtue as the root of morality and the foundation of all social bonds. In the second part of *Advice to the Privileged Orders,* Barlow explained the connection between sentiment, morality, and society: "Men are gregarious in their nature. They form together in society, not merely from necessity, to avoid the evils of solitude, but from inclination and mutual attachment. They find positive pleasure in yielding assistance to each other, in communicating their thoughts and improving their faculties. This disposition in man is the source of morals; they have their foundation in nature, and receive their nourishment from society."[18]

Because the ability to feel and the desire to connect with others was fundamentally human, it was able to overcome superficial differences and create a national community. In this way, sensibility, fostered through education and culture, could serve as an agent of national regeneration. Moreover, sensibility connected people across national boundaries. "Society" was not limited to one country, Barlow declared, but rather the "different portions of this society . . . call themselves nations." Retreat to one's own country in the face of suffering anywhere in this international society was inexcusably selfish. Barlow offered his own experience as testimony to the power of sentiment. He confessed that he often had been tempted to "relinquish the disagreeable task which I had prescribed to myself in the first part of this work [*Advice*], and, returning to my country, endeavour in the new world to forget the miseries of the old." However, his sensibility would not allow it. The "contemplation of these miseries has already left an impression on my mind too deep to be easily effaced." Since the peoples of Europe, led by the French, were struggling to educate and liberate themselves, "every person who but thinks he can throw the least light upon the subject, is called upon for his assistance; and his duty to his fellow creatures becomes more imperious, as it is increased by the probability of success." In this passage Barlow drew on the idea of universal benevolence that extended sensibility and moral sense to include all humanity. As described by the philosophers Lord Shaftesbury, Francis Hutcheson, and Richard Price, universal benevolence did not detract from but strengthened narrower attachments to country and family and prevented them from becoming parochial and selfish.[19]

After the imperial defeat in America, the concept of sensibility came under attack in Britain, both from conservatives who denounced it as effeminate and foreign and from radicals like the poet Samuel Taylor Coleridge and Mary Wollstonecraft, who saw sensibility as an obstacle to true benevolence. At the same time, the combination of sensibility and fraternity that had been forged in the War of Independence created an even closer bond between American and French revolutionaries, which found expression in the shared veneration of heroic figures like Washington and Lafayette. This shared culture of sensibility was on display in the congratulatory address that Barlow and eleven other Americans, including the war hero John Paul Jones, delivered to the National Assembly on 10 July 1790. After extolling the wisdom of patriot king Louis XVI, both "le premier *rios des Français*" and "*le premier roi des homes,*" the Americans asked "to be granted the honor of attending the august ceremony that will forever ensure the happiness of France," the Fête de la Féderation on 14 July. "When the French fought and shed their blood with us in the defense of liberty, we came to love them," the Americans avowed. "Today that the establishment of the same principles brings us closer together and strengthens our mutual bonds, we feel nothing in our hearts but the sweet sentiments of brothers and co-citizens."[20]

The president of the Assembly, Charles-François de Bonnay, himself an officer in the French army, responded by affirming the link between the American and French revolutions: "Gentlemen, in helping you to win your liberty, the French learned to know and love it. The hands that broke your chains were not made to wear them." The only difference between the two revolutions was that Americans had gained their liberty by spilling "streams of blood" while the French would attain theirs through "the progress of reason," the peaceful process of regeneration. Not only did the Assembly offer the Americans seats of honor during the upcoming celebration, but Bonnay declared Americans and Frenchmen to be "one people: united in their hearts and united in their principles." The Assembly ordered both the Americans' address and Bonnay's reply to be printed, thereby giving its seal of approval to this demonstration of cosmopolitan sensibility.

Despite pouring rain, thousands of French men and women from all over the country, as well as foreign guests, gathered on the Champ de Mars to celebrate the Fête de la Féderation. For the French, the ceremony marked the highpoint of national consensus about the achievements of the first year of the revolution. For their foreign supporters, it represented an unproblematic fusion of national and universal aspirations. The English author Helen Maria Williams, who would later become a close friend of Barlow's, expressed what many foreigners felt that summer in Paris: "This was not a time in which the distinctions of country were remembered. It was the triumph of human kind; it was man asserting the noblest principles of his nature; and it required but the common feelings of humanity to become in that moment a citizen of the world. . . . I too, though but a sojourner in their land, rejoiced in their happiness, joined the universal voice, and repeated with all my heart and soul, 'Vive la nation!'"[21]

Yet by July 1790 it was already apparent that efforts to regenerate the French nation and eradicate social, religious, and regional differences were bound to meet with opposition. Many aristocrats chose to emigrate rather than accept the abolition of their titles and orders. This was not an option for the numerous priests and their parishioners who confronted the Civil Constitution of the Clergy, a far-reaching attempt to reorganize the structure of the Catholic Church in France. When the National Assembly ordered all clergy in public service to take an oath in support of the Civil Constitution, it effectively forced them and their congregations to choose between their most deeply held beliefs and the revolution. Not only did about half the clergy of France refuse to take the oath, but the measure also fueled popular resentment against the new order in the provinces.

Such opposition raised the question of whether there were differences that were unredeemable and what to do with those who refused to assimilate. For American and French republicans, confidence in the natural harmony of society was closely connected with their fear of conflict and power. In a revealing passage from *Advice to the Privileged Orders,* worth quoting at length, Barlow claimed that in a republic the question of power would become irrelevant and its operations invisible:

Power, habitually in the hands of a whole community, loses all the ordinary associated ideas of power. The exercise of power is a relative term; it supposes an opposition–something to operate upon. We perceive no exertion of power in the motion of the planetary system, but a very strong one in the movement of a whirlwind; it is because we see obstructions to the latter, but none to the former. Where the government is *not* in the hands of the people, there you find opposition, you perceive two contending interests, and get an idea of the exercise of power; and whether this power be in the hands of the government or of the people, or whether it change from side to side, it is always to be dreaded.[22]

In the absence of power, all kinds of relations between individuals—political, commercial, and personal—would naturally fall into their proper places. Scottish philosophers like David Hume, Adam Smith, and Adam Ferguson had developed this idea of "spontaneous order." They argued that complex forms of social organization were not the result of the design of any one person. Instead, the actions of the various parts in cooperation with each other led over time to harmonious wholes of great complexity, even though the resulting whole was never intended by any of the parts. Smith's concept of the "invisible hand" of the marketplace is only one example of this theory.[23] The expectation that spontaneous order would reign once the institutional and ideological clutter of the Old Regime had been removed made Barlow and like-minded revolutionaries extremely anxious of conflict, which shattered the illusion that power had disappeared. How could republicans disdain the exercise of power and still exert influence over those who were insensible to the dictates of both the head and the heart and who insisted on allegiances other than to the nation?

Given the ambiguity of regeneration as both a natural process and a political project, it was not surprising that Barlow's answer was equivocal. On the one hand, he argued, "society itself is the cause of all crimes; and, as such, it has no right to punish them at all." In fact, punishment was merely "a confession of the inability of society, to protect itself against an ignorant or refractory member." On the other hand, after benevolent measures like education and welfare had been exhausted, the nation was entirely justified in resorting to more forceful techniques of reform. It was society's duty "in all cases to induce every human creature, by rational motives, to place his happiness in the tranquillity of the public, and in the security of individual peace and prosperity." However, "in cases where these precautions shall fail of their effect, she is driven indeed to the last extremity,—she is to use the rod of correction."[24]

The "rod of correction" was reserved for those who steadfastly refused to assimilate to the regenerated nation or even worked against it. Its manifestations could range from the deportation of refractory priests to the brutal suppression of provincial revolts to the forceful "liberation" of other nations. Still, the use of force undermined the entire concept of regeneration as a natural process that worked through persuasion and sentiment. Once force was permitted as an instrument of regeneration, it was only a small step from correcting ignorant or refractory members of society to eradicating them altogether.

In the winter of 1791 the Girondins began to call for a preemptive war against those German principalities that harbored French émigrés. In several speeches to the Jacobin Club Brissot offered three essential reasons for war: to purge France's neighbors of counterrevolutionary aristocrats, to regenerate the nation and unite it around a patriotic cause, and to test the loyalty of the king. War would significantly accelerate the nation-building process and create an international environment more hospitable to a regenerated France. Henri Grégoire also drew an explicit connection between the necessity to take the fight directly to the enemies of the republic, to "exterminate despotism, to annihilate this stupid arrogance, to purge the earth, to crush these monsters," and the desire for universal regeneration, "to reveal to all peoples their imprescriptible rights, and to emancipate the human species."[25] After France declared war on Austria in April 1792, it initially suffered a string of defeats but spectacularly turned the tide in September with the Battle of Valmy. Elated with this improbable success, the National Convention in December 1792 ordered French generals in all occupied territories to abolish feudalism, nobility, and all other kinds of privilege. The immediate aim of the decree was to put the French and their allies in control of local resources and thereby enable the French army to live off the land. Nevertheless, both opponents and sympathizers of the French Revolution regarded the order as heralding a Europeanwide and perhaps even global war of liberation.

Like his friends among the Girondins and Grégoire, Barlow believed that such a war would promote the project of national regeneration. Using none-too-subtle sexual metaphors, his poem *The Conspiracy of Kings* (1792) depicts the French army as a youthful, virile force overpowering the old and effeminate monarchs of Europe. "Men, rous'd from sloth," used their "deep-descending steel" to "teach dull nerves to feel." Liberated by France, "nations, rising in the light of truth / Strong with new life and pure regenerate youth," rallied around "The great concentred stake, the interest of mankind." The war made "Gallia's sons, so late the tyrant's sport / Machines in war and sycophants at court / Start into men, expand their well-taught mind / Lords of themselves and leaders of mankind."[26]

Such rhetoric and its underlying notion of war as an act of national renewal were already familiar to Americans from their own War of Independence, in which Barlow had served (if rather lackadaisically) as chaplain of the Third Massachusetts Brigade. Like the French revolutionaries, American patriots had understood their war with Britain as a struggle between virtue and tyranny that would pave the way to individual, national, and even global redemption. Motivated by benevolence and disinterestedness, they saw themselves as fighting not for political or military power but for a new order of perfect unity and harmony. As Charles Royster put it, "Americans could look to the future with the hope that it would differ from the past not just in detail or degree, as one country's history differed from another's, but in disposition, as the redeemed differ from the damned." In turn, the French revolutionary wars reinforced this American view of war as a unifying and purifying crusade. In 1812 the writer Charles J. Ingersoll declared that the impending conflict with Britain would do for the United States what the wars of the French Revolution had done for France, namely, promote "the grandest and most stupendous effort of national regeneration ever exhibited in history, ancient or modern."[27]

Yet the zeal among France's neighbors for regeneration at the hands of the French army left a lot to be desired. Following Barlow's address to the National Convention, Henri Grégoire invited Barlow to accompany an official delegation from the Convention on a mission to Savoy, formerly part of the Kingdom of Sardinia but newly incorporated into France as the département of Mont-Blanc. After the French army had invaded Savoy, the self-styled "Sovereign National Assembly of the Allobroges" had requested annexation by France. In a report supporting the request, Grégoire had argued that it was in France's national interest to deliver other countries from monarchy so that they could choose their own form of government. If the liberated neighbors preferred to live under a monarchy, however, France had a natural right to choose for them instead: "Free to organize themselves on their own, they will always find support and fraternity from us, as long as they don't want to replace tyrants with tyrants. If my neighbor feeds snakes, I have the right to suffocate them, for fear of becoming a victim."[28] As we will see in the next chapter, Grégoire was not alone in combining an avowed belief in popular sovereignty with a deep mistrust in the people's ability to understand their own best interests.

Encouraged by Grégoire, Barlow campaigned to be elected as one of Mont-Blanc's deputies to the National Convention. However, the Savoyard representatives who had demanded annexation had been installed by French military officials and enjoyed no popular support. Although there is little information about Barlow's time in Savoy, it appears likely that his defeat at the polls resulted directly from his close association with the French occupiers. Grégoire consoled Barlow that "if the electorate of Mont-Blanc had known their interests better, that is to say those of the *patrie,* you would have been assured a legislative seat."[29]

While in Savoy, Barlow wrote *Lettre adressée aux habitants du Piémont, sur les avantages de la Révolution française, & la nécessité d'en adopter les principes en Italie.* The only pamphlet Barlow composed in French, it urged the people of Piedmont to imitate their neighbors in Savoy and allow the French army to help them regain their liberty. Barlow depicted the French Revolution exactly as he had done in his address to the National Convention, as a force for peace and reconciliation among all nations: "The principles of this revolution are those of universal peace; and it is impossible that it should fail to produce the effect, because it takes away every motive for national hostility, and teaches the people of all countries to regard each other as friends and fellow-citizens of the world." Echoing Grégoire's appeal, Barlow promised his readers: "Purge the earth of its tyrants, and it will no more be tormented with war."[30] The pamphlet presented the most direct and therefore most jarring juxtaposition of the French Revolution's two faces as depicted by Barlow and his French associates: on the one hand, the benign image of the revolution as an educational effort, opening people's eyes to their rights and to their bonds with their "fellow-citizens of the world"; on the other hand, the martial image of the revolution mercilessly purging, annihilating, and crushing its enemies.

The uneasy coexistence of these two conceptions of the French Revolution lent a defensive tone to Barlow's letter, as Barlow was anxious to dispel misconceptions about recent events in France, especially the September

Massacres. Barlow blamed these violent incidents on "deceitful men," who, realizing that "they could not oppose [the revolution] by open force, assumed the mask of patriotism, and brought themselves into places of trust." Like Jefferson in his "Adam and Eve" letter, written around the same time, Barlow justified the blunt, but nonetheless necessary instrument of popular violence. Since the "good people" of Paris found themselves "surrounded by traitors" and could no longer know whom to trust, "even with the execution of their own vengeance, it was natural and sometimes necessary that they should assume this terrible task upon themselves. In some instances indeed the popular vengeance has been ill directed, and has fallen on innocent heads. But these instances are rare."[31]

In a letter to Jefferson in March 1793, enclosing the Piedmont pamphlet, Barlow expressed the same anxiety "lest some of the late transactions in France should be so far misrepresented to the Patriots in America as to lead them to draw conclusions unfavorable to the cause of liberty in this hemisphere." In addition to the September Massacres, Barlow was undoubtedly thinking of the execution in January of Louis XVI, whom Americans had celebrated not too long ago as their nation's savior and to whom Barlow had dedicated *The Vision of Columbus.* Barlow appealed to Jefferson as a fellow firsthand witness of the French Revolution to explain to their compatriots that "in order to form a proper judgment it is necessary to combine many circumstances that cannot be well understood by men out of the country." According to Barlow, an Italian version of his pamphlet was distributed throughout Piedmont and other parts of Italy in early 1793 but failed to galvanize support for a pro-French uprising. In the preface to the English translation in July 1794, Barlow expressed disappointment with this reception, which he, like Grégoire, attributed to the prejudices and misinformation of the people of Piedmont. But even Barlow had to acknowledge that "the manner in which French affairs were conducted that year, had a strong tendency to excite a disrelish to their cause in the minds of distant and ignorant observers."[32]

Barlow referred to the deepest crisis of the French Republic. Not only did the popular uprisings in support of the French Revolution that the Girondins had predicted fail to materialize, but in the spring and summer of 1793 the French army was forced to retreat from the Low Countries and the Rhineland, and Austrian, Prussian, Spanish, and British forces advanced onto French soil from all sides. At the same time, the resort to conscription fanned a rural insurgency in the western region of Vendée as well as op-position movements in several southern cities like Marseilles, Lyon, and Bordeaux, which became known as the "Federalist revolt." Widespread op-position to the payment of taxes forced the Paris government to rely more and more on the emission of paper money (assignats) to finance the war, leading to currency depreciation, commodity price inflation, food shortages, and subsistence riots in various parts of France. The National Convention saw no other option than to create an emergency regime, the Revolutionary Government headed by the Committee of Public Safety, which assumed the republic's executive power and became the author of all major initiatives of the Terror.

The failure of France's neighbors to welcome the French troops as libera-tors let alone to assimilate to the French nation raised doubts about the true level of regeneration among foreigners in Paris. The Revolutionary Govern-ment began to keep track of all foreigners in Paris and ordered the arrest and confiscation of property of British and Spanish subjects. Despite their special status as fellow republicans, Americans were not exempt from these laws. Alongside well-established idealized visions of the New World and admiration for American republican institutions, an image of the United States had formed in France since the end of the American Revolution that depicted Americans as ungrateful, duplicitous, opportunistic, and skirting their moral and financial obligations to their French allies. Among the is-sues contributing to this image was the lackluster development of Franco-American trade and the lengthy process it was taking for the United States to repay its huge debts from the War of Independence to French volunteer officers and the French state.[33]

After his arrival in Paris, Barlow himself had added to these resentments through his sales of land claims on the Scioto River in the Ohio Country. The frightened aristocrats looking for an idyllic refuge from the upheavals of the revolution did not realize that Scioto Associates, the group of investors Bar-low represented, did not in fact own the lands he was busy selling. Around five hundred French would-be pioneers found themselves in the Ohio Coun-try without title to the land they believed they had bought and forced to carve out homesteads from the wilderness.[34] Accounts of the reality of the Ameri-can frontier soon made their way back to Paris, where the Scioto affair gen-erated numerous outraged newspaper articles and pamphlets. In the eyes of the revolution's supporters, emigration at a time of national crisis was a

81

profoundly unpatriotic act, turning the émigrés into foreigners in the country they had abandoned. In order to counteract the pernicious example set by the Scioto émigrés, pamphleteers dusted off some well-worn stereotypes about the New World. For example, *Le Nouveau Mississippi, ou les Dangers d'habiter les bords du Scioto* (1790) revived comte de Buffon's and Cornelius De Pauw's theory of degeneration and claimed that American soil was infertile, that the climate there was cold and harsh, that Americans died young, that their women were barren at thirty, and that they were generally a lazy, apathetic people, indifferent to the arts and comforts of life.[35] Other authors found the image of haughty aristocrats and clerics on the muddy shores of the Scioto River a rich subject for satire.[36]

Eager to disprove such anti-American stereotypes, the Girondins remained confident that France could count on the support of its sister republic. Since the Americans would be unable to offer any military assistance to France, the new French minister Edmond-Charles Genet requested that the United States supply provisions to France and its West Indian colonies and open its ports to French privateers. However, not only did the Washington administration refuse to pay a substantial advancement on the remainder of the American debt, but in April 1793 it issued the Proclamation of Neutrality, which declared that the United States would remain at peace during the current war in Europe and prohibited American citizens from taking any part in the conflict. Genet's heavy-handed attempts to challenge the decision for neutrality allowed American opponents of the French Revolution to voice their disapproval for the first time in public and forced the U.S. government to demand the minister's recall.

By the time the request to recall Genet reached Paris in October 1793, it was already four months since his Girondin superiors had been purged from the Convention. In the meantime, their rivals, the Montagnards, had become convinced of the existence of a vast Girondin conspiracy dating back as far as 1791. Working in league with the British prime minister William Pitt, the Girondin conspirators allegedly had plotted to deliver France to Prussia during the campaign of 1792, to prevent the execution of Louis XVI, to destroy the republic by provoking war with most of Europe, and to incite the "Federalist revolt" against Paris in the southern provinces. Based on these charges, Brissot, Clavière, and dozens of other prominent Girondins were sentenced to death.[37]

Given that the Girondin crusade to revolutionize Europe and North America now served as evidence of a counterrevolutionary plot, it was inevitable that the Girondins' foreign supporters in Paris would be caught up in the purge. Using the exact same language as Barlow in his Piedmont letter, Robespierre in October defended a law ordering the arrest of all foreign nationals whose governments were at war with the republic by alerting the Convention to the danger posed by precisely those foreigners who made a spectacle of their love for France: "I distrust without exception all those foreigners whose face is covered with a mask of patriotism and who endeavor to appear more republican and energetic than us. It is these ardent patriots who are the most perfidious creators of our problems. They are the agents of foreign powers, for I am well aware that our enemies cannot have failed to say: Our emissaries must affect the warmest and most exaggerated patriotism to be able to insinuate themselves more easily into our Committees and into our assemblies."[38] In late December a new law expelled from the National Convention the only two foreign-born deputies, Thomas Paine and Anacharsis Cloots, a flamboyant Prussian baron and self-declared "voice of humanity." Both were arrested a few days later and Cloots was executed, while Paine narrowly avoided the same fate. Now only those born in France could represent the nation.

Historians have described this outburst of xenophobia as a retreat from revolutionary cosmopolitanism and, as for the Terror as a whole, offered two competing explanations. One focuses on the external circumstances of foreign and civil war that stirred distrust of foreigners and made national security the priority of the Revolutionary Government. The other explanation emphasizes the inherent contradictions of revolutionary ideology, particularly between the declaration of universal rights and the glorification of national sovereignty.[39] However, despite the xenophobic rhetoric, the expulsion of foreigners from the Convention, and the greater surveillance of foreigners, the Terror did not mark a break with cosmopolitan universalism. As we have seen in the previous chapter, defining political and social enemies of the revolution as alien to the nation was a well-established practice. Since the Revolutionary Government considered itself as embodying the universal principles of republicanism, it declared those who opposed these principles to be foreigners, outside the regenerated community of citizens. When orators, journalists, and pamphleteers inveighed against foreigners, they targeted the British or European peoples who refused to recognize the French as their liberators as much as French aristocrats, provincial rebels, and grain speculators.

Paine's and Cloots's foreign birth served the Montagnards as a pretext to expel two prominent political opponents. Popular xenophobia undoubtedly existed during the war, but more often than not the Committee of Public Safety deliberately appealed to it as a means of blaming unpopular policies, such as de-Christianization, on foreign agents. Even the "certificates of hospitality," which foreigners were required to obtain from the municipal authorities in Paris and carry at all times, had their equivalent in the "certificates of civic virtue" that were mandatory for French citizens. Like former nobles who could demonstrate their personal commitment to the revolution, foreigners, who "since their stay in France have provided proof of their patriotism [*civism*] and attachment to the French Revolution," continued to be tolerated.[40]

Moreover, as Michael Rapport has demonstrated, the economic crisis of the war years made the Revolutionary Government eager to retain the skills, money, and manpower of foreign workers, artisans, and entrepreneurs, including even British subjects. While Americans were arrested for not carrying proper documentation and because they were easily mistaken for Britons, Gouverneur Morris generally managed to secure their release. The Montagnard government was willing to accept American neutrality as long as trade in desperately needed food supplies from the United States continued. Ironically, it was the scandal that Genet's proselytizing for a transatlantic revolution had caused in America that convinced the Montagnards of the good intentions of the United States. Americans were among those nations, Robespierre explained in a report to the National Convention in November 1793, "whom nature and reason attach to our cause, but whom intrigue and perfidy seek to range among the number of our enemies."[41] While it was true that American support for the French cause had fallen below expectations, at least the United States had declined to join the coalition against France, as the Girondin plot had intended. The Montagnards were only too willing to comply with the American request to recall Genet, who had the good sense to seek asylum in the United States. But they took the opportunity to demand in return the recall of the American minister Gouverneur Morris, who had never made a secret of his disdain for the leadership of the French Republic.[42]

Robespierre's logic of "the enemy (the U.S. government) of my enemy (Genet and the Girondins) is my friend" was a far cry from the ever-expanding union of hearts and minds that Barlow had evoked only one year before. The appeal to sensibility as the link between the regeneration of like-minded nations had proved self-defeating. The culture of sensibility had held out the promise of a politics of authenticity, in which interests and motives would be transparent. The appeal of sensibility consisted both in its ability to connect the sensible self to society and in its power to differentiate those who declared themselves sensible from those deemed insensible. Therefore, in addition to uniting those of common feeling, sensibility could also serve as a litmus test to distinguish true patriots from selfish reactionaries. Those who were insincere were likely to betray themselves by their lack of fervor or by a misstep that those of true feeling never made.[43]

In the eyes of all friends of the revolution, Edmund Burke most certainly failed that test. "Not one glance of compassion, not one commiserating reflection" could Thomas Paine find in Burke's *Reflections:* "He is not affected by the reality of distress touching upon his heart, but by the showy resemblance of it striking his imagination. He pities the plumage, but forgets the dying bird."[44] But even in his famous denunciation of Burke's insensitivity, Paine raised the specter of mistaking real for pretended or "showy" emotions. Because they invested so much power in emotional honesty, which signified political integrity, French republicans and their foreign supporters harbored a profound, phobic suspicion that the most virtuous-looking exterior could mask a festering core of evil. The longing for transparency fed political paranoia. In this regard the ideals of regeneration and sensibility turned out to be fundamentally at odds with each other. Regeneration sought to erase traditional markers of identity in order to create a new national community. Yet it was precisely this homogenization that made it more difficult to tell if an individual put on a mask of sincerity to feign patriotic feeling. The reliance on visible signs of sensibility became part of the very problem of authenticity that it had been intended to solve.

After the outbreak of the French Revolution, sensibility had served to unite its friends and expose its enemies. But the turmoil and about-faces of the revolution rendered sensibility a more and more unreliable character witness. Instead, the war and the violent opposition to the central government within France increased the obsession with authentic representation until revolutionaries were inclined to see enemies everywhere, with disastrous consequences for the foreign patriots in Paris. The presence of foreigners not only provided convenient scapegoats for the revolution's many internal and external problems; it was precisely the efforts of some foreigners to build a cosmopolitan community by making a spectacle of their sensibility and universal benevolence that raised suspicions among the Montagnards.

During the Terror Barlow refrained from political activism and instead sought to support the republic as a merchant by procuring foodstuffs and other necessities, acquiring a small fortune in the process. Despite the potential danger to his own life, he also tried to help other foreigners like Venezuelan revolutionary Francisco de Miranda, on whose behalf Barlow testified before the Revolutionary Tribunal. When Paine was arrested, Barlow unsuccessfully circulated a petition among American residents of Paris to secure his friend's release.[45] In the spring of 1794, Barlow left Paris for Hamburg and did not return until June 1795, almost one year after Robespierre's downfall on 9 Thermidor II (27 July 1794) and the end of the Terror.

Although the Terror had claimed the lives of many of his French associates, Barlow did not regard the French Revolution as a mistake. He considered the United States as fortunate for having been spared the turmoil that France had endured and was confident that the American system of government would "furnish a great and useful example to the world." Still, Barlow insisted in a letter to his friend Oliver Wolcott that "the event of the French revolution will be such as to offer us much for imitation in our turn." Restating his argument from *Advice to the Privileged Orders,* Barlow maintained that despite the French revolutionaries' excesses and errors, "many principles for the general diffusion of information, the preservation & improvement of morals, & the encouragement of such a degree of equality in the condition of men as tends to their dignity & happiness, will certainly be established by them and will be equally necessary for us."[46]

Like everyone else who lived through the Terror, Barlow was unable to forget or rationalize the experience. Never again would he argue for the redemptive qualities of violence. Instead Barlow developed an abiding aversion to warfare, which helps explain the lengths to which he was willing to go to prevent a full-scale war between the United States and France in 1798-99. For Barlow and for many French revolutionaries, the fear of a return to the Terror became as deep-seated as that of a restoration of the monarchy.

This fear made them willing to accept and justify the growing authoritarianism of the French government after Thermidor. As we will see in the following chapter, this acquiescence was particularly paradoxical for Americans in Paris, whose sympathies for the French Republic made them extremely critical of what they regarded as the authoritarian tendencies of the Washington administration.

4

"Strange, that Monroe should warn us against Jacobins!"

THE PROBLEM OF POPULAR SOVEREIGNTY IN
THERMIDORIAN PARIS AND FEDERALIST AMERICA,
1794-1796

When the new American minister, James Monroe, appeared before the National Convention on 14 August 1794, it seemed as if no time had passed since Barlow's speech two years earlier. Outside the meeting hall of the Convention, Monroe found gathered a large crowd of friendly spectators. According to the merchant captain Joshua Barney, on whose ship Monroe had crossed the Atlantic, upon Monroe's entrance the Convention erupted in applause and shouts of "Live the Convention, Live the United States of America, our brave Brothers.". Like Barlow in 1792, Monroe felt overwhelmed "with a degree of sensibility which I cannot express." Throughout his tenure as minister in Paris, between 1794 and 1796, Monroe was determined to hang on to the spirit of his initial reception by the Convention, no matter how little it accorded with the actual state of Franco-American relations and of his own relationship with the French and U.S. governments.[1]

Monroe assured his audience that, despite the violent events of the last year, France was still on the path of republican progress established by her American brothers: "America had her day of oppression, difficulty, and war, but her sons were virtuous and brave and the storm which long clouded her political horizon has passed and left them in the enjoyment of peace, liberty, and independence. France, our ally and our friend and who aided us in the contest, has now embarked in the same noble career." Like Jefferson and Barlow, Monroe accepted bloodshed as the inevitable price of nation-building. Although he presented America as having already attained "peace, liberty, and independence," the fact that Monroe found the situations of France and the United States in 1794 at all comparable indicated that he in fact considered the American republic to be far from securely established.

The official newspaper *Moniteur* reported that the French deputies received these words with "a lively sensibility and bursts of applause." The president of the Convention, Philippe-Antoine Merlin de Douai, "in the midst of universal raptures of joy," gave Monroe the fraternal kiss and ordered his address printed in French and English. The bond between France and America, Merlin announced, was "not merely a diplomatic alliance," it was "the sweetest fraternity," and "this union shall be forever indissoluble."[2]

Monroe was blissfully unaware that the French deputies had their own motives for this rapturous welcome. The American minister had arrived in Paris only five days after the downfall of Robespierre on 9 Thermidor II (27 July 1794). The government was in such disarray that there was no one to officially receive him, forcing Monroe to present his credentials directly to the National Convention. The deputies regarded Monroe's appearance before the Convention primarily as an occasion for a demonstration of consensus on an uncontroversial issue, and as a ceremonial evocation of unity after a long period of fratricidal violence. It had little connection with French attitudes toward Monroe as an individual or with Franco-American diplomatic relations, a subject of very little concern to the government at this moment. Two years of war and one year of Terror had claimed countless lives and nearly destroyed whatever sense of unity, trust, and common aspirations remained in France after five years of permanent revolution. Now, after the fall of Robespierre, the Convention was caught between the competing imperatives of avenging the crimes of the Terror and forgiving and forgetting for the sake of national unity. Most of all, many deputies wished to end the revolution, establish the authority of the national government, and secure it against challenges from radicals and counterrevolutionaries.[3] Monroe's emotional investment in the friendship between the two republics would continue to contrast sharply with French officials' preoccupation with more pressing domestic matters.

Even worse, Monroe's speech did not reflect the attitudes of his own government. President Washington had chosen the Francophile Monroe as minister to prevent further deterioration in relations with France in light of the ongoing American treaty negotiations with Britain. In spite of American neutrality, British war vessels had begun in the summer of 1793 to seize American merchant ships headed to France, bringing the United States and its former mother country to the brink of war. Alexander Hamilton sought to use this crisis for a rapprochement with Britain, and in the spring of 1794 proposed to send John Jay to London to negotiate a treaty of amity and commerce. Cultivation of French goodwill was therefore purely instrumental to giving Jay time for his negotiations and softening the inevitable French backlash. Conversely, Monroe–who had been led to believe by Secretary of State Edmund Randolph that Jay's mandate was strictly limited to settling outstanding disputes stemming from the peace treaty of 1783–saw his task as helping to strengthen the French Republic and thereby safeguarding the United States against British attacks.[4]

By 1794, political factions had begun to coalesce in the United States around different interpretations of European events and America's place in the world. The Federalists sought to integrate the vulnerable republic into the existing international order dominated by Britain, and to keep domestic decision-making power within the hands of a national elite. They took offense at Monroe's insistence on the continued similarity between the two revolutions. Prominent Federalists, like John Adams, Noah Webster, and Fisher Ames, had come to see the French example as threatening to undermine the established social and political order in America.[5] The Republicans were committed to the alliance with France and eager to see republican principles spread throughout Europe and to extend popular political participation within the United States. The French Revolution had reopened the conversation about popular sovereignty that the Federalists had believed concluded after the Constitutional Convention of 1787. Should popular sovereignty be limited to regular elections or should there be other ways in which citizens could register their political consent or dissent? Had the American Revolution ended once and for all with the ratification of the constitution or were the people still entitled to resist government policies that they perceived as violating their rights?

By the mid-1790s, both the American and the French governments were trying to reach what has become known in the comparative study of revolutions as "Thermidor," a period when power becomes consolidated in the hands of a new elite of former revolutionaries who discard their ideology's more utopian elements.[6] But, on both sides of the Atlantic, their main obstacle to ending the revolution was their own people. Time and again, the American and French people proved frustratingly unreliable when it came to distinguishing true republicanism and their own best interests from the lies and deceptions of false patriots, counterrevolutionaries, and foreign agents. The Whiskey Rebellion, the controversy about the U.S. treaty with Great Britain negotiated by John Jay, as well as the series of uprisings that shook Paris in 1795, all confronted elites with a disturbingly unruly, seemingly irrational, potentially violent, and generally incomprehensible populace. The people appeared as both the source of legitimacy and an agent of disorder as political elites in America and France tenaciously clung to the ideal of a united, harmonious, and stable political domain. This ideal bore much resemblance to their Jacobin enemies' vision of a regenerated, conflict-free society of virtuous citizens. Thermidorians, Jacobins, Republicans, and Federalists all shared the same inability to imagine the political arena as necessarily divided into conflicting interests. Consequently, all parties continued to reject as foreign, by force if necessary, anything that disrupted the supposed unity of the nation and its political life.

Many scholars have noted the failure of the French Republic to produce a working and legitimate pluralism of opinion, association, and party, and therefore to arrive at a stable revolutionary settlement.[7] However, to many observers in the mid-1790s, including Monroe, the American republic did not appear much more stable, even in the absence of the French legacy of political strife and chronic violence that had rent the very fabric of the polity. In both republics, a similar lack of consensus over political rules and norms, and over the boundaries of political contestation, made it difficult for political actors to separate differences of opinion from efforts to subvert the regime.

This chapter examines the ideological predicaments Monroe faced in trying to be politically active in two countries at the same time, supporting the consolidation of national state power in one (France) and opposing it in the other (America). Monroe was painfully aware that the Terror had given conservative forces in the United States plenty of ammunition to attack both the French Republic and its American supporters. Therefore, he sought to explain the Terror as an aberration, but not so much of an aberration that it had irrevocably derailed or discredited the revolution. In order to prevent the French disorders from further compromising the Republican opposition in America, Monroe denounced the Jacobins, applauded the repressive policies of the Thermidorian reaction for restoring law and order, and endorsed the elitist Constitution of 1795. Thus, to safeguard the Republican opposition at home, Monroe supported policies in France that in many ways resembled those of the Federalist government. This paradoxical strategy backfired when the Federalists used his dispatches to justify their own attacks on popular political societies that they regarded as French-inspired, Republican-sponsored factions. Although Monroe was much concerned with American perceptions of the situation in France, there is no indication that he was deliberately spinning events in an optimistic way for his correspondents. He genuinely believed that the Thermidorians' authoritarian policies were necessary in France. Like other Americans in Paris, Monroe came up against the tension between universalism and particularism. The American and French republics needed to stand together to defend their shared, universal principles against internal and external enemies. Yet, as Monroe saw it, in France these enemies turned the people against the government, whereas in America they turned the government against the people. Therefore, the achievement of universal ends required the exact opposite means in each particular case.

In the month after Robespierre's fall, the National Convention quickly dismantled the central institutions of the Terror and the Revolutionary Government. Executions dropped from 1,515 in June–July to 6 in August, and by the end of that month 3,500 suspects had been released from prison. Over the following months, Monroe, with the help of Consul General Fulwar Skipwith, managed to secure the release of several Americans who were still in prison, most prominently Thomas Paine.[8]

What proved more difficult than halting the machinery of the Terror was explaining how it had been created in the first place. Was it possible to dismantle the Terror without repudiating the aims and accomplishments of the revolution in whose name it had been perpetrated? In the national debate about this question, which preoccupied the press, pamphlets, and the Convention, four possible explanations of the Terror quickly emerged. One, put forward by conservative theorists Joseph de Maistre and Louis-Gabriel de Bonald, attributed the bloodshed to historical forces inherent in the revolution and the radical rationalism of the philosophes, forces beyond the intention, control, and responsibility of individuals. Another, favored by those directly involved in the Terror, blamed the exigencies of foreign and civil war and sought to put the Terror in perspective as an unfortunate detour in the progress of the revolution, caused by excessive zeal in the struggle against its many enemies. A few moderate authors, like Benjamin Constant and Madame de Staël, tried to stake out a moral perspective that carefully distinguished between individual responsibility and historical circumstances, between the necessary revolution and an unnecessary Terror. But the most popular explanation simply argued that the Terror was entirely the work and responsibility of the monstrous tyrant Robespierre. As his former colleague on the Committee of Public Safety, Bertrand Barère, memorably put it in his self-defense: "Is his grave not wide enough for us to empty into it all our hatreds?"[9]

Eager to cleanse the revolution of its bloody stains, Monroe quickly passed on the demonization of Robespierre to his correspondents in America. In his first report to Edmund Randolph, Monroe did his best to match the hyperbolic language of the resurfaced French right-wing press, which denounced Robespierre as the "new Catiline," the "new Cromwell," the "new Nero," and a "vile monster": "It was his spirit which dictated every movement, and particularly the unceasing operations of the guillotine. Nor did a more bloody and merciless tyrant ever wield the rod of power. His acts of cruelty and oppression are perhaps without parallel in the annals of history." Republicans in America greeted these accounts with relief, especially as their arrival coincided with the aftermath of the Whiskey Rebellion and the nervous anticipation of Jay's Treaty. "Our comfort," Jefferson responded to Monroe, "is that the public sense is coming right on the general principles of republicanism, and that it's success in France puts it out of danger here." Jefferson also immediately adopted the scapegoating of Robespierre in his own correspondence: "This ball of liberty, I believe most piously, is now so well in motion that it will roll around the globe," he wrote to Tench Coxe. "What a tremendous obstacle to the future attempts at liberty will be the atrocities of Robespierre!"[10]

Such vilifications left unexplained how Robespierre had ever been able to rise to such unlimited power. How did it reflect on the French nation that it had allowed itself to be so misled? Monroe turned the problem on its head and argued that the conspiracy of Robespierre, by its very treachery and its ultimate discovery, proved the French people's progress: "[Robespierre] was believed by the people at large to be the foe to Kings, nobles, Priests, etc., the friend of republican government regardless of money and in fact devoted to their cause. Under this impression, he perpetrated acts, which without perceiving the cause, had gradually spread a gloom over the whole republick. But as soon as they saw him in opposition to the Convention, the cause was known, his atrocities were understood, and the people abandoned him with demonstrations of joy rarely seen." According to Monroe, the frequency with which the revolution had devoured its children was in fact a sign of the regenerative power of the French nation to rid itself of leaders who strayed from the path of righteousness. Now that the "last tyrant" was gone, "perfect tranquility" reigned throughout the republic, and the "whole community seemed to be liberated from the most pestilent scourge that ever harassed a country."[11]

The tranquility proved short-lived. *La Queue de Robespierre* (Robespierre's Tail), a popular pamphlet published in late August, declared that "it was not possible for Robespierre to do all that evil alone," and named the names of those who formed the murderous reptile's tail. The political atmosphere was rife with suspicion, resentment, and the desire for revenge. Monroe acknowledged to Jefferson that "it seemed improbable he [Robespierre] should have been able to carry every thing in the committee of p[ublic] safety and by means of it in the Convention &ca without more associates than [Louis de] St. Just & [Georges] Couthon, who were executed with him." Yet Monroe confidently declared that he could "readily conceive that a man may gain an influence in society powerful enough to controul every one & every thing." The American minister remained convinced of "the certainty with which the revolution progresses toward a happy close, since the preponderance of those Councils which are equally distinguished for their wisdom, temperance and humanity, continues to increase."[12]

This description certainly corresponded with the self-image of the Thermidorians—an unstable coalition of moderate Montagnards, former terrorists like Jean-Lambert Tallien and Louis Fréron, and deputies of "the Plain" (deputies in the Convention who had not been affiliated with either Girondins or Montagnards) temporarily united in opposition to Robespierre—who saw themselves as bringing about reconciliation, restoring harmony, and ending the revolution. Many prominent figures in the Thermidorian reaction were in fact regular guests at Monroe's dinner table. Like his mentor

Jefferson, Monroe proudly remembered in his memoirs how the French politicians treated him as an equal: "The conversation was free and unreserved and [Monroe's] participation in it admitted as a right, common to him on principle, as well as to them."[13]

Monroe's rosy view of the revolution's progress reflected not only his own selective vision, but also the information provided by his French interlocutors. When he presented the Thermidorians' views to Randolph as "resting upon the interests and the wishes of the great mass of the French people," he drew this conclusion "from those data the revolution itself has furnished, as well as from my own observations since my arrival (the latter of which, it is true, has been confined to a small circle)." This small circle included leading Thermidorians like François-Antoine de Boissy d'Anglas, Tallien, Antoine-Clair-Thibaudeau, and Antoine-Christophe Merlin; army generals like Jean-Charles Pichegru, Jean-Victor Moreau, and Louis-Lazare Hoche; and future Directors Jean-François Reubell, Paul Barras, and Louis-Marie La Revellière-Lépeaux. Monroe announced to his Republican friends that he was "personally acquainted" with "the leading members of the preponderating party," and "from what I have seen of their conduct, for some time past, in publick and private life, . . . I consider many of them as among the most enthusiastic admirers and advocates of publick liberty I have ever known."[14]

Monroe's dinner receptions were part of a general revival of social life and sociability after the end of the Terror. The intense political polarization of the early 1790s had largely extinguished the open-minded and polite conversation of salon culture. The Montagnards had been hostile toward all vestiges of the Old Regime, and particularly toward gatherings at private residences, which they regarded as nests of counterrevolutionary conspiracies. During the Terror, the only places where traditional sociability was still practiced were prisons such as the Luxembourg. After Thermidor, sociability remained circumscribed by lack of resources and residual fears of attracting too much attention to oneself. Rather than in private salons, social life was concentrated in balls, restaurants, gardens, theaters, and cafés.[15]

In keeping with this trend, and in order to cultivate his personal ties and the bond between the two republics, Monroe staged an elaborate Fourth of July garden party in 1795 with two hundred guests, including Americans and members of the diplomatic corps, the various government committees, and the National Convention, as well as officers of the French army. The

American tourist William Dallam of Maryland noted in his journal that the dinner opened with a procession to the tune of "Yankee Doodle" and "several patriotic hymns." During the meal, Merlin, as president of the Convention, proposed a toast to the United States, and Monroe responded with a salute to the "republic of France." Dallam pronounced the celebration "a superb entertainment," marked by "the greatest harmony and jocularity. Many of the company were merry and gave us very enlivening songs after dinner."[16]

Such harmonious scenes stood in sharp contrast to the discord within the National Convention. Upon visiting the legislature, Boston merchant Thomas Perkins was "astonished at the intemperance which discovered itself in a debate which took place there. . . . The two parties showed themselves *pro* and *con.;* and their gestures and tones would have led one to suppose that they would be at fisticuffs every moment." Perkins concluded disapprovingly, "This kind of management in a legislative assembly is most certainly wrong and disgraceful; at least, it appears so to an American spectator." In fact, however, the behavior of representatives and senators on the floor of Congress struck American and, especially, British observers as no less chaotic, contentious, and undignified.[17]

The continuing power struggles in the Convention convinced Monroe that the real origins of the Terror were to be found not only in the depravity of Robespierre but also in the evils of party conflict, in particular, in the past and present machinations of the Jacobin Club of Paris. In his dispatch to Randolph of 16 October 1794, Monroe included a lengthy history of "the Jacobin Society," which "furnishes a lesson equally instructive to public functionaries and to private citizens."

Until the fall of the monarchy, Monroe explained, the Jacobin Club was "the cradle of the revolution" and "the organ of the public sentiment," without which "most certainly the Republic would not have been established." After the proclamation of the republic, however, the club had "neither sufficient virtue nor inclination" to give up the power it had gained during its opposition to the king, so that "the same Society which was heretofore so formidable to the despotism [was] now brandishing the same weapon against the legitimate representation of the people." It was just a matter of time before it became "the creature of Robespierre and under his direction the principal agent in all those atrocities which have stained this stage of the revolution. It was by means of this society that he succeeded in cutting off the members of the two succeeding parties of Brissot and Danton, and had finally well nigh ruined the Republic itself." Still, as many "deserving characters" had merely joined the Jacobin Club out of fear, "the preponderating party in France [the Plain], and the world at large, should now look with indulgence, and indeed with forgiveness, upon the conduct of many of those who seemed at the time to abet his enormities."[18]

As it turned out, the "lesson" contained in Monroe's history of the Jacobin Club was open to several conflicting interpretations. His intention was to demonstrate that the Jacobin Reign of Terror was not representative of the will of the French people or the nature of the revolution, but was, in fact, conceived and implemented by a minority faction. Monroe explained to James Madison that he wanted to set the record straight on the Jacobins, lest their crimes "injure the cause of republicanism every where by discrediting popular complaints and inclining men on the side of government however great its oppressions might be." Far from being the voice of the people, the Jacobin Club had by 1793 in effect become "the government of France, and the principal means of retarding the revolution itself; by it all those atrocities which now stain & will always stain certain stages of the revolution were committed: and it had obviously become the last pivot upon which the hopes of the coalisd [coalition] powers depended." This analysis reflected the common republican belief that extra-parliamentary political associations created internal divisions, served as channels of foreign influence, and weakened the nation against attacks from the outside. In his portrait of the Jacobins as a minority faction that had taken over the government, Monroe likely expected his readers to discover resemblances to the Federalists in the Washington administration.[19]

However, events in America made it possible to interpret Monroe's lessons in a very different way. In February 1795, Monroe received a letter from Madison reporting Washington's condemnation of "certain self-created societies," namely, the Democratic-Republican Societies of western Pennsylvania. In a congressional address, the president had accused them of fomenting resistance against the federal excise tax in the so-called Whiskey Rebellion, and of disseminating "suspicions, jealousies, and accusations of the whole government." The Democratic-Republican Societies had indeed strongly condemned the tax, but they were not directly responsible for the attacks on tax collectors that accompanied these protests. Precisely because the protesters claimed to resist an illegitimate law in the name of the revolutionary tradition of 1776, Washington (himself a great absentee landowner in Pennsylvania) and his cabinet felt it necessary to restore the government's authority with a disproportionately large military campaign. For Washington, the Republican-sponsored protesters were not merely opposing his administration's policies but posing a threat to the entire system of government. In Madison's view, the executive was trying to tar all opposition with the brush of treason and deny the legitimacy of *all* voluntary political organizations critical of government policies. "The game," Madison explained to Monroe, "was, to connect the democratic Societies with the odium of the insurrection–to connect the Republicans in Cong[res]s with those Societies–[and] to put the P[resident] ostensibly at the head of the other party, in opposition to both."[20]

In response, Monroe belatedly told Madison about the critical account of the Jacobin Club he had sent to the secretary of state in October, and defended his motives for writing it, clearly anticipating that it might play into the Federalists' hands. He now claimed that the dispatch had been meant to highlight the differences between the Jacobin Club in its corrupt later form and the innocuous American opposition groups, like the Democratic-Republican Societies, it had originally inspired: "It is easy for designing men to turn the vices of one society somewhat similar in its origin . . . ag[ai]nst all others, altho' the parallel may go no farther than the stage in which they all had merit."[21]

As Monroe feared, his history of the Jacobins had arrived at a particularly opportune moment for the Washington administration. Although the text of Jay's Treaty would not reach Philadelphia until 7 March 1795, and its exact terms would be kept a closely guarded secret until July, the Republican press was already preparing its attack on the treaty in late February. In this context, Monroe's critique of the Jacobin Club provided a welcome reminder–by a well-known Republican supporter of the French Revolution no less–of the dangers of all "self-created societies." Without asking for Monroe's permission, the administration decided to publish extracts from the dispatch in the *Philadelphia Gazette.* "Your history of the Jacobin societies was so appropriate to the present times in our own country," Randolph slyly informed Monroe, "that it was conceived proper to furnish the public with those useful lessons; and extracts were published, as from a letter *of a gentleman in Paris to his friend in this city.*"[22]

Extracts from Monroe's letters to Randolph of 16 October, 7 November, and 20 November 1794 appeared in the *Philadelphia Gazette,* the *New York Herald,* and the *New York Daily Advertiser* in late February and early March 1795. Both New York papers identified Monroe as the author. Representative Fisher Ames savored the irony of Monroe's inadvertent support for the government's censure of opposition parties. He hoped that more papers would reprint the letter and reveal its author, as "it would greatly assist the antidote, to know that it was sent from one who had swallowed the poison and was cured. Strange, that Monroe should warn us against Jacobins! So the world turns round." Like many Americans, Ames habitually called all French revolutionaries "Jacobins," regardless of the fact that the current regime was aggressively anti-Jacobin. Madison had to inform his friend that he had become the unwitting tool of the Federalists: "The question agitated in consequence of the President's denunciation of the Democratic Societies, will account for this use of your observations. In N. York where party contests are running high in the choice of a Successor to [Governor George] Clinton who declines, I perceive the use of them is extended by adroit comments, to that subject also. It is proper you should be apprized of these circumstances, that your own judgment may be the better exercised as to the latitude or reserve of your communications."[23]

Federalists did not have to distort Monroe's dispatches to claim that they corroborated the conventional anti-party creed shared by American and French republicans alike, according to which official government institutions were the only legitimate and entirely sufficient representations of popular sovereignty. Monroe had used the Jacobins as an illustration of that belief to show that their Reign of Terror was an illegitimate aberrations of the French Revolution. Yet this effort to rehabilitate the French Revolution helped cast the same shadow of illegitimacy on political associations in America, including Monroe's own Republicans. Having approved of the closing of the Jacobin Club of Paris in November, Monroe found himself on the same side as the Federalist "friends of order" who demanded that Congress crack down on French-inspired political clubs in the United States.[24]

C ontrary to Monroe's predictions of harmony and tranquility, the political and economic situation in France deteriorated rapidly during the winter and spring of 1794-95. The value of the assignats (the paper money currency) plummeted; there was widespread agitation for higher wages in state-run armaments workshops; and basic commodities, especially bread and fuel, were scarce and sold at prices far higher than the legal *maximum* (the price control on basic commodities). Monroe minimized the mounting crisis in his letters to the State Department and the Republican opposition alike. "Bread is scarce in some quarters," he acknowledged to Madison, "but the people are beyond example patient under it. I do not think a real distress is to be apprehended, but if such were to happen, I am convinc'd the yeomanry wo[ul]d emulate by their fortitude, the bravery of their compatriots in the army."[25]

The extent to which Monroe exaggerated the social harmony reigning in the French capital and the forbearance of its inhabitants can be measured by comparison with the observations of Thomas Parkin, the twenty-one-year-old son of a wealthy Baltimore merchant, who traveled in England and France between November 1794 and August 1795. On his first visit to Paris, in January 1795, Parkin noted "a great want of unanimity in political opinion." The sight of working-class women debating politics in the street astounded the young American: "I saw a woman who kept a coffee-house tear the national colors down from her door, stamp and spit on them and execrate the Republic and the Convention because bread was scarce." Parkin made no attempt to synthesize the broad range of political opinion he encountered during his four months in Paris. But even as a short-term visitor, he could not help noticing the deep political and social divisions in Paris that Monroe was so eager to dismiss.[26]

The winter weather deepened the simmering discontent. In December 1794, just as the Convention announced the closing of the arms workshops and abolished the *maximum* in an effort to end the Jacobins' controlled economy, one of the coldest winters of the eighteenth century hit France. Rivers froze and roads became impassable, rendering almost impossible the transport of what little supplies existed. Most of that year's indifferent harvest went to the army, and the Convention was forced to introduce bread and meat rations. As these rations became ever smaller, prices skyrocketed. With the poor starving and freezing to death in the streets, popular resentment against the Convention grew in the sections of Paris. Further fueling these resentments was the Thermidorians' anti-Jacobin campaign. Fréron used his newspaper *L'Orateur du Peuple* to encourage the vigilantism of the *jeunesse dorée* (gilded youth), reactionary youth gangs in extravagant clothing who roamed the streets in search of suspected Jacobins to beat up, or sans-culotte meetings to disrupt. On 12 November they ransacked the Jacobin Club's meeting place at the Palais Égalité (formerly Royal), which provided the Convention with a welcome excuse to ban the club as an incitement to public disorder. Monroe applauded the measure in a dispatch to Randolph, since "that body was constantly at work to undermine and impair the regular and constituted authority of the government."[27]

While Monroe devoted his attention to painting the French Republic as internally stable, victorious on the battlefields across Europe, and committed to its fraternal alliance with the United States, disturbing rumors reached Paris in December that John Jay had concluded a treaty of commerce with Britain. Based on Randolph's misleading instructions, Monroe had assured the French that Jay had no power to negotiate any such treaty. He could not believe that his government would jeopardize its union with France, whose military campaign had severely weakened Britain, and embarrass its minister before his French hosts to enter into a connection with the archenemy of the American people. Consequently, in early 1795 Monroe redoubled his efforts to demonstrate to the secretary of state and the president "the good disposition of [the National Convention] and of the nation generally towards us," as evidenced by the lifting of all commercial restrictions. "In my judgment no region of the world presents such an opening to the enterprize of our countrymen as this does," a fact that Monroe wished "was more generally known." Still, French concerns about Jay's Treaty persisted, and so as not to disturb the newly restored harmony between the two republics, the American minister continued to downplay its significance to the Committee of Public Safety. To his own government Monroe provided detailed updates about French advances in Holland and Spain, as well as negotiations with Prussia, which he predicted would leave Britain entirely isolated.[28]

By the beginning of March, the Convention was no longer able to guarantee regular bread rations, and on some days whole districts were without any supply of bread at all. Although the Convention passed decrees to remedy the food shortages, workers in the city's eastern districts began to discuss the need for a new uprising. At the same time, the anti-Jacobin campaign reached its peak with the impeachment of former Committee of Public Safety members Barère, Jean-Marie Collot d'Herbois, and Jacques Billaud-Varenne, and Marc Vadier, the former president of the Committee of General Security. Bread riots in the former radical sections now combined with calls for the Constitution of 1793, but after their persecution under both Jacobins and Thermidorians, the sans-culottes lacked the leadership and institutions that could have coordinated direct actions. Nonetheless, on 12 Germinal III (1 April 1795) a crowd of several thousand people occupied the National Convention for four hours, demanding bread and the Constitution of 1793, but dispersed empty-handed after reinforcements of the National Guard arrived. In response, and in flagrant violation of its own rules guaranteeing accused deputies the opportunity to defend themselves, the Convention that same evening condemned Barère, Collot d'Herbois, Billaud-Varenne, and Vadier to deportation to Guiana. It also banned large gatherings, ordered the arrest and disarmament of sans-culotte activists, and arrested sixteen Montagnard deputies who were accused of being behind the uprising.[29]

The uprising came only a few weeks after Monroe had assured Randolph at great length that the French people did not deserve "the reputation for turbulence and licentiousness, often ascribed to them in foreign countries." The prison massacres of September 1792 were perpetrated not by the people of Paris, Monroe claimed, but by outside agitators, "brought from a considerable distance, Marseilles, and some even from Italy, put in motion by some secret cause not yet fully understood." In fact, Parisians "were struck with the same horror that we were when we heard of it on the other side of the Atlantic." Likewise, during the purge of the Girondins from the Convention on 2 June 1793, the citizens occupying the Convention had been the innocent dupes of "Robespierre, Danton, &c.," and "knew nothing of the object for which they were convened, or the purpose to which they were to be made instrumental." Monroe deemed these historical revisions and reflections on "the character and disposition of the people" to be indispensable for Randolph "to judge of the future fortune of the Revolution," as the "success of the Revolution depends of course upon the people." Fortunately, Monroe concluded, "the great mass of the French nation through all the vicissitudes of the war, and succession of parties, was always on the side of the revolution." Still, the long-winded explanations that Monroe had to employ to clear the French people's name raised the question of how the popular will was to be known if even the mobilization of thousands in widely celebrated events only disguised the designs of a few.[30]

Monroe's similarly improbable explanation for the Germinal uprising was lifted directly from the pages of *Moniteur.* Dismissing the desperate scarcity of bread as a mere "pretext" to "excite a general sympathy," he regarded the occupation of the Convention as a joint conspiracy of Jacobins and royalists, "heretofore opposite classes of society, but united now for the common purpose of disturbing the public tranquility," murdering "the leading members of the preponderating party," and reviving the Reign of Terror. The failure of the insurgents, Monroe predicted, would be "productive of good," as it reinforced the power of the reigning "moderate party," which was "the avowed patron of humanity, justice and law, and equally at variance with the opposite extremes of aristocracy and anarchy."[31]

Although Monroe continued to predict that from now on "perfect tranquility" would reign in the capital, the uprising opened his eyes to some extent to the suffering around him. Bread rations had continued to diminish through April, and by the beginning of May they were down to two ounces. Monroe was allowed two pounds of bread a day for a household of fourteen people, but with foreign currency he was able to buy flour on the black market for forty dollars specie per barrel. He admitted, "The accounts which we have of the distress of the aged, the infirm, and even of children are most afflicting." Still, "calmness and serenity are seen everywhere," and the uprising must have been "excited by the animosity of contending parties, and most probably encreased by foreign influence."[32]

This time, it took only three days for Monroe to be proven wrong. On 1 Prairial (20 May), Paris workers again invaded the Convention hall, killing and decapitating the young deputy Féraud. They demanded, in addition to the end of food shortages and the Constitution of 1793, the release of imprisoned Jacobins, the revival of an independent Paris commune, and the arrest of returned émigrés. The intimidated deputies pretended to grant some of these demands before the National Guard forcibly drove the sansculottes from the hall after nine hours.

After another confrontation between twenty thousand protesters and forty thousand Guardsmen the next day, the Convention moved to crush the revolt once and for all. It arrested eleven Montagnard deputies accused of collaborating with the insurgents and ordered the army to surround the working-class district of Saint-Antoine, where they disarmed the residents and arrested over three thousand suspects. Thirty-six, including the six deputies, were executed on the guillotine. The effectiveness of the government reaction, which relied on skills honed during the Terror, contrasted sharply with the aimlessness and ineffectuality of the crowd.[33]

In his report on the uprising of Prairial to Randolph, Monroe fully approved of its violent suppression: "Its success, if it had succeeded, would have revived the reign of terror, and most probably carried all the aristocrats, with the leading men of the preponderating party to the scaffold." Moreover, "these convulsive shocks" would have a beneficial effect on the writing of the new constitution by inclining the Convention to strengthen the power of government, including "a division of the legislature into two branches" and "an organization of the executive and judiciary upon more independent principles." Monroe proudly added that the new constitution would thus be based "upon those principles indeed which exist in the American constitutions, and are well understood there. Should this be the case, the republican system will have a fair experiment here; and that it may be the case, must be the wish of all those who are the friends of humanity every where." The establishment of universal principles abroad justified the use of means that Monroe would have condemned at home.[34]

Monroe was eager to allay concerns in America that the French Revolution might have strayed too far from the American path and descended into chaos. He minimized the impact of two consecutive uprisings and urged Jefferson to arrange publication of his optimistic "Sketch of the State of Affairs in France." There Monroe once again predicted the revolution's fast-approaching "happy close, under a government founded upon principles which when completed and resting firm, must cause a similar revolution every where." Monroe also sent copies of this letter to Aaron Burr, George Logan, Robert R. Livingston, and John Beckley, and asked them to have it published anonymously in the *Aurora,* so that "the community at large may be more correctly informed of the progress of the revolution than they have heretofore been or can be from the English prints." However, Monroe's letter to Logan fell into the hands of the new secretary of state, Timothy Pickering, who forwarded it to President Washington as "proofs of sinister designs," along with the cabinet's recommendation for Monroe's recall.[35]

Due to his close ties to the Thermidorians, Monroe—like Jefferson, Morris, Paine, and Barlow before him—was asked for advice on a new French constitution, most likely by the head of the constitutional commission, Boissy d'Anglas. He gladly complied with the commission's request for a "digest" of America's national and state constitutions.[36] In 1789, the radical rejection of the past and of the examples of other nations like England and America had dominated the debate about the French constitution. In

1795, the constitutional commission was eager to draw lessons both from France's own recent violent history and from America's experience with a bicameral system. The most important lesson seemed to be that popular sovereignty, which in 1789 had been proclaimed to be unlimited, in fact required legal, moral, and institutional restraints to prevent the return of the Terror and the revolution from starting again.

A pamphlet by Adrien de Lezay-Marnezia, a young journalist from an émigré background (his father was one of the unfortunate Frenchmen enticed by Barlow to emigrate to the Ohio Country in 1790), explicitly argued that in 1789, and again in 1793, French legislators had followed the wrong American model. Lezay imagined himself embarking on a tour of the United States accompanied by Samuel Adams (although Lezay appears to have had Samuel's cousin John in mind), which culminated in an encounter in Boston with Benjamin Franklin, generally regarded in France as the author of the Pennsylvania constitution. In the ensuing argument about the constitutions of Massachusetts and Pennsylvania, Adams inevitably emerged victorious, pointing out that if men already knew how to govern themselves, as Franklin evidently assumed, no government would be necessary at all, and that of the thirteen American states, eleven enjoyed order and tranquility, with the exception of Georgia and Pennsylvania, the only two with unicameral legislatures.[37]

While retaining the unicameral legislature of the Constitution of 1791, the unimplemented Constitution of 1793 had gone much further in establishing political and social equality, by promising universal manhood suffrage and proclaiming the rights to work, subsistence, and even insurrection. In stark contrast, the Constitution of 1795 gave France for the first time a bicameral legislature, to be chosen through a complicated system of limited, indirect suffrage and with highly restrictive property and age requirements for officeholders. It also bestowed considerable authority on the Executive Directory, consisting of five men who were responsible for the external and internal security of the republic. No fewer than five separate articles banned extra-parliamentary political associations. Finally, the constitution amended the declaration of rights with a list of civic duties. Whereas in 1789 natural rights had served as the foundation of political authority (rather than as a limitation of government power, as in the American case), now the attending duties were meant to limit the popular sense of entitlement and provide the government with legitimate grounds for suppressing sedition.[38]

At this moment, Federalists in America were similarly trying to dissociate the concept of popular sovereignty from its revolutionary denotation and redefine it as the basis of citizens' duty to obey their government. Washington articulated this new definition most succinctly and powerfully in his Farewell Address: "The very idea of the power and the right of the People to establish Government presupposes the duty of every Individual to obey the established Government." Thus, ironically, just as Washington was warning his countrymen of the dangers that factious partisanship and "passionate attachments" to France posed to national unity and independence, he put forward a similar understanding of popular sovereignty as the French legislators'. Like the American Constitution of 1787, the new French constitution promised stability at the price of limiting popular involvement in the decision-making process. Political elites on both sides of the Atlantic hoped that the absence of disruptive interventions from the people in the everyday business of governing would help foster the image of a unified and stable nation, an image that could then become reality as representatives got on with the work of nation-building.[39]

Despite Monroe's contribution, the only authority Boissy d'Anglas cited in his introduction of the proposed constitution to the Convention was John Adams on the need for the balance of powers. Like Lezay, Boissy d'Anglas mistakenly referred to the vice-president as Samuel Adams, but was faithful to the constitutional doctrine of Adams's *Defence of the Constitutions of the United States* (1787). One might have expected Monroe to resent the tribute that the French lawmakers paid to the Federalist Adams. Instead, Monroe was delighted with the Convention's "unanimous" agreement on a bicameral legislature, "after the model of the American constitutions," and declared that this model was "certainly of greater importance to the preservation of their liberty than any other that has been spoken of."[40]

However, a new round of revolts in the fall of 1795 confronted Monroe directly with the paradox of trying to create a republican government of the people and for the people, but as little as possible by the people. A supplementary decree to the constitution, known as the Two-Thirds Law, stipulated that two-thirds of those elected to the new national legislature had to be drawn from those who had served in the current National Convention. If the requisite number of veteran deputies was not chosen in the electoral assemblies, the Convention was to appoint the rest from its own ranks. The Convention presented this blatant attempt to perpetuate its power as a means of ensuring continuity and stability. Monroe willingly accepted these rationales and reported to Madison that the deliberations on the constitution in Paris were "conducted with calmness & perfect good temper."[41]

With a turnout of only one-fifth of eligible voters, the new constitution was ratified. However, the anti-Jacobin campaign had allowed royalists to gain uncontested control in many sections of Paris. Now the Two-Thirds Law dashed their hopes for a dramatic power shift in the new legislature. Shortly after the results of the votes were announced, on the morning of 12 Vendémiaire IV (4 October 1795), seven sections declared themselves to be in insurrection and mobilized their National Guard units. The following day, the guards and crowds marching on the Convention clashed with regular troops, commanded by the young general Napoleon Bonaparte, in a pitched six-and-a-half-hour battle with hundreds of casualties. It was the first time the army had been used to put down unrest in the capital since the Réveillon riots of April 1789. When the National Guard, along with the sectional assemblies that had controlled it, was abolished on 10 October, the army became the supreme instrument of government at home as well as abroad.[42]

Monroe's shock and confusion about the seemingly unending cycle of violence are reflected in a long, convoluted letter to Secretary of State Timothy Pickering. The paradox that Monroe was struggling to explain was that, on the one hand, he had to acknowledge that getting rid of the Two-Thirds Law "would have secured the elections in favor of the royalists." On the other hand, he clung to the belief that the armies, "the great bulk of the citizens of Paris," and "the farmers or cultivators" were all in favor of the revolution. Already during the debate over the Two-Thirds Law, the deputy Thomas-François Jouenne had pointed out the same inconsistency in the Convention's policy, which claimed to represent the people's will, yet feared that counterrevolutionary sentiment was rife among the people and distrusted the choices they might make.[43]

Republicans in America faced a very similar predicament when the massive popular protests against Jay's Treaty quickly turned to acceptance in the spring of 1796. It was axiomatic that, as Jefferson put it, "the great body of our *native* citizens are unquestionably of the republican sentiment." Still, the line between genuine patriots and what Jefferson liked to call the "foreign and false citizens" proved disturbingly fluid when a great number of supposedly Republican citizens put economic interests before ideological purity in supporting the ratification of Jay's Treaty.[44]

In trying to explain how so many Americans could have been duped into support of the "Anglican, monarchical aristocratical party," Republicans blamed the corrupting influence of British trade and dependence on foreign credit, as well as the lies spread through the British and Federalist press. As we have seen in previous chapters, the definition of political opponents as "foreigners" had become commonplace on both sides of the Atlantic in the early 1790s. By the middle of the decade, political elites, grappling with the unpredictability of the new kind of popular politics practiced in the United States and France, increasingly relied on this equation of lines of partisan division with the boundaries of national identity to sustain their faith in the capability of the people to govern themselves.[45]

In order to maintain the belief that the people of Paris consented to the new constitution, Monroe had to deny that they had been free agents in the recent uprising. The number of actual Parisians who had participated in the riot was "inconsiderable," Monroe claimed, and the crowd who had fought in the streets had in fact been "composed of adventurers from other regions, and in some instances even forcigners." The revolt in the sections was the result of the designs of "artful men" who had managed "to prevail over the ignorant, and seduce them into error." Royalists throughout the country had extended the persecution of "the subaltern, and perhaps wicked agents of the former reign" to terrorize "many of the soundest patriots, and best of men" into abstaining from voting or voting for royalist candidates. The pendulum had swung from the government reaction against Jacobin terrorism to royalist terrorism against the government.[46]

On the bright side, Monroe believed that the uprising had "unmasked" the royalists and their secret designs, which would certainly "open the eyes of the community." At the same time, he hoped for a similar unmasking of the Federalist enemies of the American republic during the debate over Jay's Treaty. Political heresy on the part of the people could only be the result of deception and misinformation, never of irredeemable corruption, let alone of a diversity of equally valid viewpoints. Once the truth was revealed and the enemy unmasked, the people would once again rally around the standard of the one true republican faith.[47]

After the experience of three consecutive uprisings in the space of half a year, Monroe welcomed with a sigh of relief the inauguration of the Directory on 27 October 1795. Despite the turmoil of the last month and the problematic election, France was now finally approximating the American example. As he reported to Pickering, "When I observe that the scene, which was exhibited upon this great occasion, resembled in many respects what we see daily acted on our side of the Atlantic, in our national and state assemblies, you will have a better idea of the tranquility and serenity which reigned throughout, than I can otherwise describe." While this paean might appear ironic, given the intense battles that had been fought in American national and state assemblies over Jay's Treaty, it genuinely reflected Monroe's belief that "tranquility and serenity" were the natural condition of the political realm.[48]

To this end, it might be necessary to exclude large parts of the people from the political process, to protect the republic from its citizens and the people against itself. Monroe bestowed particular praise on the constitution's transfer of all military and police powers of the state to the executive, removed from any influence of the legislature and the public. In Monroe's view, the French needed a strong hand to steer clear of either anarchy or monarchy. At the same time, in true republican fashion, Monroe denied that in a republic any power had to be exercised at all: "Intemperate zeal too is restrained, but the restraint is always easy, indeed it is a self-one, or rather it does not exist, when the administration possesses the confidence of the People and wields the government according to their wishes."[49]

Monroe's political career was nearly destroyed by his attempt to be an active partisan in two rapidly evolving political landscapes at the same time, all in the name of non-partisanship. After Randolph's forced resignation as secretary of state in August 1795, his successor, Timothy Pickering, and Secretary of the Treasury Oliver Wolcott, along with Alexander Hamilton, worked to convince Washington to recall Monroe from Paris. The ratification of Jay's Treaty and the absence of an official French protest made the continuance of a Republican in such an important diplomatic position both unnecessary and potentially dangerous, especially after Pickering intercepted a copy of Monroe's "Sketch of the State of Affairs in France," which he regarded as disparaging the administration's foreign policy. The recall was a devastating blow to Monroe's personal reputation and to the future of Franco-American relations. For the next year, and really until the end of his life, Monroe tried to defend his honor and conduct as minister to France, first in a 473-page documentation of official correspondence between himself and the executive, titled *A View of the Conduct of the Executive in the Foreign Affairs of the United States Connected with the Mission to the French Republic* (1797), and later in his unfinished retirement memoirs, written between 1827 and 1830.

When Monroe took his leave from France, in an official ceremony on 30 December 1796, he expressed the same warm devotion to the French Republic and faith in its bond with the United States as during his appearance before the National Convention when he first arrived. The Terror and the upheavals he had witnessed during his tenure, he declared, had only made the republic stronger.[50]

In the Directory's reply to Monroe's farewell address, Paul Barras drew a sharp distinction between the U.S. government, which submitted "to the wishes of its ancient tyrants," and "the good people of America," who "will always possess our esteem" and whose "true interests" Monroe had represented. But like Monroe's depiction of the Parisian populace as both the foundation and the main threat to the revolution, the distinction between the good American people and their bad government, which was often repeated in the French press, cast doubt on the very concept of popular sovereignty that the two republics were supposed to exemplify.[51]

Monroe could take some consolation in the fact that seventy members of the American community in Paris presented him with a testimonial in which they praised his conduct and disapproved of his recall. But, as he was aware that the Federalists were blaming Americans in Paris for the belated French protests against Jay's Treaty, he was reluctant to accept the tribute, lest it would be used to further discredit him. Four months earlier, at the celebration on July 4th, a toast to Washington had led to a scuffle between American critics and supporters of the president, and Monroe was deeply embarrassed in front of his prominent French guests. Moreover, as he had anticipated, the Federalist press in America elevated the dispute into a full-fledged brawl and used the incident as confirmation of the president's wisdom in recalling Monroe. As relations between France and the United States edged toward war, the American presence in Paris seemed more likely to further divide than reunite the two republics.[52]

5

The End of a Beautiful Friendship

ANTI-COSMOPOLITANISM, ANTI-AMERICANISM,

AND PUBLIC DIPLOMACY, 1796-1799

In "Political Reflections," an essay published anonymously at the height of the Quasi-War between the United States and France in February 1799, James Madison wrote that recent events in the French Republic could not "be too much pondered and contemplated by Americans who love their country."[1] Of course, there were those who sought "to caricature the scene as to cast an odium on all Republican government." But even among republicans there was sharp disagreement about what lessons should be drawn from reports, whether true or not, that the French executive body, the five-man Directory, had "erected itself into a Tyranny, actuated by its own ambitious views, in opposition to the sentiments and interests of the nation." Madison's own interest lay in ascertaining "the true causes of the abuses in France, as so many rocks to be shunned" by the American republic. The Federalists, however, appeared to him engaged in the "strange endeavor" of inferring "from the vices and usurpations charged on the French government, the propriety of a blind and unqualified reliance on the infallibility of our own."

If the real or exaggerated exigencies of war could turn the French Republic from a representative government with separate powers into a dictatorship dominated by the executive, what would prevent the same thing from

111

happening in the United States? For Madison, the true lesson of the French example was "that in no case ought the eyes of the people be shut on the conduct of those entrusted with power." The Federalists, on the other hand, in the name of defending America against French tyranny, were adopting the exact same measures–increasing the power of the executive and the military, curtailing civil liberties, and branding any dissent as unpatriotic–that had corrupted the Directory. But if there was one universal truth in the "whole field of political science," it was that "*the fetters imposed on liberty at home have ever been forged out of the weapons provided for defence against real, pretended, or imaginary dangers from abroad.*"

For all its sagacity, Madison's essay was as much a product of the political battles of the time as the Federalist policies it condemned. But it suggests an overlooked irony of the confrontation between the administration of John Adams and the Directory: the similarity in attitudes toward popular politics between the two regimes. Both distrusted popular politics but ambivalently tried to use them to their own ends. Both tended to conflate their own rule with the very principle of republican government. Therefore, they had little tolerance for organized, legal opposition and considered public criticism as an attack on the republic itself. As repressive as the Alien and Sedition Acts were, the Directory went much further in stifling and persecuting all opposition, most notably in the coups d'état of 18 Fructidor (4 September 1797) and 22 Floréal (11 May 1798). The two regimes' common insecurities also expressed themselves in their fear of the subversive presence of foreigners. One group that attracted the suspicion of both regimes, and that therefore allows us to explore these parallels, were Americans in Paris.

In 1798 there were more Americans in Paris than ever before. In 1791, William Short had celebrated the Fourth of July with fewer than twenty Americans. The outbreak of war in Europe in 1792 had drawn increasing numbers of merchants, speculators, and adventurers to the French capital. In 1795, close to a hundred Americans attended James Monroe's elaborate Independence Day fête. By the end of 1797, the number of Americans had grown to more than two hundred and fifty. Most were merchants from New England who sought to take advantage of the food shortages in France and Saint-Domingue, demand redress for ships and cargoes impounded in French harbors or seized by French privateers, sell American lands, speculate in French currency, or buy real estate.[2]

While war among Europeans was good for American business, open conflict between the United States and France was not. Therefore, Americans in Paris witnessed the deterioration of Franco-American relations with great concern. Since Monroe's recall in 1796, diplomatic negotiations between the two republics had completely broken down, and had been replaced by undeclared warfare on the high seas. The Directory had refused to receive Monroe's successor, Charles Cotesworth Pinckney, and hundreds of American ships had been captured by French privateers in the Caribbean or confiscated in French ports.

There had been hope for improvement in 1797, when the new president, John Adams, sent three commissioners to Paris to restore amicable relations while preserving American neutrality. The envoys, John Marshall, Elbridge Gerry, and Pinckney, had arrived in Paris in October 1797 on the heels of a political upheaval. After the coup d'état of 18 Fructidor, the "second Directory" was even more committed to an aggressive foreign policy, and more dependent on the army, than the previous regime. Preoccupied with plans for an invasion of Britain, the French government was also in desperate need of money. Consequently, the agents of French Foreign Minister Charles-Maurice de Talleyrand-Périgord had informed the American envoys that there were a number of preconditions before any official negotiations could begin. The agents, Jean Hottinguer, Pierre Bellamy, and Lucien Hauteval, had demanded that the U.S. government assume all private American claims against the French Republic, grant a loan of thirty-two million Dutch florins, offer an apology for President Adams's belligerent speech to Congress of 16 May 1797, and pay a bribe of fifty thousand pounds to Talleyrand. The American envoys had refused, not because they were outraged at the demand for bribes, but because it was far from certain that they would receive anything in return. In March 1798, Marshall and Pinckney, who had fallen out with Gerry over how to proceed in the absence of official negotiations, left France. On 3 April, Secretary of State Timothy Pickering presented Marshall's dispatches from Paris to Congress, substituting the letters X, Y, and Z for the names of the French agents. Soon after, the full text of the reports was available in pamphlets and newspapers to readers all across the United States.[3]

Even before the enormous publicity generated by the XYZ dispatches, a number of prominent Americans in Paris had decided to intervene and reverse the decline of Franco-American friendship. After trying unsuccessfully to mediate between the three American envoys and the French Foreign

Ministry, they turned their attention to the political scene in America. In letters to friends and allies in the United States, spokesmen of the American community in Paris, like Joel Barlow and Consul General Fulwar Skipwith, explained that France wanted to avoid a full-scale war and was eager to renew diplomatic negotiations. At the same time, the prominent Jeffersonian George Logan traveled to Paris on his own initiative to persuade the Directory that reconciliation with America was possible and in France's best interest.

These mediation attempts provide a fresh perspective on early American diplomacy. Since the American Revolution, in the absence of a well-established diplomatic corps, private Americans abroad sometimes had been called upon to informally represent American interests, or had assumed this task on their own initiative. Moreover, the letters written by Americans in Paris were similar to previous efforts by official American representatives in Europe to influence public opinion at home and abroad.

Like Federalist contemporaries, historians have dismissed the Americans in Paris as "a gang of hustlers," who, owing to their commercial interests, "had a selfish stake in peace."[4] It is true that Americans in Paris sought to profit from the war in Europe and the unstable French economy. In fact, their business practices, such as speculation in the fluctuation of the French currency, caused outrage and resentment in Paris. However, it is precisely the similarity of the perceptions of Americans in Paris, in the United States and France, that sheds new light on the fate of the cosmopolitan ideal at the end of the 1790s.

The interventions of Americans in Paris helped fuel a heated debate in the United States about the boundaries of the national community and the limits of private political activism in foreign countries. Contrary to standard accounts of a universal surge in popular patriotic fervor after the XYZ Affair, the controversy surrounding Americans in Paris highlights the difficulties that Federalists encountered in manufacturing a nationalist consensus.

Federalist newspapers and politicians derided the Americans in Paris as meddlers or denounced them as traitors in collusion with Jacobin agents and the "French party" in the United States. Yet there were two ironies about the Federalists' anticosmopolitan campaign. First, Federalist attitudes toward the Americans in Paris were remarkably similar to those held by many Frenchmen. For the Federalists, these "French Americans" exemplified the corrosive influence of the French Revolution on the American character.

For the French, the Americans in Paris embodied everything they had come to resent about Americans in general: their greed and shady business practices, their lack of gratitude to France, and their continued subservience to Britain. While for the Federalists these Americans were too much attached to France, the French regarded them as not loyal enough. Both sides saw American cosmopolitans as unreliable, untrustworthy, and motivated by selfish financial interests rather than universal benevolence. Second, by attacking the Americans in Paris in print, the Federalists gave unprecedented publicity to their activities and thereby inadvertently elevated their importance in Franco-American relations. The Directory adroitly played on this dynamic and used the American mediators to seek rapprochement with the Adams administration while allowing the Republican opposition to take credit for the peaceful resolution of the crisis.

When Marshall, Pinckney, and Gerry arrived in Paris, many longtime American residents of the city felt that they knew more about the French government's procedures and personnel than the envoys, and they freely offered their advice. For example, Barlow and Skipwith cautioned that the new arrivals would need to be patient since the Directory was preoccupied with affairs in Europe and likely to prolong the negotiations as much as possible.[5] James Cole Mountflorence, who worked for the American consulate in Paris, offered his services as intermediary between the envoys and the Foreign Ministry, as he had good relations with the baron d'Osmond, one of Talleyrand's private secretaries, and was also a trusted source of information for Pinckney.[6]

Such private intervention was not without precedent. During the colonial era, the British government, when formulating its American policy, frequently consulted with private individuals from the colonies who were staying in London. Americans in London with access to government ministers acted independently from the official colonial agents and without formal authority. As Julie Flavell has shown, when the colonial agencies became defunct in late 1774, these Americans became the only remaining channel of communication between Britain and her North American colonies. Private colonists like William Lee, Stephen Sayre, Josiah Quincy Jr., and Ralph Izard, by default, assumed the tasks of representing the Patriot position to members of the North administration and opposition politicians, sending intelligence to Patriot leaders in the colonies and putting the case for colonial resistance before the British public through newspaper articles and pamphlets. In the eyes of Americans in Paris, Talleyrand's refusal to officially receive the envoys made similar kinds of private intervention both necessary and legitimate.[7]

The French penchant for informal negotiations in private conversations and at dinner parties irritated Marshall and Pinckney but provided an opportunity for private Americans to become involved. The merchant Nathaniel Cutting boasted, "I have frequently had *unofficial* communications with some individuals connected in the French government; now and then I have had the honor to converse with the American Envoys." The artist John Trumbull was invited to meet Talleyrand at a dinner party at Madame de Staël's and later visited the minister at his office to discuss the state of negotiations.[8]

Marshall and Pinckney were deeply suspicious of these "French Americans." Pinckney thought that the Americans in Paris were conspiring with the French to aggravate the division between Gerry and the other envoys. He noted that the "American Jacobins here pay him [Gerry] a great court," and that "every art is used by Talleyrand and French Americans here to detach Mr. Gerry from his colleagues." Similarly, after a visit by Edward Church of Boston, who had extensive property interests in Paris, Marshall described him sarcastically as "an American I believe *by birth,* who had been consul of France."[9]

Unsuccessful in their attempts to mediate between the envoys and the French Foreign Ministry, Barlow and Skipwith turned to influential friends in America for help. Again, they were following common practice. During and after the American Revolution, official American representatives had engaged in public diplomacy–the attempt to influence opinion in other countries through well-placed letters, pamphlets, or newspaper articles. Historians have traced the origins of public diplomacy to the efforts of the restored European monarchies to control public opinion after the French Revolution, but American representatives were practicing public diplomacy even before the fall of the Bastille. Having observed the power of public opinion in their own country, American diplomats hoped that information management might compensate somewhat for the United States' glaring lack of economic and political influence in Europe.[10]

Benjamin Franklin was the first master of public diplomacy. During his stay in France from 1776 to 1785, Franklin worked tirelessly to bring French and European opinion onto the side of the American struggle for independence by funneling information to sympathetic publications like the *Affaires de l'Angleterre et de l'Amérique* and by encouraging the translation and distribution of American state constitutions. Similarly, Franklin's successor, Thomas Jefferson, provided the *Gazette de Leyde* with pro-American news items throughout his tenure as minister to France. In 1795, James Monroe sought to influence American public opinion by asking political allies at home to publish his optimistic, and therefore "more correct," reports on the French Revolution. In 1797, Charles C. Pinckney printed a pamphlet in Amsterdam (where he and his family had moved after their expulsion from France) based on a report on Franco-American relations by Timothy Pickering, and sent a copy to every member of the French legislature. French newspapers protested that the High Federalist Pinckney's appeal to a foreign legislature to challenge its executive was not all that different from the activities of the Federalist bête-noire, Edmund Genet.[11]

As in Monroe's case, the target of Barlow and Skipwith was opinion in the United States, which they feared had been poisoned by British and Federalist misinformation and propaganda. They did not see themselves as spokesmen for the French Republic, but as American patriots who were trying to save their country from the misguided policies of its own government. Barlow wrote a letter to his brother-in-law, Senator Abraham Baldwin of Georgia, to set the record straight on the true origins of Franco-American estrangement. In case Congress adjourned before the letter could reach Baldwin, Barlow also sent a copy to Vice President Jefferson, "trusting in your prudence to make such use of it only as may do the most good to the cause of truth, & the least mischief to me." This indicates that the letter was of a "public-minded" nature but intended to be circulated among political allies only. Skipwith likewise addressed a letter on the subject to Jefferson, and both he and Barlow entrusted their messages to William Lee, an American merchant in Paris who was returning to America.[12]

Barlow's and Skipwith's letters highlighted the central role that Americans in Paris had played in Franco-American relations. Using the language of sensibility familiar from his earlier writings, Barlow depicted the falling-out between the United States and France as the product not of geopolitical calculations, but of a great, unrequited love. The main characters in this tragic tale were the Americans on the ground in Paris, who represented the United States to its French devotees.

The French revolutionaries of 1789, Barlow wrote, had looked up to the American example for having solved "the frightful problem of representative democracy," and had regarded America with "the most extravagant affections." If American policymakers had "properly nourished" these affections, the result would have been "confidence without bounds." Instead, "slighted or answered with indifference," these feelings turned into "a jealousy uncontrolled by the rules of justice & blind to the light of truth." Gouverneur Morris, "personally detested by all the leaders in the revolution," had destroyed the goodwill that Jefferson's presence had generated earlier, with his "invectives against every principle of liberty" and by serving as "the banker, protector & correspondent of the most obnoxious emigrants." Monroe and other "Americans in Paris, of characters far more respectable than that of Morris"—Barlow likely had Thomas Paine and perhaps himself in mind—had tried to repair the damage. However, after Monroe's recall, "for the apparent crime of preventing a war," and the election of Adams, the French had concluded that American hostility toward them had been "nationalized." Deeply wounded, they were "determined to fleece you of your property to a sufficient degree to bring you to your feeling in the only point in which it was presumed your sensibility lay, which was your pecuniary interest."

Barlow and Skipwith insisted on the bond between the American and French republics, based on the shared principles of their revolutions and on America's continued obligation to France for its support of the War of Independence. The recent negotiations had failed, they argued, because the hostility of Marshall and Pinckney toward the French Revolution made them unfit to represent the United States. The only policy that could save the American republic from a French invasion, Skipwith advised, was to "confess some of our errors, to lay their sins heavily upon the shoulders of a few persons who have perpetrated them, to modify or break the English treaty with Jay, and to lend France as much money, should she ask it, as she lent us in the hour of distress." For good measure, Barlow added that Congress should have sent President Adams to the "Mad-house" for "borrowing the cant of Edmond Burke" while ostensibly trying to negotiate a treaty with France. Both letters were blatantly one-sided, denouncing American insensitivity while excusing French attacks on U.S. commerce. But they accurately reflected the attitudes of other Americans in Paris. Mary Pinckney found that many of her compatriots "are amazingly fearful of hurting the feelings of this government, but are ready to find fault with their own–if an indecent paragraph against this government appears in our papers, where the press is free, they snort with anger and fear, but they can read violent tirades against us in the french papers without any emotion."[13]

This partiality stemmed in some cases from previous experience in France. Despite the Directory's lack of popular legitimacy and its dependence on the army, many Americans in Paris regarded it as the only bulwark against a return of either the Terror or the monarchy. Especially those who had lived through the Terror were willing to give the Directory the benefit of the doubt when it claimed that it was curtailing civil liberties and nullifying election results for the sake of law and order. For example, Thomas Paine publicly justified the coup d'état of Fructidor as dictated by "the supreme law of absolute necessity" to save the republic from a royalist conspiracy. Paine insisted that even the coup could be seen as following the blueprint of the American Revolution: "At one time congress invested general Washington with dictatorial powers. At another time the government of Pennsylvania suspended itself and declared martial law." The Directory gratefully received copies of his pamphlet from Paine and immediately authorized a French translation.[14]

Moreover, Paine, Barlow, and Skipwith were not the only Americans for whom loyalty to the French Revolution was an expression of American patriotism. If reports of the Terror raised doubts among American Republicans about the nature of the French Revolution, most were unwilling to admit to them, for fear of playing into the hands of their political opponents. By the time Barlow's and Skipwith's letters reached the United States, cosmopolitan patriotism had come under severe attack in the wake of the XYZ Affair. Historians have used the natural metaphors of a "great explosion of national feeling" or a "wave of patriotism" to describe the public reaction to the publication of Marshall's dispatches. According to the standard account, Americans everywhere united behind the Adams administration and against French belligerence. Francophiles publicly repudiated their former positions. Congress formally abrogated the Franco-American Alliance of 1778, imposed an embargo on trade with France, and authorized the construction of warships as well as the creation of a Navy Department. American nationalism took on new characteristics, such as nativism, xenophobia, and the exaltation of American moral superiority, which culminated in the Naturalization and Alien Acts of 1798.[15]

Conversely, Seth Cotlar has argued that this "explosion of national feeling" was far from a natural phenomenon, but instead the product of a carefully orchestrated "cultural offensive" by the Federalist Party. Rather than tapping into a preexisting well of widespread anti-Jacobinism, Federalists worked hard to manufacture a nationalist consensus through the press, pamphlets, rallies, and mass petitions.[16] Having learned their lesson from the controversy around Jay's Treaty, Federalists styled themselves as champions of publicity during the XYZ Affair and turned the charges of secrecy and conspiracy back on the French and their Republican supporters. The xenophobic, deferential, and explicitly anti-revolutionary vision of American politics that Federalists disseminated for the first time on a grand scale in 1798 succeeded in putting their Republican opponents on the defensive.

Still, although Federalists enjoyed electoral gains in the South and doubled their margin in the House in the congressional elections of 1798–99, they lost the governorship of Pennsylvania and representation in the key states of Pennsylvania, New Jersey, and Maryland. Federalists continued to bemoan the American people's insufficient national sentiment. Joseph Hopkinson, author of the song "Hail Columbia," reported to Secretary of the Treasury Oliver Wolcott from New York: "It is a mortifying fact, my dear sir, that the federal spirit of this city is not worth a farthing." George Cabot noticed the same lack of outrage in other parts of the country. "It is impossible," he lamented, "to make the people feel or see distinctly that we have much more to fear from peace than war." He was convinced that "war, open and declared, would not only deprive our external enemy of his best hopes, but would also extinguish the hopes of internal foes." Like the Girondins in 1792, Federalists looked to war as a panacea that would purge the nation of its enemies on the inside and unite it against those on the outside.[17]

Cosmopolitanism was a particular target of the Federalist "cultural offensive" because it was said to undermine the ties of nationhood that preserved social order and to open the nation to foreign subversion. Federalist authors and speakers urged their fellow citizens to see themselves as part of a historically grown community with strong ties of customs, values, and blood. While the Alien and Sedition Acts of 1798 resulted in few actual persecutions, their real significance lay in codifying this new exclusive language of nationhood.[18] Barlow's and Skipwith's letters posed a direct challenge to this new nationalist consensus.

Skipwith's letter never reached its destination. At the same time that he and Barlow gave their letters to William Lee in Paris, Talleyrand sent to the United States an open letter to the American envoys for publication in American newspapers. Trying to shift responsibility for the crisis from himself and the Directory to the Adams administration, Talleyrand restated French grievances against the United States and suggested that he would be willing to negotiate with more conciliatory envoys. Marshall and Pinckney immediately composed a rejoinder, and made sure that copies made their way to America as quickly as possible. Negotiations between France and the United States were now conducted as much in the American public sphere as in Parisian government chambers and salons.[19]

The Federalist press had long been eager to prove that the Republican editor Benjamin Franklin Bache was in direct correspondence with the French government. When Bache's *Aurora* published Talleyrand's message on 16 June 1798, Federalists charged that Bache had received it directly from the French minister and that he and his paper were part of a network of French agents in the United States. A few days later, the *Gazette of the United States* and other papers claimed to have found additional evidence in a packet, bearing the official seal of the French Foreign Ministry and addressed to Bache, that William Lee had carried across the Atlantic. When questioned by Oliver Wolcott about the mail he had brought over from France, Lee turned over several letters, including the one from Skipwith, but not Barlow's. To allay suspicions that he was an agent of Talleyrand, Lee also issued a public statement disclaiming any knowledge of the contents of the letters he had received in France. The interception of the mail became the subject of a bitter newspaper battle between Bache and his opponents, and Bache's published comments during the controversy led the government to charge him with seditious libel even prior to the passage of the Sedition Act.[20]

Barlow's letter did reach its addressee, but then fell into the hands of the wrong public. Soon after Senator Baldwin began to discreetly circulate the letter among other Republicans, it was stolen. Earlier, Baldwin had allowed Congressman Matthew Lyon to make a copy of the letter, provided that he would not publish it. In September, Lyon proceeded to regularly read the letter aloud on the campaign trail in western Vermont, where, according to the testimony of two young Federalists, it elicited violent reactions from the audience. Then the letter appeared as a pamphlet whose author was described only as "an American Diplomatic Character in France" but who was quickly identified as Barlow. Lyon claimed that his wife had given his copy of the letter to another printer in his absence and that he had tried to prevent its publication. In fact, Lyon was eager to test the recently passed Sedition Act and publication of Barlow's letter constituted part of his indictment. His case was the first under the new law, and he was sentenced to four months in prison and a fine of one thousand dollars. As he had intended, Lyon became a martyr for freedom of the press, and from his cell he successfully ran for reelection to Congress.[21]

Meanwhile, Barlow's letter was widely reprinted and vigorously denounced in Federalist newspapers. The *Columbian Centinel* declared that it undoubtedly had been written in Talleyrand's office while the French foreign minister, "arch apostate, sat at the elbow of the duped American and dictated every word. A greater quantum of folly, arrogance, egotism, and falsehood could not be condensed within equal limits." The letter constituted a betrayal, "compared with which that of *Judas Iscariot* is but a foible."[22]

Accusations of atheism and blasphemy were standard in anti-Jacobin propaganda but had particular resonance in Barlow's case, owing to his involvement in the publication of Paine's *Age of Reason* (1794). Many of Barlow's old friends in Connecticut, now prominent Federalists, homed in on this connection. Richard Alsop combined Barlow's alleged atheism and his rootless cosmopolitanism in the kind of doggerel for which Barlow and the Connecticut Wits had been renowned a decade earlier: "This 'Jack-at-all-trades, good *at one*' / This ever-changing, Proteus mind / In all his turns, thro' every wind / From telling sinners where they go / To speculations in Scioto / From morals pure, and manners plain / To herding with Munroe and Paine / From feeding on his country's bread / To aping X, and Y, and Z / From preaching Christ, to Age of Reason / From writing psalms, to writing treason."[23]

In an open letter to Barlow published in the *Commercial Advertiser*, Noah Webster explicitly denied that the United States owed anything to France. On the contrary, the Franco-American alliance of 1778 had in fact unnecessarily prolonged the war with Britain. Closing on a personal note, Webster publicly ended his decades-long friendship with Barlow: "One more word, Sir, from an old friend who once loved and respected you. The contemptuous manner in which you speak of the President and the Senate of America is a striking proof of the effect of atheism and licentious examples on the civility and good manners of a well-bred man."[24] Another old friend, Senator

James Watson of New York, responded to a private letter from Barlow, who had argued that a war between the republics would "disgrace the principles of both their revolutions," by declaring that he was happy to see Americans recover from "our preposterous predilection for France." In fact, it was "indispensable to our national existence that we should be cured of that idolatry to France of which we were guilty in the early stages of our revolution." Barlow had reappeared as an embarrassing reminder of those "early stages," and judging by the intensity of the attacks on him, many Federalists feared that their compatriots might not have fully outgrown them.[25]

Such attacks were not limited to Barlow. In the *Philadelphia Gazette,* Samuel Hopkins declared that all Americans in Paris were, with a few exceptions, "the fugitives of America, and the dregs and out-laws of Europe. I need not observe, that they and their connections here [in Paris] have been the most active despoilers of our commerce–the most inveterate calumniators of our country and our government–nor that they have continually contradicted and embarrassed all our public missionaries, except Mr. Monroe." Watson likewise accused the Americans in Paris of putting their own financial interests above the interests of their native country: "It has been said that some Americans in Paris have shown by calculation, that to pay the gratuity of fifty thousand sterling and the loan of thirty millions of florins would be cheaper than a war." This "renegade arithmetic" proved how much French influence had corrupted their morals, as it was "something worse than is used when a man sets a price upon his integrity or a virgin upon her chastity."

Alongside treason and atheism this was the most common charge against Americans in Paris. Mrs. Pinckney, like her husband and John Marshall, believed that beneath the flowery rhetoric it was greed that inspired the "French Americans'" overzealous defense of French policy: "In short they would have their own government and its ministers to consider what may affect their fortunes in France and act accordingly." The dismissal of the cosmopolitan ideals professed by Barlow and other Americans in Paris as a cover for selfish ambition followed logically from the new Federalist dogma that only national allegiances could count as authentic motives.[26]

Ironically, this last Federalist accusation was also regularly found in French newspapers and pamphlets. Both the Federalists and the French regarded the Americans in Paris as unreliable and insufficiently loyal to their side, and both attributed this lack of loyalty to selfishness and greed. In his letter, Barlow failed to acknowledge that Gouverneur Morris had been far from the only American in Paris who had contributed to the buildup of French resentment against the United States. While Morris certainly had created much furor within political circles, it was the everyday behavior–their business practices and ostentatious lifestyles–of prominent Americans in Paris (including Barlow) that reinforced anti-American stereotypes among the French public.

In early 1796, Donatien-Marie-Joseph de Rochambeau, son of the celebrated French general, alerted Tench Coxe, the assistant secretary of the treasury, to a change in French attitudes toward America.[27] Having recently returned to Paris from a trip to the United States, Rochambeau no longer found "among the French that cordial attachment for the Americans which they had at the close of the last war." In part, this shift was due to Jay's Treaty and the American rapprochement with Britain at the expense of France. At least equally resented, however, was the great number of Americans in Paris who speculated in the depreciation of the French currency, the assignat, or lent their names to that "scandalous commerce," as well as the fraudulent business practices of American land sellers. Frequent reports of the avarice of American merchants in France were compounded by similar complaints from French refugees in the United States who had fled the revolution in Saint-Domingue. Whereas Federalists accused Americans in Paris of loving France too much, the French thought that Americans were not grateful enough. According to Rochambeau, there was widespread "astonishment that Americans are estranged from France just as the French Revolution had taken a Republican cast." After all, like the French, the Americans had also scrapped their first constitution and persecuted and banished the Tory "aristocrats" from the new republic. And, unlike the French, they had done so under far more favorable circumstances, supported by a powerful ally rather than surrounded by hostile armies. For both republics, liberty had not been achieved without struggle, but now the Americans seemed to prefer to forget how similar their past troubles were to those presently engulfing France.

Police spies who haunted the streets, markets, and theaters of Paris confirmed Rochambeau's impressions. Their job was not to identify criminals and counterrevolutionaries, but to study the mood of the public and submit daily reports to the Central Bureau of Police and the Ministry of the Interior.

On 22 Brumaire V (12 November 1796), an informer reported: "There is much talk about the American strangers who here engage in the most flagrant *agiotage.*" *Agiotage* was originally a general term for financial speculations of all kinds, but during the revolution it had acquired connotations of greed, usury, war profiteering, and parasitic and unpatriotic behavior. *Agioteur* was also used to describe those traitors who hid behind a "mask of patriotism." "We will mention only Judas Iscariot," declared a sans-culotte paper, "who was exposed as a traitor, an *agioteur.*"[28]

Since Americans had already experienced the collapse of their own currency at the end of the War of Independence, they were quick to profit from the falling value of the assignat by buying goods and property with devalued assignats and reselling them against hard currency such as gold and silver.[29] Flush with paper money, Americans bought up prize pieces of real estate all over Paris. Skipwith at one point owned five townhouses on the Left Bank, and Edward Church and William Rogers won several houses in the National Lottery whose owners had emigrated or had been executed. By the same means, the middling merchant William Vans became the owner of the Hôtel de Senneterre on the Rue de l'Université, which was ten times the size of anything he would have been able to afford back home. These investments were not entirely without risks, however. Just as Thomas Griffith tried to sell for specie a house in the Rue de Richelieu he had bought for "a large sum of assignats," a new paper currency, the mandats, was introduced. The new currency "fell in value as soon as it appeared, but, having been made legal tender, my purchaser took advantage of it, and thus my hopes of a successful speculation in real estate cost me dear."[30]

The lifestyle of the American nouveaux riches is reflected in Mary Pinckney's description of a typical day in the life of fellow Charlestonian Henry Middleton: "Mr. Middleton hates London, & England, & loves Paris. He says it is the most agreeable place in the world. Every odd day he attends [physicist Jacques] Charles lectures from ten till near two, & immediately after [Antoine-François de] Fourcroys lectures on chemistry from 2 till four. He makes notes–he corrects them–he learns french & italian–he finds out pictures–he buys a few–he sometimes goes to a subscription ball, & often to plays–he amuses himself, not in a dissipated, but in a philosophical manner." At a time when poverty was still widespread in Paris, Americans were far from discreet about their new wealth. The merchant Richard Codman threw extravagant parties, described by Mary Pinckney as the most lavish of the time, in his elegant townhouse and his chateau on the outskirts of Paris, which he had restored at staggering cost. The festivities were well attended by Frenchmen and Americans and included dining, concerts, and dancing.[31]

In combination with the larger political issue of Jay's Treaty, reports of Americans in Paris cheaply buying old estates and speculating in the depreciation of the French currency were bound to reinforce anti-American stereotypes: Americans put money before everything else; therefore they had no scruples about profiting from the misfortune of their old French allies and collaborating with their enemies, and they would always remain British colonials at heart. Some Americans tried to counter these stereotypes in print. In 1795, the radical republican John Skey Eustace and the self-described Federalist Thomas Griffith sought to refute the charge of American subservience to Britain and to highlight the opportunities for expanded Franco-American trade, but their defensive tone was unlikely to change the minds of many French readers.[32]

As official relations between France and the United States deteriorated, Americans in Paris became increasingly concerned about their safety. Shortly after his arrival in Paris, John Marshall reported: "Mr. Putnam an American citizen has been arrested and sent to gaol under the pretext of his cheating frenchmen. By those Americans who have mentioned the subject to me this is understood to be a mere pretext. It is considered as ominous towards Americans generally." Thomas Griffith likewise remembered that during this time, "American property was subject to many risks, and our persons were in danger." Particularly alarming was a decree of 9 Germinal V (29 March 1797) stipulating that passports issued by U.S. ministers or consuls would no longer be valid, which meant that Americans had to leave France unless they could obtain a *carte de sûreté*. Griffith was arrested several times for failing to renew his residency permit.[33]

However, this decree did not reflect a particular hostility toward Americans, but rather the general insecurity of the Directory, which felt surrounded by domestic and foreign enemies. In fact, the Directory rejected the recommendation of Minister of Police Charles Cochon de Lapparent to banish all Americans from France. Moreover, the Directory was likely aware that despite all the popular resentment against Americans, at no point did public opinion support a war against the United States. In fact, there was some criticism of the Directory for needlessly antagonizing the Americans, as well as concern that a war would result in the loss of France's West Indian colonies.

Still, as the Directory prepared for an invasion of Britain, it again became increasingly suspicious that the British government might use agents claiming U.S. citizenship to circumvent French laws against enemy aliens. A decree of 8 Ventôse VI (26 February 1798) defined as British all English-speaking individuals, unless they had documentary proof that they were Americans.[34] Like their Federalist counterparts in America, the embattled Directory considered aliens and immigrants as guilty of subversion until proven innocent.

Studies of the origins of French anti-Americanism in this period that argue that it is rooted in French cultural anxieties and political pathologies ignore the behavior of Americans that Parisians observed on a daily basis. Admittedly, Americans in Paris would have had a difficult time living up to the idealized images of "the American" that Parisians encountered in the theater and in the lore about Benjamin Franklin and "the good Quaker." Still, as Barlow suggested, it was not inevitable that the "most extravagant affections" that the French projected onto America would turn into the opposite. Dreams of Frenchmen and Americans facing the conspiracy of kings side by side on the battlefield were bound to be disappointed. But it was the Americans' single-minded pursuit of their business interests in France during a period of intense social and political conflict that nourished enduring generalized resentments against America.[35]

In addition to the parallels between Federalist and French attacks on Americans in Paris, there was a second irony in the print warfare against the American Jacobins. By denouncing Barlow and others as traitors to a narrowly defined American nation, Federalist politicians and newspapers gave their activities broader publicity than ever before. This inadvertently created the impression among some readers that these Americans were indeed important players in the transatlantic relationship.

Federalists had always had a conflicted relationship with the popular politics that seemed to be turning their way in 1798. As David Waldstreicher and others have pointed out, the new forms of mass mobilization, which the Federalists used to launch their "cultural offensive" against Jacobinism and the Republican opposition, were at odds with their ideal of a deferential, politically passive citizenry. Federalists were aware of this contradiction and worried that trying to beat the Republicans at their own game of print warfare might demean their party and the federal government. Still, national security seemed to require that Federalists dirty their hands with the Jacobin tool of character assassination. Barlow's friend-turned-nemesis Noah Webster declared, "The friends of govt must be active & vigilant–they must lay aside that delicacy about characters which men of honor observe in ordinary cases–they must expose the *real characters public & private,* of the leaders of opposition."[36] But while exposing their nefarious character and designs, the denunciation of American Francophiles also exposed a greater audience to their views and activities.

When George Washington, who had recently been appointed commander in chief of the Provisional Army, received a letter from Joel Barlow imploring the former president to use his influence for a peaceful resolution of the conflict with France, he immediately contacted his successor, John Adams. Washington was unsure whether and how to respond. He knew Barlow only by reputation as a poet and diplomat, but recently there had been much in the press about his exploits and close ties with the Directory, so perhaps he could be an important mediator. Adams was incensed at this suggestion. He responded that he had resolved to reopen negotiations, but vehemently denied that Barlow's advice, or that of any other American in Paris, had influenced his decision in any way whatsoever. Barlow was certainly not worthy of a response: "The wretch has destroyed his own character to such a degree, that I think it would be derogatory of yours to give any answer at all to his letter. Tom Paine is not a more worthless fellow."[37]

Federalists' repeated highlighting of the close links between the French government, Americans in Paris, and French-loving Republicans in America also played into the hands of the Directory. The occasion was the spectacular peace mission of the Philadelphia merchant-farmer George Logan. A scion of one of the oldest Quaker families in Pennsylvania, Logan was a friend and supporter of Jefferson's, had published newspaper articles and pamphlets against the Hamiltonian economic program, and in 1785 had been elected to the Pennsylvania Assembly. When a Democratic Society had formed in Philadelphia in 1793, shortly after Genet's arrival, Logan had served on its Committee of Correspondence. Disturbed by the Federalist agitation around the XYZ Affair, Logan traveled to Europe in June 1798 to head off war with France.[38]

The Federalist press at once seized upon the voyage of a prominent Republican to France as evidence of a treasonable plot. "There cannot be the least question," declared the *Philadelphia Gazette,* "but the Doctor, from his *inordinate* love of *French liberty,* and hatred of the *sacred constitution* of the United States, has gone to the French directory, fraught with intelligence of the *most dangerous tendency to this country.*" Logan's "infernal design" had to be "the introduction of a French army, to *teach us the genuine value of true and essential liberty* by re-organizing our government, through the brutal operation of the bayonet and the guillotine." On the floor of Congress, Robert Goodloe Harper of South Carolina announced that an event had taken place that "would lead to the discovery of a treasonable correspondence, carried on by persons in this country with France, of the most criminal nature." Moreover, Logan's departure coincided with Bache's publication of Talleyrand's letter, which lent additional credibility and urgency to these allegations.[39]

Once in Paris, Logan found that Gerry, the last remaining envoy, had already left France. After consulting with Skipwith and Barlow, Logan decided to stay on and try to persuade the French authorities to lift a recently imposed embargo on American trade, and to release a number of American sailors who had been imprisoned as Englishmen. Not all Americans in Paris welcomed his unauthorized intervention. Two days after Logan's arrival, James Cole Mountflorence, who now served as an informant for the staunchly Federalist American minister to the Batavian Republic, William Vans Murray, sent a letter to Talleyrand warning the minister against "criminal and unaccredited negotiations" with an agent of "the party of the opposition."[40]

Logan's mission could not have come at a worse moment for Talleyrand. By mid-May 1798, published copies of Marshall's dispatches had reached Britain, where they were reprinted for distribution throughout Europe. The reports accused Talleyrand of personal corruption—a charge that came as no surprise to most readers, but that had never before been so widely publicized. Fearful for his position, Talleyrand denounced X, Y, and Z as renegade agents who at no point had acted in his name. In an elaborate defense submitted to the Directory, the minister blamed the episode on the American envoys, "picky men, shy and stubborn," who lacked any understanding of the workings of diplomacy and its fluid boundaries of public and private conversations. How could he be expected to deal with "negotiators who, angered at not being received officially, neglected the opportunity of meetings in society and nowhere presented themselves to the minister"?[41] At the same time, Talleyrand discussed his readiness to receive new American envoys with Richard Codman, an American merchant with Federalist leanings, and with Skipwith, no doubt hoping that they would convey the reformed French attitude to their correspondents in the United States.[42]

Talleyrand feared that Logan's arrival in Paris might jeopardize his covert efforts to reopen negotiations with the United States through William Vans Murray, and went out of his way to reassure Murray that the Directory would not treat with an unaccredited agent.[43] However, Logan managed to secure audiences with all three Directors, who enthusiastically welcomed his mission. At a dinner party, Director Philippe-Antoine Merlin de Douai and Logan shared a toast to the United States and the "speedy restoration of amity between them and France." According to his own account, published in the *Aurora,* Logan told the Directors that he attributed the falling-out between the two republics to the intrigues of British Prime Minister William Pitt. Pro-British propagandists in America were using earlier "atrocities" of the French Revolution and the recent attacks by French privateers to stigmatize "every friend to France and republican principles" as an enemy of the United States. He also appealed to French economic self-interest to respect American neutrality and thereby increase trade in French harbors.[44]

Shortly after meeting with Logan, the Directory announced the lifting of all restrictions on American trade and a ban on privateering. The decision to avoid war with the United States had already been made before Logan's arrival, for a variety of geopolitical reasons, including the specter of an official Anglo-American alliance, the fear of losing French colonies in the West Indies, the failure of a French-sponsored insurrection in Ireland, Nelson's annihilation of the French fleet off the coast of Egypt, and the economic damage that war would cause for France's satellite republic in the Netherlands. Nonetheless, the Parisian press, from the republican *Le Bien Informé* to the conservative *Publiciste,* credited "le brave L—n" with bringing about the end of the embargo. Within a few days, the same report appeared in the *Gazette de Leyde,* now titled *Nouvelles Politiques Publiées a Leyde,* one of the most widely read and respected newspapers in Europe.[45]

Without informing Talleyrand, whom they treated with undisguised contempt since the XYZ scandal, the Directors took Logan's much-publicized mission as an opportunity to make a gesture of goodwill to the Adams administration while at the same time allowing the Republican opposition to claim that one of their own had facilitated this rapprochement.[46] Federalist observers in Europe saw through this maneuver, and in their indignation tacitly acknowledged its effectiveness. Thomas Boylston Adams, the president's youngest son, wrote from Berlin to the merchant Joseph Pitcairn in Paris on the raising of the embargo:

> Wonderful act of justice & generosity! Why, all the ships embargo'd in their ports don't amount I dare say to *a dozen*. . . . Certainly, however, the vessels caught in the snare, made in point of value no object to the generous Directory; but an *Embargo raised* as a proof of pacific intentions, reads just as well in a newspaper, when only one ship or even a fishing schooner is released by it, as if all the British navy were the prize renounced. You must know too, that for the raising of this embargo the merit is claimed by *several* pretenders, neither of which, probably brought it about.[47]

In order to prevent Murray from breaking off negotiations over the Logan mission, Talleyrand and his agent, Louis-André Pichon, had to devise the contorted argument that the report of Logan's success emanated from an "anarchical" newspaper in Paris (meaning *Le Bien Informé,* co-edited by Paine's close friend, Nicolas de Bonneville) and had been supplied by "the *Americans* at Paris." However, trying at the same time to absolve the prominent Republican Logan, Talleyrand claimed that the source of the false rumor that the Directory had negotiated with Logan was Thomas Paine, with whom Logan himself had supposedly disavowed any connection. Murray remained unconvinced by these denials and surmised that the Directory had allowed the reports about Logan to be published in order to court Republican opinion in the United States. Republicans in America were indeed only too happy to credit Logan with bringing about the peaceful resolution of the crisis. The *Aurora* published a slew of letters from anonymous Americans in Paris written during Logan's stay in the city, all calling for peace and praising Logan as a "true patriot" and "friend to humanity." Jefferson declared, "Logan's enthusiastic enterprize was fortunate, as it prevented the effect which our actual hostilities on their vessels would have produced."[48]

When George Logan returned to the United States in November 1798, his official reception was hostile. Timothy Pickering, George Washington, and

John Adams all censured his mission. By receiving Logan after the rejection of the official envoys, the Directory had rubbed salt into the wounded American national pride. Washington noted bitterly to Logan that it was "very singular" that "he who could be viewed as a private character; unarmed with proper powers; and presumably unknown in France; should suppose he could effect what these gentlemen [the envoys] of the first respectability in our Country, specially charged under the authority of the Government, were unable to do." In an address to Congress on 12 December, Adams declared, with obvious reference to Logan and other Americans in Paris, "Although the officious interference of individuals without official character or authority, is not entitled to any credit, yet it deserves to be considered whether the temerity and impertinence of individuals affecting to interfere in public affairs between France and the United States should not be inquired into and corrected."[49]

Within days, a committee formed within the House of Representatives to follow up on the president's suggestion and consider an amendment to the Sedition Act that would have made it illegal for any citizen to "usurp the Executive authority of this Government by commencing or carrying on any correspondence with the government of any foreign prince or state relative to controversies or disputes between such prince or state and the United States." However, Republican representatives put up unexpected resistance to the new law, also known as the Logan Act, and the ensuing debate lasted for three weeks.[50]

In the course of the debate, Robert Harper, one of the chief proponents of the law, produced an anonymous letter to Talleyrand, which he claimed was written by Logan. However, Republican Albert Gallatin of Pennsylvania persuasively countered that the author was in fact the Federalist merchant Richard Codman. The author of the letter described himself as "a firm friend to the principles of the French Revolution." He warned the French foreign minister not to walk into a trap laid by "the enemies of France and America," who sought to persuade the French that if they launched an attack on the United States they could count on the active support of the Republicans. In fact, "the very idea strikes all true Americans with horror." Rather than playing into the hands of Britain, France should, "by a great and magnanimous conduct . . . draw back those wandering affections which Intrigue and misunderstandings have estranged for a moment and leave the true American character to blaze forth in the approaching elections."

Clearly, the "true American character" included both patriotic unity in case of an outside attack and cosmopolitan solidarity with other nations founded on similar political principles. Gallatin gleefully noted, "The clamour which gentlemen have thought proper to raise about this paper, when the public knows the fact, may recoil on themselves."[51]

Moreover, Harper inadvertently revealed the thin line between friendly advice and intervention in official foreign policy. Responding to arguments that the law would criminalize any harmless social interaction with foreigners, Harper declared that if he were in France even after the law had been enacted and if Talleyrand invited him to dinner and asked for his opinion on the relations between the two countries, he would not hesitate for a second to speak his mind. Republicans were quick to pounce on this statement. Gallatin responded that what Federalists seemed to object to was not Americans offering their advice to Frenchmen, but rather the nature of their advice: "What does this amount to, connected with what has been said about the existence of a dangerous combination of men–a French party in this country, and other expressions of the same import? Does it not mean that the law is to attach to a certain description of men, and not to others? . . . If a man is a federalist, he will be innocent, but if he is an anti-federalist he will be guilty."[52] Targeting the paradox of Federalist anti-French publicity, Gallatin argued that it was the Federalists who endangered the United States, by constantly assuring the French in the press and in Congress that a "French party" that would welcome them with open arms really existed. By contrast, Logan and others had merely tried to act as mediators, combining love of their country with knowledge and appreciation of other nations in their desire to preserve peace.

Despite this spirited defense of the cosmopolitan ideal, the House passed the Logan Act on 17 January 1799 by a vote of 58 to 36. The law barred citizens from all contact with agents of foreign governments without official authorization, thereby rendering illegal a decade of American participation in the French Revolution. The law also put an end to the practice of private individuals informally representing American interests abroad. This colonial tradition had become an embarrassment to a national government trying to win the respect of the European powers.[53]

Only nine days after Adams denounced his "officious interference," Logan was elected to the Pennsylvania Assembly with a resounding majority. The *Aurora* exulted, "The election of Dr. Logan is the best reply which could have been given by the *people* to the President." James Monroe predicted that the Federalist persecution of Logan would backfire, to the benefit of the Republicans: "The enterprise of Logan with its consequences will not hurt any in his political sentiments, while the attempt to make it instrumental to that end will have its advantages. The ill humour shewn by the head and all the members of the opposit party, at an interference forbidden by no law, prompted by benevolent motives, & wh[ich] was useful to the publick, is a circumstance wh[ich] will tend to shew the views of that party."[54]

Barely two weeks after signing the Logan Act into law, Adams announced his nomination of William Vans Murray as minister to negotiate with the French government. Like the Directory, Adams had many reasons to seek an accommodation that had little to do with the interventions of any American in Paris. War with France would further increase the already considerable influence of Alexander Hamilton over Adams's cabinet and the growing U.S. army. In his letter about Barlow, Washington had noted that peace was "the ardent desire of all the friends of this rising Empire," which signaled to Adams that the former president would not oppose the reopening of negotiations. Finally, Adams had received reliable information from many different sources in Europe—including his sons John Quincy and Thomas Boylston, William Vans Murray, and Elbridge Gerry, as well as Richard Codman and George Logan, and, despite all of Adams's protestations, Joel Barlow—that the French government was genuinely seeking a peaceful resolution and was willing to make amends for the disrespectful treatment of the envoys.[55]

Adams's unexpected turnabout shocked and dismayed the Federalists. Theodore Sedgwick lamented: "Had the foulest heart & the ablest head in the world, been permitted to select the most embarrassing and ruinous measure, perhaps, it would have been precisely the one which had been adopted." Adams's and Hamilton's respective followers quickly turned on each other with the same severity that had previously been reserved for Jacobins. Still, it was the party as a whole that had become a victim of its own publicity. After months of alarmist rhetoric about an imminent French attack and the subversive activities of American Jacobins, the Federalists had boxed themselves in with an all-or-nothing, war-or-surrender, foreign policy. The government already faced a popular backlash against the new taxes required for the expansion of the military, as well as resistance against the Alien and Sedition Acts, some of which was expressed in the language of natural rights and international revolution. But Sedgwick was correct that nothing could have damaged Federalist credibility more than to suddenly reverse policy toward France, especially along the lines suggested by prominent Republicans like Logan.[56]

The published documents, speeches, pamphlets, newspaper articles, and letters to the editor that made up the public diplomacy of the XYZ Affair proved to be a double-edged sword for both the French and American governments. The publicity of the XYZ Affair embarrassed French officials and made American popular support for the Adams administration appear more unified than it actually was. But public diplomacy also allowed the Directory to play the two American parties off against each other, and to hand a public relations success to the Republican opposition.

Do the Americans in Paris deserve any credit for averting a war between the two republics? Barlow certainly thought so. In an open letter "to His Fellow Citizens," Barlow denounced the Logan Act and refused to accept "that it is a crime in a private citizen to serve his country." While he and "a few other men, not commissioned for the purpose, have hitherto prevented a war," the Adams administration had done "little for America but increase her debt, and nothing for Europe but imitate her follies."[57] Americans in Paris did not shape the decisions of either the Directory or John Adams, but they struggled hard to keep communications between the two sides open. Even though neither French nor American officials entirely trusted what these Americans had to say, their letters and newspaper articles kept the history of Franco-American friendship and alternatives to war in the public sphere. Once Talleyrand and the Directory decided that the time for serious accommodation with the United States had come, Americans in Paris were available and ready to serve as go-betweens. Still, even as the cosmopolitan ideal embodied by the Americans in Paris appeared vindicated, the controversy over their interventions demonstrated to their Republican allies what a burden the party's ideological attachment to France had become.

6

From Sister Republics to Republican Empires

THE JEFFERSONIAN DIVORCE FROM FRANCE
AND THE LOUISIANA PURCHASE, 1800–1805

The turn of the century coincided with significant regime changes in
both the American and the French republics. In France, the coup of 18
Brumaire VIII (9 November 1799) toppled the Directory and established
an executive Consulate under the overriding authority of the First Consul,
General Napoleon Bonaparte. In the United States, following an acrimonious and turbulent election, Thomas Jefferson was inaugurated as the third
president in March 1801. Like many new heads of state, Napoleon and Jefferson were eager to distinguish their regimes from those of their predecessors, especially as their means of coming to power cast a shadow on their
legitimacy. "Nothing, in history, resembles the end of the eighteenth century; nothing, at the end of the eighteenth century, resembles the present
moment," Napoleon Bonaparte declared on 18 Brumaire. Shortly after his
own inauguration, Jefferson announced to Joseph Priestley: "we can no longer say there is nothing new under the sun. for this whole chapter in the
history of man is new. the great extent of our republic is new. it's sparse habitation is new. the mighty wave of public opinion which has rolled over it is
new. but the most pleasing novelty is it's so quickly subsiding, over such an
extent of surface, to it's true level again."[1]

As it turned out, neither Napoleon nor Jefferson was exaggerating. No one could have predicted in 1799 that only five years later Napoleon would crown himself as Emperor of France. In Jefferson's case, the unprecedented peaceful transfer of power from one political party to another overshadowed a more gradual but nonetheless profound transformation. By proclaiming the uniqueness of the American republic, Jefferson also implicitly dissociated it from its French counterpart. The Republicans' unwavering support for the French Revolution, despite its extreme volatility, had become too much of a liability. The increasing intensity of the controversies connected to the French Republic–from Genet's mission, Jay's Treaty, and Monroe's recall, to the XYZ Affair–convinced Jefferson and other Republicans that they would either lead to civil war or drag the United States into the European conflagration. Even before the XYZ Affair, Jefferson had recognized the need for a separation from France in a letter to Elbridge Gerry urging him to accept the nomination as an envoy: "Our countrymen have divided themselves by such strong affections to the French and the English, that nothing will secure us internally but a divorce from both nations. And this must be the object of every real American, and it's attainment is practicable without much self-denial. But for this, peace is necessary."[2]

By 1801, peace between the United States and France had come through the Convention of 1800, negotiated by John Adams's second mission of envoys, and an armistice between France and Great Britain was on the horizon. Jefferson's correspondence in 1800–1801 with Americans in Paris eager to see the United States join a new league of armed neutrality sponsored by Napoleon, reflected his attempt to redefine Republican ideology for a post-revolutionary age. The question remained of how much "self-denial" the divorce from France would require on the part of Republican Francophiles. How could Republicans distance themselves from the French Revolution without repudiating the universal principles that had sustained the bond between the sister republics?

Jefferson's letter to Priestley hinted at a solution to this quandary. In addition to the power and moderation of American public opinion, the new president highlighted the "great extent of our republic," and its "sparse habitation," as distinguishing the New World from the Old. The imaginary clean slate of the American West, soon to be vastly expanded through the Louisiana Purchase, offered an alternative canvas onto which Republicans could project the universalist aspirations they previously had invested in the French Revolution. However, as they formulated their visions for nation-building on the western frontier, the French Revolution remained a constant and problematic reference point for Republicans, especially for those who had experienced it firsthand. Was the lesson to be drawn from the turmoil of the French Revolution the superiority of decentralized government or, conversely, the need for a strong state that could guide its citizens in the difficult task of self-rule?

The coup of 18 Brumaire and the rise of Napoleon Bonaparte as First Consul represented a mixed blessing for the Republicans. On the upside, Napoleon was eager to negotiate a comprehensive settlement to the Quasi-War. During the protracted negotiations of the Convention of 1800, the Federalist envoys decided that they had to abandon one of their two main goals, the settlement of claims for damages done to American commerce, to obtain the other, a definitive end to the Franco-American alliance of 1778. Republicans gleefully observed the embarrassment that the Convention caused their opponents. After first rejecting it, Federalists in the Senate reconsidered, following the advice of Alexander Hamilton that it would be "better to close the thing where it is than leave it to a Jacobin Administration to do much worse." The Federalists thereby relieved their Republican successors of the obligations of a burdensome alliance and allowed them to loosen their ideological attachment to France without having to acknowledge it openly. Without so much as mentioning the Convention, Jefferson could announce in his first inaugural address the policy of "peace, commerce, and honest friendship with all nations, entangling alliances with none." Turning his back on the "exterminating havoc of one quarter of the globe," the president instead looked westward on "a chosen country, with room enough for our descendants to the thousandth and thousandth generation."[3]

On the downside, Federalists were able to welcome 18 Brumaire both as a restoration of order and a purge of Jacobins and as confirming their predictions that the anarchy of the French Revolution would inevitably result in a dictatorship. The three Federalist envoys charged with negotiating the Convention of 1800, William Vans Murray, Chief Justice Oliver Ellsworth, and Governor William R. Davie of North Carolina, vied with each other for Napoleon's attention and approval. Asked by Napoleon what Americans thought about 18 Brumaire, Murray enthused that the "friends of order and rational liberty" had "rejoiced at it bringing F[rance] back to reason" and that only "the Jacobins c[oul]d not like it, as it concentrated the powers and gave a Senate for Life." Murray added in his diary that unless Napoleon would "give back his power to L[ouis] 18, I wish for the peace of the world he may keep it as long as he lives!"[4]

Napoleon had carefully prepared the ground for this Federalist-Brumairian meeting of the minds by declaring ten days of national mourning in honor of George Washington, whom the French press had painted as a British lackey for the past four years. During a grand ceremony at the Temple de Mars on 20 Pluviôse VIII (9 February 1800), Louis Fontanes delivered a much-celebrated funeral oration that drew numerous, none-too-subtle parallels between the late liberator of America and the present savior of France: "As a rule, in the wake of great political crises an extraordinary personage must appear who by the very ascendancy of his glory shall restrain the audacity of all parties and restore order in the midst of confusion."[5]

Federalists on the other side of the Atlantic echoed these sentiments. Congressman Robert Goodloe Harper explained in a letter to his South Carolina constituents that "a despotism more complete [than the Consulate] never existed," but at least it was "the despotism of one man of sense, who may find it in his interest to govern well, and in his power to govern with steadiness." Napoleon's regime was by far "the best for France, that has existed there within ten years," and the First Consul deserved the gratitude of Americans because he had suppressed "an anarchical democratical despotism."[6]

By contrast, Republicans had initially dismissed the news that Napoleon had participated in a coup d'état against the Directory as "highly ridiculous." After finding the reports confirmed, Jefferson worried that the takeover would set a pernicious example for the upcoming American elections, both to his followers, who had "to be made sensible that their own character & situation are materially different from the French," and be reminded to adhere to the will of the majority in every eventuality; and to the Federalists, led by "our Buonaparte," Alexander Hamilton, who "surrounded by his comrades in arms may step in to give us political salvation in his way."[7]

Exacerbating this predicament were the efforts of Americans in Paris to align the United States with Napoleon's foreign policy in Europe. One reason why Napoleon had been so keen on reconciliation with the United States was his plan to bring together America and the nations of northern Europe (Sweden, Denmark, Prussia, and Russia) in a league of armed neutrality in order to challenge Britain's control of the seas. As an advertisement of its role as the champion of neutral rights, the French government, in October 1800, hosted a magnificent fête in celebration of the Convention of 1800, at Môrtefontaine, Joseph Bonaparte's chateau north of Paris. Attended by the First Consul and almost two hundred dignitaries, the fête included fireworks, a concert, two plays, and a state dinner, during which the three consuls offered toasts to the Americans and Frenchmen who had died fighting for American independence, to Washington's successor, and, finally, to "the union of America with the northern powers to give respect to the freedom of the seas." A detailed account of the event, including the toasts, was published in the *Moniteur,* which in the same issue carried a lengthy essay extolling the benefits that Europe would derive from forming an armed defense against British maritime supremacy.[8]

Several prominent Americans in Paris enthusiastically supported this strategy. Much like their Federalist compatriots, Republicans in Paris welcomed the stability that the Consulate promised to bring to France after the turmoil of the Directory period. Joel Barlow assured his brother-in-law, Senator Abraham Baldwin: "Our administration is now better than it has ever been, & you know that *administration* is all, during a revolutionary war." In a surprising statement from the author of *Letter to the National Convention,* Barlow added, "It has always been my opinion that they ought to have less to do with constitutions till tranquility comes." The merchant Nathaniel Cutting admitted to Jefferson that the Consulate was autocratic, but, unlike its predecessor, it was capable of controlling "the inordinate rage of contending Factions." The young painter John Vanderlyn–a protégé of Aaron Burr who had encouraged him to become the first American to train at the Académie de Peinture et de Sculpture in Paris, rather than in London–likewise appreciated the new order that encouraged the French to forget politics and refocus their attention on the finer things in life. "Without mentioning anything Political," he wrote his brother in November 1800, "I believe I may tell you that Paris enjoys harmony & tranquility & not only the necessities but even the luxuries of life. Arts & Sciences are much attended to & the gay folks think of nothing but pleasure."[9]

The inclusion of the popular General Bonaparte in the Consulate lent some credibility to the shopworn justification that the most recent regime change represented the will of the people and was necessary to safeguard the revolution's achievements at a moment of crisis. American Republicans had long admired Napoleon's military talents, and had counted on his seemingly endless string of victories to contain Federalist belligerence. In 1797, Fulwar Skipwith had even favorably compared the modest, self-sacrificing Napoleon with George Washington wallowing in the adulation of the young girls of Trenton. Thomas Paine waxed lyrical that France, surrounded by enemies on all sides, was "like the burning bush, not only unconsumed, but erecting her head and smiling above the flames. She throws coalitions to atoms with the strength of thunder–Combat and victory are to her synonymous."[10]

Moreover, the First Consul enjoyed the support of many intellectuals, known for their close association with the United States, who regarded Napoleon as a statesman-philosopher not unlike Jefferson. Among them were Lafayette, J. Hector St. John de Crèvecoeur, Pierre-Jean-Georges Cabanis, Grégoire, Volney, and (more reluctantly) Destutt de Tracy; the last four even received appointments to the Senate.[11] In light of France's preponderance in Europe, its unrelenting hostility toward Britain, and its apparent interest in cooperation with the United States, the Republicans in Paris resolved to seize the moment and persuade the man who they hoped would become the next American president to join forces with the First Consul in the cause of neutral maritime rights.

Within a week after the signing of the Convention of 1800, Barlow, Paine, and Cutting wrote to Thomas Jefferson–Paine and Cutting for the first time in three years. They all took a dim view of the official envoys–"three more useless rascals never came upon public business," Paine fumed–who had refused to meet with Skipwith or Barlow, on the grounds that the two men "had not the confidence of the executive." Undeterred, Paine had visited Ellsworth and lectured him that even if the commissioners managed to negotiate a treaty with France, it would constitute the same "surrender of the rights of the American flag" as Jay's Treaty, "for the principle that Neutral ships make Neutral property must be general, or not at all." Barlow dismissed the negotiations as "a constant scene of mystery, distrust & ill humour," while Cutting predicted that the best that could come of them was a breach in Anglo-American relations, which would *"eventually* prove advantageous to our rising Empire," as Britain had acquired too much influence in the United States already.[12]

Cutting also anticipated that the "military Genius of Bonaparte" would soon bring lasting peace to Europe, and that if Britain refused to negotiate, the northern naval powers would form a league of armed neutrality. He sincerely hoped the United States would join this association for the protection of neutral commerce, since British arrogance and lawlessness "put Algerine Marauders to the blush!" Paine enclosed no fewer than three manuscripts on the subject of neutral rights with his first letter, and sent two more on 6 and 16 October. Barlow conveyed an imprint of the second part of his open letter, *Joel Barlow to his Fellow Citizens of the United States,* which contained a "Memoir on Certain Principles of Public Maritime Law," through Zephaniah Swift, an old friend who had served as secretary to the commissioners. A few months later, Jefferson received yet another recommendation from Paris, this time from William Short, to take advantage of this "unexpectedly favorable" moment and to carefully consider joining an alliance of neutral nations. Encapsulating the dilemma with which all these letters confronted Jefferson, Short argued that the United States should "keep themselves disentangled from European politics," while insisting at the same time that "procuring a permanent system of neutral maritime rights, should be a polar star of our Government in all their foreign relations."[13]

Paine and Barlow made the most comprehensive cases in favor of joining forces with other neutral nations. In order to give their appeals more weight, both authors emphasized their close ties to the current French regime. Paine claimed that he had composed the first, untitled manuscript, "in consequence of a question put to me by Bonaparte," namely, whether France, after signing a peace treaty with Austria, should take steps toward negotiations with Britain. The second enclosure, entitled "On the Jacobinism of the English at Sea," Paine had translated into French with the help of the journalist Nicolas de Bonneville, printed as a pamphlet, and distributed among the foreign ministers in Paris and members of the French government. As Paine proudly noted, the *Moniteur* had published an abstract in September.[14]

Barlow explained in his pamphlet that he had formulated the plan for a "Maritime Convention" at the request of "one of the members of the French government," for use in the framing of the new constitution. Although the issue had been set aside for future consideration in the new legislature, Barlow assured his readers that, "by what I can discover of the prevailing disposition of this government, the principles therein contained are gaining ground, and will probably one day be enacted." While Barlow admitted to Jefferson that his "Maritime Convention" might appear "chimerical," he predicted that the "approaching interval of peace" would present an opportunity to publicize the concept in America and present it to other nations interested in free maritime trade. This in turn would encourage some of the "most influential members" of the French government, who were waiting for an occasion to enact measures for the protection of neutral commerce.[15]

What Paine and Barlow advocated in the writings they sent to Jefferson was nothing less than "a new code of Public Law, or *Law of Nations.*" The wars of the French Revolution had exposed the old law of nations, based on a balance of power and codified in treaties, to be a mere pretext for a "system of robbery and murder," as Barlow had put it earlier. Paine categorically declared that treaties could not create laws, since they did not bind non-signatories, were often contradictory, and were unenforceable even among the parties forming them. Law had to be grounded in first principles, in natural rights, justice, and equality, or it did not deserve its name.[16]

The issue of neutral rights in wartime stood at the center of the law of nations because it was a question of national self-determination. A belligerent that searched a neutral nation's ships for contraband not only ignored that nation's sovereign decision to remain neutral, it usurped the right to legislate for that nation's citizens and to police and punish them according to its own laws. In order to protect themselves against these violations of their sovereignty, Paine and Barlow proposed, nations should voluntarily relinquish a part of their sovereignty to an international body, which Barlow called a "Chancery." This body would be endowed with the exclusive power to adjudicate international disputes over maritime commerce and enforce the new law of nations by imposing fines and, if necessary, economic embargoes against nations found guilty of misconduct. The main target of these reprisals was, of course, Britain, whose status as a great maritime power Paine and Barlow depicted as entirely dependent on the willingness of other nations to trade with it: "Were the neutral nations of Europe, together with the United States of America, to enter into an association to suspend all commerce with any belligerent power that molested any ship belonging to that association, England must either lose her commerce, or consent to the freedom of the seas." Both Paine and Barlow described this association as an "unarmed neutrality" that would be more practical, more virtuous, and more powerful than any attempt to confront the British Navy militarily.[17]

For Barlow, the association of neutral powers was merely a step toward a federation of all European nations based on the American model. According to Barlow, the term "nation" had neither geographical nor numerical limits, and it seemed, indeed, "the tendency of civilization . . . to diminish the number of nations, and to increase their size and prosperity." Still, the travails of the French Revolution had demonstrated that the only durable way to establish representative government over as large and diverse a nation as France was to turn it into a federation of twenty or more republics. Barlow acknowledged in a footnote that in French politics the term "federalism" had come to mean the opposite of what he was proposing here, namely, the division of the French nation into separate regional entities. He assured his French readers that the federation he envisioned for France and Europe would not compromise the unity of the French Republic, but in fact strengthen it by allowing for its unlimited expansion. Barlow recommended the same system of federal republicanism for France's neighbors, "as fast as they become free," until all of Europe could form "a great union of Republics; which might assume the name of *the United States of Europe.*" As the war in Europe drew to a close, Barlow hoped to see "the moral force of nations take [the] place of their physical force, the civilization of states keep pace with that of individuals, and their commercial relations established on the principles of peace."[18] In his optimism, Barlow chose to ignore the glaring contradiction in his plan for a United States of Europe, namely, that federal republicanism would somehow both increase the power and size of the French nation and guarantee the freedom and independence of its neighbors.

Some historians have suggested that Paine and Barlow might have acted as mouthpieces for French officials, or even Napoleon himself. But reforming the law of nations to include more protections for neutrals and free trade had been a cornerstone of American foreign policy since Independence. Paine and Barlow had argued for an alliance of neutrals and economic sanctions against England for years. Moreover, at this moment, other prominent Republicans, like Robert R. Livingston and William Barton, were also calling for a new law of nations. Still, it is certainly true that Paine's and Barlow's writings in 1799–1800 matched perfectly with the benevolent self-presentation of the French government.[19]

One of the most successful vehicles of this self-presentation was *De l'etat de la France à la fin de l'an VIII,* an anonymous work written by the career diplomat Alexandre d'Hauterive, who had advised Talleyrand during the XYZ Affair and now served as the director of the North American and Russian Correspondence Divisions in the French Foreign Ministry. Composed and printed within six weeks to coincide with the signing of the Convention of 1800, the book ignited much debate in Europe and the United States. Its appeal to the neutral maritime powers to unite with France against the common enemy Britain and its call for a "federative" navigation act was in perfect accord with Paine's and Barlow's tracts. Hauterive's claim that France was capable of unlimited expansion, and was therefore in a position to give Europe a new federal constitution, likewise bore a striking similarity to Barlow's *Letter.* Both Hauterive and Barlow depicted the power of the French Republic as not merely military, but as residing in its political principles, formed and tested in the crucible of the revolution, and in France's ability to bring civilization to Europe and beyond. The significance of *De l'etat de la France* consisted not in its originality, but in the fact that Hauterive, as even his foremost critic, the conservative Prussian journalist Friedrich von Gentz, acknowledged, "represents the prevailing opinions, the prevailing sentiments, the prevailing bias of a significant group of writers and merchants in all European nations."[20]

Barlow and Paine did not deny that their proposals were primarily designed to curb Britain's preponderant naval power and therefore inevitably favored French interests. In their view, the interests of France and those of the neutral nations were identical: France's interest was to increase and protect free commerce, while Britain's interest was to monopolize and control it.[21] In fact, precisely because a league of neutral nations would have benefited the French Republic at a time when its own navy had effectively ceased to exist, Napoleon's commitment to neutral rights was (for the moment) genuine. It was despite France's best efforts that the league of armed neutrality that Sweden, Denmark, Prussia, and Russia formed in mid-December 1800 fell apart only a few months later. The assassination of Czar Paul I in March 1801 removed the most powerful member of the league, and the crushing blow that the British Navy delivered to the Danish fleet at Copenhagen in April demonstrated its weakness. In envisioning a new Franco-American collaboration, the Americans in Paris did not misjudge the objectives of the First Consul, but, rather, those of their own president, Thomas Jefferson.

Having just narrowly won a bitterly divisive election, the Jefferson administration was anxious to insulate the strained American union from the vagaries of European politics. Jefferson firmly believed that only a policy of strict neutrality and avoiding even the impression of any pro-French bias could preempt a resurgence of the Federalists. Moreover, the success of the slave revolution in Saint-Domingue had significantly diminished Republican sympathies for the French Revolution. Especially after Gabriel's Rebellion, an abortive slave uprising in Virginia in 1800, southern slaveholders, who had shared the enthusiasm for the revolution during the previous decade, began to decry the subversive influence of leveling and atheistic French ideas.[22]

Ironically, the strategy that Republicans pursued in consolidating their authority bore great similarity to that of the Consulate from which Republicans were ostensibly trying to distance themselves. Both the Jefferson administration and the Consulate defined their new regimes against the far right (aristocratic Federalists and royalists, respectively) and against plebian "Jacobins" on the left. The specter of "Jacobinism" in particular served to unite a political mainstream where all were Republicans and all Federalists, or all Brumairians. By simultaneously reaching out to former partisans (moderate Federalists in America, Catholics and émigrés in France), both regimes hoped to damp down the recriminations and rivalries of the past decade. For the Consulate, this reconciliation from above formed part of a larger project of depoliticizing society, which it rigorously enforced through the prohibition of political clubs, press censorship, and police surveillance. Napoleon's expansionist foreign policy (in the guise of the civilizing mission described in Hauterive's book) contributed to this project by diverting public attention away from domestic politics and uniting the nation in support of a glorious cause.[23]

By contrast, the Jefferson administration did not have access to the repressive arsenal of the Consulate in domestic affairs. Meanwhile, its declared retreat from European politics left a gaping ideological void for Republicans, as the French Revolution had played a major role in transforming the party from an opposition faction into a national movement. Jefferson's answers to Paine, Barlow, and Short, written only a few weeks after his inauguration, reflect both confidence in the recovered unity of the American nation and uncertainty about how to reconcile the nation's dissociation from Europe with its universalist ethos and ambitions.

In his reply to Paine, Jefferson informed him of the publication of his manuscripts, which "contain precisely our principles, & I hope they will be generally recognized here." Jefferson did in fact distribute Paine's *Compact Maritime* among political allies in Virginia, as part of his ongoing effort to develop the "republican soundness" of public opinion. Moreover, he put Paine's application for the position of indemnification commissioner in France (sent between manuscripts on 4 October 1800) near the top of one of the earliest lists of offices and possible appointments that formed the basis of his patronage policy. Nonetheless, Jefferson explained that because the new administration was determined "to avoid, if possible, wasting the energies of our people in war & destruction, we shall avoid implicating ourselves with the powers of Europe, even in support of principles we mean to pursue." In fact, the new president welcomed "the return of our citizens from the frenzy into which they have been wrought partly by the ill-conduct in France, partly by artifices practiced on them." In other words, the Federalists and the Directory deserved equal blame for the troubles of the past three years.[24]

Similarly, Jefferson thanked Barlow for his "excellent 2d. letter," whose sound principles would hopefully "make their way." The pamphlet proved to Jefferson that even from a distance Barlow had understood that "the revolutionary movements in Europe, had by industry & artifice, been wrought into objects of terror even to this country, and had really involved a great portion of our well-meaning citizens in a panic which was perfectly unaccountable, and during the prevalence of which they were led to support measures the most insane." Now that the citizenry was recovering from its temporary "derangement," party divisions were melting away. The election of 1800 had only confirmed Jefferson's belief in the natural homogeneity and unanimity of the body politic, which had finally been cured of the false patriots as of a disease.[25]

Jefferson gave the same account to William Short, and assured him that "no endeavors will be spared on my part to reunite the nation in harmony and in interest." He acknowledged that it would "indeed be advantageous to us to have neutral rights established on a broad ground." But since "no dependence can be placed in any European coalition," an alliance "would be a much greater evil than a temporary acquiescence in the false principles which have prevailed." Nevertheless, Jefferson emphasized that the American republic had neither abandoned its principles nor lost its missionary zeal. Reiterating his conviction that its growing population would sooner rather than later turn the United States into a great power, he promised Short that the "day is within my time as well as yours when we may say by what laws the other nations shall treat us on the sea. and we will say it."[26]

Jefferson urged Paine, Barlow, and Short to return home, and developments in Europe made his evocation of a post-Federalist utopia increasingly appealing to the expatriates. By the summer of 1801, the failure of the league of armed neutrality had become undeniable. Alternative ways of containing the British threat to neutral maritime trade, like the French invasion of Britain that Paine had championed for several years, or the submarine constructed by Barlow's protégé, Robert Fulton, held little promise of being realized in the near future. Without a maritime convention or the submarine, Barlow wrote glumly to Jefferson, "the prospect for civilization is frightful," as all nations, including the United States, were bound to engage in a naval arms race that would force them to "turn pirates abroad & tax gatherers at home."[27]

Meanwhile, the political climate in France became increasingly inhospitable to radical republicans like Paine. Soon after 18 Brumaire, Paine found himself under police surveillance. He was put on notice that "the police are informed that he is behaving irregularly and that at the first complaint against him he will be sent back to America, his country." Paine's irregular behavior included his close friendship with Nicolas de Bonneville, to whose popular daily paper *Le Bien Informé* Paine contributed regularly. After Bonneville had run a satirical portrait of future consul Sieyès in 1798, the hypersensitive Directory had suspended the paper. Paine had interceded with the Directory on Bonneville's behalf, vouching for his personal and political reliability, which might have contributed to the eventual reinstatement of Bonneville's printing privileges. However, when *Le Bien Informé* compared Napoleon to Oliver Cromwell the day after 18 Brumaire, Paine was unable to prevent the authorities from briefly arresting Bonneville and, this time, not only shutting down the paper, but also confiscating the presses.[28]

Yet due to the shared emphasis of the Consulate and the Jefferson administration on moderation and reconciliation, Paine found himself similarly out of place in the American political landscape. When Jefferson's invitation to Paine to return to the United States on the government warship *Maryland* became known in July 1801, it provided the Federalists with a welcome opportunity to launch an all-out attack on the new president. Jefferson had hoped that upon his arrival in America Paine would "find us returned generally to sentiments worthy of former times," sentiments that Paine had promoted "with as much effect as any man living," and for which he was due "to reap the rewards in the thankfulness of nations." On the contrary, news that the president had welcomed home "that living opprobrium of humanity, Tom Paine, the infamous scavenger of all the filth which could be raked from the dirty paths which have been hitherto trodden by all the revilers of Christianity," unleashed a flood of histrionic anti-Paine diatribes that betrayed the Federalist editors' delight at having been handed such an easy target. In addition to pouncing on Paine's alleged atheism, personal immorality, and insults to George Washington, Federalists used the transnational character of his political activism—which Jefferson had praised as Paine's highest achievement—to define him as a foreign, un-American agitator: "Our government has so long permitted foreign convicts and renegades to go on, with impunity, in insulting the nation and dictating public measures, that they now seem to consider this country as the natural right and common property of all those who have shewn themselves pre-eminent in baseness and impiety, of whatever nation they may be."[29]

Republican newspapers initially mounted a half-hearted defense of Paine's right to free expression no matter how distasteful his views. But leading Republicans quickly realized that inviting Paine had been a blunder, and that the strong emotions his name still managed to arouse ran counter to their vision of a moderate, non-revolutionary, and unified American polity. When Paine finally arrived in Baltimore, on a private vessel, on 30 October 1802 and traveled to Washington, the Republican newspaper editor James Cheetham remembered his reception as "cold and forbidding. Even Mr. Jefferson received him with politick circumspection; and such of the members of congress as suffered him to approach them, did so from motives of curiosity. *Policy* dictated this course."[30] Just as the Consulate had tolerated Paine's presence in Paris due to his usefulness as an anti-British propagandist, the Jefferson administration allowed Paine's writings to appear in its semi-official organ, the *National Intelligencer,* if it suited its purposes. Yet the importance that both regimes placed on consolidation and political harmony left little room for the most prominent transatlantic pamphleteer of the 1790s.

While they had not misrepresented Napoleon's contingent support for neutral rights, the letters from Paine, Barlow, Short, and Cutting helped to create a false impression of the Consulate in the minds of Jefferson

149

and his secretary of state, James Madison. Reviving the league of armed neutrality was not the only reason for Napoleon's pursuit of a settlement with the United States in 1800. It was equally important to him to complete the negotiations before it became known that he was aiming to restore the French empire in North America. The First Consul's highest priority was to reassert control over the most valuable of the French colonies, Saint-Domingue. In order to rid the recolonized Saint-Domingue of its dependence on trade with the United States, Napoleon planned to occupy Spanish-owned Louisiana, which would supply all essential provisions for the reconstructed plantation society. French Louisiana would also serve as a barrier to the waves of American settlers moving westward, or absorb them as French citizens. Moreover, the French government was pressuring Spain to cede all or part of the Floridas, which would give France control of the Gulf of Mexico. On 9 Vendémiaire IX (1 October 1800), the day after Franco-American negotiations had concluded, Napoleon's minister to Spain signed a secret agreement for the retrocession of Louisiana to France, thereby putting in jeopardy the settlement achieved only twenty-four hours earlier.[31]

When the first rumors of the retrocession reached Washington, in late May 1801, Jefferson and Madison assumed, based on the information they had received from the Americans in Paris, that the Consulate was well disposed toward the United States, and therefore the two nations would be able to find a mutually acceptable agreement with regard to navigation on the Mississippi and the right of deposit in New Orleans. Americans were not worried primarily about the military threat France posed to the United States or that French Louisiana would block American expansion. The greater concern was that France might use its control over the Mississippi to convince western settlers to desert the union and form a separate American nation beyond the Appalachians. By its very existence, this rival American nation would be far more ominous to the future of the union than a French colony. Jefferson and Madison believed that it would be sufficient to convince the Consulate that the new Republican regime was fundamentally different from its Anglophile Federalist predecessor and that it would never allow any part of the mouth of the Mississippi to fall into British hands—a fear that they speculated had prompted the French to reacquire Louisiana. Accordingly, at his first audience, the new American minister, Robert R. Livingston, assured Napoleon of the sincere interest of the United States in harmonious relations with France. He congratulated the French Republic on the recently signed preliminary peace treaty with Britain, and "on having for its first Magistrate a chief, who united to the most splendid civil & military talents, possesses a spirit of patriotism & humanity which stops the progress of war, even in the full career of Victory, when the interests of his country & the happiness of Mankind call for peace."[32]

In sharp contrast to this official line, Livingston was astounded to find that every aspect of the French government's monthly audience for foreign ministers and ambassadors had "a military appearance." A few weeks later, Livingston concluded that the Consulate had "nothing that can be called republican in its form & still less in its administration." Moreover, "the change in politicks of the united States is not what they [the Consulate] would have wished." Napoleon himself had "severely commented" on Jefferson's inaugural address. The First Consul might have been reacting to a translation of the speech in the opposition paper *Décade Philosophique,* the organ of the pro-American French "idéologues" whose initial support for Napoleon had helped convince the Americans in Paris of the Consulate's legitimacy. Highlighting Jefferson's defense of freedom of the press and political pluralism, the *Décade* noted, "All those called to govern republics could if necessary draw from this speech useful lessons." Livingston also reported that Napoleon, when informed that the Institut National des Sciences et des Arts planned to elect Jefferson and British playwright Richard Brinsley Sheridan as members, had "sent them word that the choice of either would be improper, that they were both Jacobins." Given these attitudes, the prospects for negotiations on Louisiana were bleak. Although Livingston quickly learned that the retrocession was "a very favorite measure" with the French government, neither Foreign Minister Talleyrand nor Minister of Finance François de Barbé-Marbois would even acknowledge the existence of a Franco-Spanish treaty.[33]

It was in response to these discouraging reports that Jefferson wrote his second-most-famous letter on Franco-American relations (after the "Adam and Eve" letter) on 18 April 1802. Although ostensibly a private letter to Livingston, its intended audience was the Frenchman who carried it across the Atlantic, Pierre-Samuel Du Pont de Nemours, a merchant and economist with business interests in the United States and connections to the Consulate. Jefferson instructed Du Pont to read the letter so that he could "impress on the government of France the inevitable consequences of their taking possession of Louisiana."[34]

Jefferson asserted that France's acquisition of Louisiana "completely reverses all the political relations of the U.S. and will form a new epoch in our political intercourse."[35] Previously, Americans had regarded France as their *"natural friend,"* whose "growth therefore we viewed as our own, her misfortunes ours." But France's claim to New Orleans threatened to change all that: "There is on the globe one single spot, the possessor of which is our natural and habitual enemy. It is New Orleans, through which the produce of three-eights of our territory must pass to market." By "placing herself in that door," France had assumed an "attitude of defiance" toward the United States. Not only was it "impossible that France and the U.S. can continue long friends when they meet in so irritable a position," but the French occupation of New Orleans would seal "the union of two nations who in conjunction can maintain exclusive possession of the ocean. From that moment we must marry ourselves to the British fleet and nation." Jefferson here evoked the specter of an anarchic world much like that dreaded earlier by Barlow, in which all nations must "turn pirates abroad and tax gatherers at home." On one level, this prediction was a combination of damage control and strategic bluffing. Acting on his own initiative, Livingston had already contacted the American minister in London, Rufus King, and urged him to secretly encourage British opposition to the transfer of Louisiana. Jefferson's letter tried to preempt the potential embarrassment should these efforts become known, and at the same time to use the threat of an Anglo-American alliance without actually involving Britain.[36]

Still, as a whole, the letter is much more conciliatory than this often-quoted passage suggests. While asserting the inevitability of an Anglo-American alliance, Jefferson also went out of his way to emphasize repeatedly "the strong sympathies still existing in the minds of our citizens" for France. He offered a compromise solution that would allow France to retain Louisiana, as long as it ceded New Orleans and the Floridas to the United States. And Jefferson refrained from commenting on the autocratic and militaristic character of French domestic politics that Livingston had described in such detail. As in his responses to Paine, Barlow, and Short, Jefferson sought to redefine the United States' relationship with France in a way that protected American national interests but at the same time preserved the universal principles that had previously united the two republics. Instead of proclaiming revolutionary solidarity with the French republic, engaged in a universal struggle for "the liberty of the whole earth," Jefferson now depicted two powerful, independent nations that for all their mutual sympathies could never exist peaceably as neighbors, because both were expanding empires.

Jefferson openly acknowledged that he was not opposed in principle to the foreign occupation of New Orleans. Spain could have retained the mouth of the Mississippi "quietly for years" because of its "pacific disposition" and "feeble state." By contrast, France, given the "impetuosity of her temper" and "the energy and restlessness of her character," and the United States, "energetic and enterprising as any nation on earth," were bound to clash. In a war between the United States and France, the Americans would prevail, for the same reason that the French Republic had defeated one coalition of European monarchies after the other, namely, that "however greater her force is than ours compared in the abstract, it is nothing in comparison of ours when to be exerted on our soil." The United States had become in North America what France was on the European continent: the hegemonic power whose strength was based on its republican principles that made every citizen "meet invasions of the public order as his own personal concern," as Jefferson had put it in his inaugural address.

The notion that the United States and France had permanently parted ways to follow their own particular national destinies was also reflected in other letters from Jefferson to French correspondents, in which he revived the explanatory model of national character: "I shall say nothing of your country, because I do not understand either it's past or present state, nor foresee it's future destiny," he confessed to Volney two days after writing to Livingston/Du Pont. "Those on the spot posses alone the facts on which a sound judgment can be formed. Believing that forms of government have been attempted to which the national character is not adapted, I expect something will finally be settled as free as their habits of thinking & acting will permit. My only prayer is that it may cost no more human suffering."[37]

In an attempt to strike a balance between cultural relativism and political universalism and to explain how the American and French republics could be both similar and completely different, Jefferson turned to Montesquieu's distinction between the forms and the principles of government. In an earlier letter to Du Pont, Jefferson explained: "What is practicable must often countroul what is pure theory, and the habits of the governed must determine in a great degree what is practicable. Hence the same original principles, modified in practice according to the different habits of different nations, present governments of very different aspects. The same principles reduced to forms of practice accommodated to our habits, and put into forms accommodated to the habits of the French nation would present governments very unlike each other."[38]

The common original principles of the American and French republics were popular sovereignty and national self-determination–principles for which Jefferson had been willing to see "half the earth desolated." With the election of 1800, which Jefferson would later describe as, "as real a revolution in the principles of our government as that of 76 was in its form," the United States had arrived at its national destination, the perfect match of principle and form. But Jefferson held out the hope that France would slowly follow in America's footsteps, perhaps even under the leadership of Napoleon: "I have no doubt but that a great man, thoroughly knowing the habits of France, might so accommodate to them the principles of free government, as to enable them to live free. But in the hands of those who have not this coup d'œil, many unsuccessful experiments I fear are yet to be tried before they will settle down in freedom & tranquility."[39]

The official American representative "on the spot," Robert Livingston, had noted as early as January 1802 that, although an impending purge of the legislature caused "some murmurs & discontents," the Consulate generally was "pleasing to the people." He speculated that Napoleon needed Louisiana to compensate for the loss of Egypt, to defuse domestic discontent through imperial expansion, and to keep the army occupied. The French appeared glad to trade freedom of speech and a free press for stability, equality of opportunity, and imperial splendor: "The patriots here grumble but the people are satisfied they have run through all the changes & they see something like the ancient pageantry–while Liberty & equality & 'le palais du peuple' written upon every public building [are] sufficient to assure them that they combine the energy of the old government with the freedom of Roman citizens." Such observations led Livingston to the same conclusion that his friend and fellow New York patrician, Gouverneur Morris, had reached more than a decade earlier: if the French were happy under an autocratic government, who was to say that this was not the best regime for them? As Livingston wrote to Morris: "I am well satisfied from what I have seen that it is idle to think there is one form of government adapted to all the world. Manners habits & wants are as much to be consulted in forming a government as the elevation of the pole is in setting a sun dial." The American government was not a universal model, and even its own creation had been contingent upon particular circumstances. Americans should consider themselves fortunate, Livingston argued, "for having seized perhaps the only moment in which our habits & manners qualified us for freedom."[40]

Even Republicans who were less willing to accept the cultural relativism of national character regarded the French as having come full circle. A plebiscite in late summer 1802 overwhelmingly approved Napoleon's appointment as First Consul for Life. Faced with the paradox that Napoleon's reign appeared to grow more popular the more autocratic it became, Barlow sourly noted: "Bonaparte has thrown back the progress of civilization & public happiness about one age." For Barlow, the only explanation was a resurgence of the kind of false consciousness that he had identified in *Advice to the Privileged Orders* as one of the pillars of the Old Regime. When bells and cannon fire rang out throughout Paris in celebration of Napoleon's birthday in August, Barlow wrote in disgust to his wife: "High mass & Te Deum all over France, more powder burnt than would serve to conquer half Europe, & this is to conquer only the French people."[41]

The Consulate for Life was only the last in a series of measures that completed the consolidation of Napoleon's reign: he had purged parliamentary opposition; signed the Concordat with the Catholic Church; achieved peace with Britain in the Treaty of Amiens; and bound the political elite to his person through an amnesty for émigrés, the creation of lists of notables, and the Legion of Honor. In 1802, the French Revolution finally had come to an end.

Fortunately for Republicans, it was only a few months later that the Louisiana Purchase opened up a new vista for their universalist nation-building ambitions. In April 1803, James Monroe joined Livingston in Paris. The previous October, the Spanish intendant at New Orleans had suspended the American right of deposit, causing a storm of outrage among western settlers. Federalists, who had earlier been so enamored with Napoleon's energetic government, had called for an immediate military response and the seizure of New Orleans. Instead, Jefferson had appointed Monroe, who since his return from France had served as governor of Virginia, as special envoy to France and Spain. Federalists in the Senate had strongly objected to this choice, since, as William Plumer of New Hampshire explained, it was "well known that Monroe when he was recalled from France by Washington was in friendship with the Men whom Bonaparte considers as Jacobins & enemies to him." But in addition to Monroe's contacts in Paris (he knew personally the second and third consuls, Jean-Jacques Regis de Cambacérès and Charles-François Lebrun), his defense of western interests as a congressman in the 1780s had made him popular on the frontier. Jefferson had calculated correctly that Monroe's appointment would sufficiently calm the settlers to buy the administration more time for negotiations.[42]

The acquisition of the entire Louisiana territory from France was something Livingston and Monroe had neither sought nor expected. Showing no interest in territory west of the Mississippi, Madison had instructed the two diplomats to purchase all or part of New Orleans and, if possible, either East or West Florida, or both. However, the same developments that Madison hoped would force the French government to make these relatively small concessions–the imminent resumption of war between France and Great Britain and France's failure to reconquer Saint-Domingue–convinced Napoleon to abandon his plans for an empire in the West altogether. Without Saint-Domingue, and without the Floridas, which Spain refused to relinquish, Louisiana was more a liability than an asset to France, given its vulnerability to attack from British Canada. Selling Louisiana to the United States would keep the territory out of British hands, bring in much-needed funds, and help ensure American neutrality in the coming war.[43]

The addition of an area whose boundaries remained uncertain but which at least doubled the size of the United States was bound to dazzle and trouble the American imagination for years to come. As the first Americans to grapple with the news, the Republicans in Paris found it remarkably easy to transfer the universalist aspirations they had projected on the French Revolution to the uncharted wilderness of the American West.

Even before the Purchase, some of the most ardent supporters of the French Revolution, like Barlow and Monroe, had shifted from trying to export the American brand of republicanism to proposing that the United States instead should demonstrate the practice and benefits of nation-building by example. The more the United States was able to perfect its domestic republican order, the more other nations would be inclined to imitate it and to accommodate American interests abroad. In his second *Letter,* Barlow called on his fellow citizens to separate the English, Spanish, and French colonies still remaining on the North American continent from their mother countries–not by conquest, but by setting "such an example of rational liberty and public happiness, as they cannot fail to admire, and must therefore wish to partake." Once the European colonies in America joined the United States, the "projected empire" would be of unprecedented and frightening magnitude. Barlow asked his readers to share his faith in the federal union–a league of self-governing republics and thus an empire unlike any other in history, based on consent, not coercion–and assured them that there was "no knowing yet to what extent it may be carried." Similarly, Monroe declared that Jefferson's election, in conjunction with Napoleon's ascension to power, rendered the beginning of the nineteenth century "more favorable to the cause of liberty, than any former epoch of time. America & France in republican hands can advance the cause with effect. France by arms, America by form of example."[44]

Having concluded the Louisiana Purchase without authorization from Washington, Monroe and Livingston justified their actions by arguing that it would insulate America from "the European World & its concerns, especially its wars & intrigues"; enable the United States to "take a more imposing attitude" in relation to other nations; and at the same time strengthen the "Bond of our Union." Monroe exulted to Madison that the Purchase "secures to us every thing which is essential to the sovereignty of our Country to the peace prosperity & happiness of our people." By enabling Americans to expand and solidify the federal republic, which was both a model nation and a model state system, it also had the potential to transform the nature of international relations: "The period therefore may not be remote when our pacific system will be placed on a solid and secure basis; when that strict & impartial justice & respect for their rights which we observe in our intercourse with other nations, will be reciprocated to us by them all."[45]

Barlow hailed the Louisiana Purchase as a singular opportunity to rid the United States of slavery. Like many abolitionists in Britain, France, and the United States, Barlow believed that New World slavery was a declining institution that was bound to wither away before the forces of moral and economic progress. Denying slavery space for expansion by banning it from the newly acquired territory, he wrote to Alexander Wolcott, "would be one of the most powerful means of eradicating slavery from the U. States; which in every point of view, moral, political and economical, is perhaps the greatest blemish and may become the greatest scourge of our country." Such a policy would send a signal to the entire hemisphere and "probably be the means of eradicating [slavery] from Spanish America and the Islands as from the U.

States." Emphasizing the potential of the Purchase for initiating the abolition of slavery also served to distinguish the American republic from its French counterpart, which in May 1802 had taken the unprecedented step of ordering the reinstitution of slavery and the slave trade in its colonies (after the National Convention had been forced to abolish it in 1794 in response to the insurrection on Saint-Domingue).[46]

While this might seem hopelessly naïve, given that the Louisiana Purchase would pave the way for the westward expansion of slavery, many other Americans looked to the West for a solution to the intractable problem of slavery. In the aftermath of the revolution on Saint-Domingue and Gabriel's Rebellion, Jefferson and Monroe had discussed whether freed slaves or those who became dangerous to white society could be "colonized" north of the Ohio or in the Louisiana territory, which they believed was still held by Spain. The Louisiana Purchase revived interest in western colonization among other prominent Virginians. But in addition to the basic impracticability of such schemes, Jefferson cautioned that a black colony would sooner or later present an obstacle to white expansion and spoil the vaunted harmony of "a people speaking the same language, governed in similar forms, & by similar laws" by introducing an intolerable "blot or mixture."[47]

The hemispheric abolition of slavery was only one of the benefits Barlow ascribed to the Louisiana Purchase. It marked the beginning of a new age, in which American national and imperial power would guide the world toward peace and prosperity. The American settlement of Louisiana would forever remove, Barlow predicted, "the causes of war and every strong temptation to deviate from economy and justice and the steady pursuits of sober and well-protected industry by which alone our institutions can be preserved, improved and probably extended by example to other countries."[48]

Republicans in America likewise celebrated the Louisiana Purchase as the harbinger of an age of perpetual peace by removing the United States from European conflicts and strengthening the bonds between the frontier and the federal government. Federalists objected that the acquired territory was too large to be governed effectively as a republic and that the Purchase would break up the union through either the establishment of independent nations in the West or the destruction of the Constitution's original sectional balance. While many Republicans shared these concerns, others countered, in the words of Senator John Breckinridge of Kentucky, that the "Goddess of Liberty" could not be contained by geographical boundaries.

Expansion would not weaken the union, he argued; on the contrary, "the more extensive its dominion the more safe and more durable it will be."[49]

In his second inaugural address, Jefferson acknowledged the mixture of hope and fear that expansion inspired, even among his supporters, by rephrasing Barlow's declaration about the unknown limits of federal republicanism as a question: "But who can limit the extent to which the federative principle may operate effectively?" Contrary to the axiom in contemporary political science (most famously articulated by Montesquieu) and Federalist policy, that territorial expansion was only feasible if the power of the central government increased accordingly, Jefferson argued that expansion would actually lessen the need for centralized government, since it both stimulated national sentiments and created a safer neighborhood along the republic's borders: "The larger our association, the less it will be shaken by local passions; and in any view, is it not better that the opposite bank of the Mississippi should be settled by our brethren and children, than by strangers of another family? With which shall we be most likely to live in harmony and friendly intercourse?"[50]

As Republicans pondered the future of the expanding American empire, the history of the French Republic remained a constant reference point, but its lessons were ambiguous. On the one hand, Napoleon's coup d'état confirmed the wisdom of decentralized government and of relying on the states as a bulwark against the consolidation of power. The "true barriers of our liberty in this country are our state-governments," Jefferson explained to Destutt de Tracy in 1811. By contrast, "the republican government of France was lost without a struggle," and Napoleon was able to usurp power because "the party of 'un et indivisible' had prevailed; no Provincial organizations existed to which the people might rally under authority of the laws, the seats of the Directory were virtually vacant, and a small force sufficed to turn the legislature out of their chamber, & to salute it's leader Chief of the nation." On the other hand, the French experience also suggested that nations could and needed to be molded from above, through the application of state power, even if teaching former subjects to become republican citizens was a long, arduous, and potentially bloody process. In a letter to Cabanis written shortly after receiving news of the Louisiana Purchase in July 1803, Jefferson wistfully recalled their meetings at the salon of Madame Helvetius: "In those days how sanguine we were! And how soon were the virtuous hopes and confidence of every good man blasted! How many excellent friends have we lost in your efforts toward self-government, *et cui bono*?" But not all was lost, since after Napoleon's regime had given the French "as great a portion of liberty as the opinions, habits, and character of the nation are prepared for, progressive preparations may fit you for progressive portions of that first of blessings, and you may in time attain what we erred in supposing could be hastily seized and maintained, in the present stage of political information among your citizens at large."[51]

The concept of progressive preparation for self-government under executive leadership in accordance with national character found ready application in Louisiana. Article III of the Louisiana Purchase treaty stipulated that the territory's inhabitants "shall be incorporated in the Union of the United States, and admitted as soon as possible according to the principles of the federal Constitution to the enjoyment of all the rights, advantages and immunities of citizens of the United States." However, the territory's heterogeneous Creole population aroused deep suspicions among Republicans and Federalists alike. Jefferson acknowledged, "Our new fellow citizens are as yet as incapable of self government as children," while the Federalist Fisher Ames dreaded the incorporation into the union of a "*Gallo-Hispano-Indian omnium gatherum* of savages and adventures." Other Federalists argued that it was better to forestall expansion into the region or to rule it as a colony. However, the Republican majority was prepared to grant the president extraordinary powers for nation-building, at least on a temporary basis.[52]

Dispensing with the process for territorial governance and state-formation established in the Northwest Ordinance of 1787, Jefferson argued that Congress should extend civil rights in Louisiana, "in proportion as [it found] the people there ripen[ed] for receiving these first principles of freedom." To this end, he drafted the Louisiana Governance Act, which Congress passed largely unchanged in March 1804. While the law was in effect for only one year, it provides a link between Republican attitudes toward the French Revolution and western expansion. Just as Jefferson and other Republicans had believed that they could school the French in the theory and practice of republicanism, they now directed their educational efforts toward frontier settlers.[53]

The Governance Act provided for local, but not popular government, in the form of an "Assembly of Notables," an institution that Jefferson hoped would be "familiar & pleasing" to the French inhabitants of Louisiana. This executive council of local property owners appointed by the governor (who in turn was chosen by the president) did bear a striking resemblance to the body of the same name that convened in Paris in early 1787, and that Jefferson had then considered "productive of much good in this country," by preparing the French people to receive "as much liberty as they are capable of managing." Like its French predecessor, the Louisiana Notables would facilitate an orderly transition from executive autocracy to popular sovereignty.[54]

Speaking in support of the law, Representative Samuel Mitchell of New York assured those opposed to the incorporation of Louisianans that the new citizens would be required to "serve an apprenticeship to liberty; they are to be taught the lessons of freedom; and by degrees they are to be raised to the enjoyment and practice of independence." William Plumer commented sarcastically that had "such a bill been passed by federalists, the Democrats would have denounced it as *monarchical;* but when enacted by the *exclusive friends* of the people, it is pure *republicanism.*" Gouverneur Morris likewise concluded that the Republicans had "done more to strengthen the executive than Federalists dared think of, even in Washington's day."[55]

Among the vocal supporters of this policy of out-Federalizing the Federalists was Thomas Paine. Soon after news of the Louisiana Purchase reached the United States, he offered Jefferson his views on what needed to be done to make Americans out of French Louisianans. Paine simply assumed that "the present inhabitants know little or nothing of election and representation." Therefore, they were "not in an immediate Condition to exercise those powers, and besides this they are perhaps too much under the influence of their priests to be sufficiently free." Paine recommended that Congress should establish a "*Government provisoire*" for between three and seven years, until the population was "in train to elect their state Government." Among the most urgent measures was the establishment of schools to teach English in order to replace French and Spanish as the official language. On the same day, in a letter to John Breckinridge, Paine offered to move to New Orleans and help out with the nation-building effort there: "They are a new people and unacquainted with the principles of representative government and I think I could do some good among them." Over the previous decade, Paine had seen himself as engaged in a similar mission in France. Despite his disappointment with the outcome of the French Revolution, Paine's suggestions for Louisiana reflected the influence of French nation-building and its concern with language as a unifying force.[56]

In September 1804, residents of Upper Louisiana, including Frenchmen, Americans, and Spaniards, protested congressional restrictions on slavery in their territory and petitioned for the institution's unlimited expansion. In his outraged response, an open letter "To the French Inhabitants of Louisiana" published in the *National Intelligencer,* Paine drew on his expertise as a participant-observer of the French Revolution to argue that the French in Louisiana (whom he held solely responsible for the petition) had shown themselves as yet unfit for republicanism. Paine reminded Louisianans that, "without any merit or expence in obtaining it," they were already enjoying "the blessings of freedom," and would over time be granted more rights, "in proportion as you become initiated into the principles and practice of the representative system of government." But they had to understand that Americans were determined not to repeat the mistakes of the French Revolution: "You see what mischief ensued in France by the possession of power before they understood principles. They earned liberty in words but not in fact. The writer of this was in France through the whole of the revolution, and knows the truth of what he speaks; for after endeavoring to give it principle he had nearly fallen a victim to its rage."[57]

In a letter to Jefferson, Paine counseled against elevating the territory's residents to a level of equality with U.S. citizens until there were "a sufficient number of American settlers to be trusted with Constitutional Powers." It was important not to grant the French in Louisiana any measure of self-government, because they were clearly "a troublesome set" and likely to take any concession as encouragement to ask for more: "I observed in the french revolution that they always proceeded by stages and made each stage a stepping stone to another." One way to Americanize these troublesome French was to change the territory's name. Advocating the use of French methods in order to avoid French results, Paine pointed out that "France has lost the names and almost the remembrance of provinces by dividing them into departments with appropriate names."[58]

Paine warned Jefferson against permitting slavery in Louisiana, for even "besides the immorality of it," this would be a "certain way of preventing population and consequently of preventing revenue." He recalled that in Paris Jefferson had told him "of a plan of making the Negroes tenants on a plantation, that is, allotting each Negroe family a quantity of land for which they were to pay to the owner a certain quantity of produce." The time had come to put this plan into action, Paine argued, which would allow free blacks to become productive plantation cultivators, although he nowhere implied that they would become citizens as well. However, the desire to preserve and expand slavery, which for Paine demonstrated that French Louisianans were not yet Americans, was in fact shared by Republicans throughout the South, including President Jefferson. Ironically, Paine also denied the inhabitants of Louisiana full citizenship rights on the grounds they had failed to liberate themselves: "We fought for liberty when you stood quiet in slavery." Defenders of slavery frequently used the exact same argument to prove that African American slaves neither desired nor deserved freedom, since they were not willing to fight for it.[59]

How profoundly the outcome of the French Revolution had changed Paine's understanding of the American Revolution, which he had famously described as "the cause of all mankind," became apparent in his strictures to the inhabitants of Louisiana: "We obtained our rights by calmly understanding principles, and by the successful event of a long, obstinate and expensive war. But it is not incumbent on us to fight the battles of the world for the world's profit."[60] From now on, America fought for itself, not mankind. If it decided to allow other, less deserving people to partake in "the blessings of freedom," it would be on America's terms, and the recipients of its largesse could be expected to be grateful, a lesson that the French inhabitants of Louisiana had yet failed to grasp.

Paine was not the only Republican convinced that the federal government needed to assert its authority on the frontier as forcefully as the French had done throughout Europe. Even as staunch a states' rights advocate as John Randolph advised Secretary of the Treasury Albert Gallatin to print a "thousand copies of Tom Paine's answer to [the Louisianans'] remonstrance" and to distribute "them by as many thousand troops; who can speak a language perfectly intelligible to the people of Louisiana." Under the Jefferson administration, Republicans increasingly distinguished between a domestic republic, on the one hand—defined by the voluntary allegiance of the people and the autonomy of the states—and, on the other hand, an imperial republic on the western frontier, where the central government had a free hand to clear the way for civilization and to protect the nation from internal disorder and foreign threats. In this Republican empire, the idea of the nation as a harmonious "family" of shared sentiments, common interests, and universal principles served to render the power of the federal state invisible, since that power was ostensibly directed only against those outside the nation: Native Americans and Europeans.[61]

Notwithstanding Republicans' avowed disassociation from France, these conceptions of nation and state power grew directly out of their engagement with the French experience of nation-building and political conflict over the previous decade. Jefferson and other Republicans had witnessed in France the power of popular mobilization under the banner of the nation, as well as the effectiveness of defining political opponents as outsiders to the nation. Yet they had also observed the dangerous malleability of the boundaries of nationhood, which could turn insiders into outsiders virtually overnight. Dismissing all internal divisions as superficial and temporary, and identifying the boundaries of nationhood with the physical boundaries of the nation, promised to stabilize the powerful but explosive force of nationalism. Once again, while regarding themselves as teachers of republican principles, Americans were in fact applying the lessons they themselves had learned from France.

Epilogue

Historians have often told the story of the United States and France in the late eighteenth century as one of inevitable disenchantment, in which exclusionary yet realistic nationalisms supplanted a well-meaning yet utopian cosmopolitanism. But looking at the age of revolution from the vantage point of Americans in Paris suggests that nation-building and universalism were complementary rather than competing forces during this period. The efforts of Americans to apply their revolutionary expertise in Paris highlight the central role of cosmopolitanism in the construction of the new national communities in the United States and France. Only through appeals to universal principles could American and French revolutionaries unify their diverse populations and transform royal subjects into citizens in a process of national "regeneration." Moreover, nationalists needed to think in cosmopolitan terms because their nation's future depended on a hospitable international environment and on recognition by other nations.

However, as the French Revolution unfolded in unpredictable twists and turns, cosmopolitan patriots faced two fundamental challenges. First, they had to grapple with the inherent tension in cosmopolitan ideology between universalism and particularism. American and French revolutionaries believed that their respective nations offered a universal model to the rest of the world. But they were equally convinced that each people had to develop according to its particular manners and customs. Second, in both the United States and France, nation-builders had to invent the rules of a new political culture in which "the people" figured both as the source of legitimacy and as a potential agent of disorder.

American and French elites subscribed to the ideal of a united, harmonious, and stable political domain. When factions nevertheless formed in each country around domestic and foreign policy issues, the ensuing conflicts were exacerbated by the definition of the nation as based on supposedly universal, but in fact highly contested and evolving principles. Each faction identified itself as speaking for the nation and its underlying principles, and branded its opponents as "foreigners." This exclusion from the nation in turn justified the use of political violence, which many American and French revolutionaries came to see as the inevitable price of nation-building.

The harrowing experience of the Terror convinced American Republicans in Paris that the pursuit of universal ends might require particular means in each country and led them to justify the increasing authoritarianism in France. At the same time, fear of the subversive presence of literal and political "foreigners" caused some American Federalists and officials of the French Directory to argue for more-restrictive concepts of national belonging. As relations between the United States and France deteriorated, the activities of Americans in Paris became the object of a heated debate over the boundaries of the national community and the primary locus of political allegiance. Yet Federalist efforts to manufacture a nationalist consensus faced a resilient tradition of revolutionary cosmopolitanism. Once in power, Republicans chose to dissociate themselves from the French Revolution, in the interest of consolidating their own regime. Although America and France shared certain universal principles, they argued, these principles had to assume different political forms as each nation followed its own destiny. Just as the Federalists and their ostensible antithesis, the Directory, had similar attitudes toward popular politics and foreigners, Thomas Jefferson's and Napoleon Bonaparte's pursuit of a post-revolutionary order had much in common. Neither American nor French nationalism became any less universalist, even as the two countries appeared to develop in opposite political directions at the beginning of the nineteenth century. The universalism that had inspired American and French revolutionaries and forged a

bond between sister republics now found expression in national expansion-
ism across the North American continent and Europe, respectively.

The French Revolution reinforced the idea that France was a "universal
nation" that represented the apex of civilization and was charged with res-
cuing other peoples from tyranny and ignorance. Despite the strong resistance of France's European neighbors against being rescued, and the loss
of all conquered territories after Napoleon's final defeat, this national self-
understanding continued to dominate debates about France's place in the
world throughout the nineteenth century, developing into the ideology of
the nation's *mission civilisatrice*. The idea of the "universal nation" proved
so enduring in part because it reflected an anxiety that, as a nation, France
could not do without the confidence and unity that only military conquest
and colonization were able to provide. French nation-building at home required imperial expansion abroad.[1]

The French Revolution also confirmed the idea of American exceptionalism, which held that the New World was providentially separated from
the turmoil of the Old World. However, national sentiment remained weak,
and the American union seemed constantly on the verge of disintegration
along regional and partisan lines. As a remedy, Jeffersonian Republicans
argued that territorial expansion would facilitate national consolidation.
A growing union would instill national pride, increase national power and
resources, and create a safer neighborhood along the republic's borders.
Critics of territorial expansion countered that the United States would not
be able to assimilate or subjugate the heterogeneous populations inhabit-
ing the continent without compromising its republican values. However,
proponents of a Manifest Destiny felt confident that backward peoples had
no right to stand in the way of progress, and that the American empire, by
its very nature, would exercise its power only for good. U.S. nation-building
and the advance of civilization would be one and the same. The redefinition
of the Atlantic revolutions' universal principles as embodied exclusively by
the American and French nations marked the logical, if ironic culmination
of the two revolutions' cosmopolitan nation-building projects.

The fact that these parallels between the experiences of the American
and French nations have been overlooked is testimony to the success of Federalist historiography. Beginning in the late 1790s, Federalists realized that
to counteract the influence of the French Revolution in the United States,
they had to redefine the American Revolution as entirely different from its

European successor. Since the Federalists' beliefs were no less universalist than the principles of their opponents (as the case of Gouverneur Morris shows), they looked for allies among the conservative movement in Europe that had emerged in reaction to the French Revolution. When the American minister to Berlin, John Quincy Adams, met Hauterive's critic, Friedrich von Gentz, in 1800, he immediately recognized the value of translating Gentz's comparison of the French and American revolutions for an American audience. In a letter to Gentz, Adams explained: "It cannot but afford a gratification to every American attached to the honor of his country to see its revolution so ably vindicated from the imputation of having originated, or been conducted upon the same principles as that of France." Thus, even American exceptionalism remained Eurocentric, explaining American difference in European terms.[2]

In his work, Gentz contrasted the defensive, limited, and local nature of the American Revolution with the offensive, expansionist, and global character of the French Revolution. One of the reasons why his approach held so much appeal to Federalists was that Gentz went out of his way to deny that Paine and other cosmopolitans should be considered at all representative of the American Revolution. "Never did it enter the head of any legislator, or statesman in America," Gentz proclaimed, "to combat the lawfulness of foreign constitutions, and to set up the American revolution, as a new epocha in the general relations of civil society." In sharp contrast to the French, the "wise moderation" of American revolutionaries led them to refrain "from every thing that may be called proselyting and propagandism." Gentz insisted that, despite all its virtues, the American Revolution did not offer any kind of example applicable to Europe.[3]

Republicans failed to offer a coherent and compelling counternarrative. Around 1796-97, Joel Barlow began to sketch a history of the French Revolution, but his inability to either ignore or explain the events of the Terror presented an insurmountable obstacle. His account was meant to demonstrate that "revolutions in favor of representative democracy ought to be encouraged." However, even in his outline, Barlow considered it necessary to add numerous qualifications to this simple message. While the French Revolution might be considered a failure, Barlow conceded, "the fault was not in the inherent nature of the operation, but in the manner of conducting it. The mistakes that may have been committed ought to be clearly pointed out, the causes of the failure detailed in a most candid & critical examination;

so that other nations, or a future generation here, need not be unnecessarily deterred from a like attempt, whenever they shall feel themselves able to avoid the errors and secure the advantages held up to view in this example."[4]

Despite their loss of political power, it was the Federalists' interpretation of the two revolutions that proved enduring to the present day. According to this consensus view, the American Revolution was a unique and comparatively bloodless affair whose objectives had been entirely achieved by the time of Washington's inauguration in 1789. Nonetheless, whenever news of popular uprisings in foreign countries has reached the United States, American observers have been apt to temporarily regard their revolution as an ongoing and exportable tradition that can serve as an exemplar to oppressed peoples elsewhere.

This ambiguity has shaped American reactions to foreign revolution for the last two hundred years. Americans regularly both affirm and deny the relevance of the American revolutionary model for other nations. Most Americans approve of movements for national self-determination in principle, and indeed welcome foreign revolutions with hopeful enthusiasm. But to maintain American support, a revolution has to be conducted with a minimum of violence and social upheaval and a scrupulous regard for property rights. Such unrealistic expectations, based on sanitized images of the American Revolution, have led to inevitable disappointment. Drawing on notions of national character and race, Americans have concluded that other nations are inherently incapable of following the American model *and* that the perceived failure of foreign revolutions stems from not following that model closely enough.[5]

It is all too easy to deride the double standard of revolutionaries who advocate revolutions only for people who do not really need them. But it would be disingenuous not to acknowledge the powerful and enduring appeal of the idea that America can regenerate the world in its image, and be in turn periodically regenerated by seeing its best features adopted by other nations. Neither the allure nor the folly of this notion was lost on the founder most closely associated with it, Thomas Jefferson.

In an 1821 letter to John Adams, Jefferson expressed his profound anxiety over the Missouri Compromise and the likelihood of civil war. Turning to the ongoing wars of independence in South America, Jefferson declared that while he had wished the Hispanic Americans well, he had always suspected that they were "not yet sufficiently enlightened for self-government." Still, he remained confident that in time they would become "sufficiently trained by education and habits of freedom to walk safely by themselves," and he suggested some specific measures that would speed this process along. At the end, Jefferson must have been struck by the incongruity of the two parts of his letter, for he noted with a self-awareness that often eluded him and other cosmopolitan patriots, "You see, my dear Sir, how easily we prescribe for others a cure for their difficulties, while we cannot cure our own."[6]

Notes

Abbreviations

AAECPE-U	Archives du Ministère des Affaires étrangères, Correspondance Politique, Etats-Unis
AN	Archives Nationales
Diary	Gouverneur Morris. *A Diary of the French Revolution.* 2 vols. Ed. Beatrix C. Davenport. Boston, 1939.
GM	Gouverneur Morris
GMP	Gouverneur Morris Papers, Library of Congress
HSP	Simon Gratz Collection, Historical Society of Pennsylvania
JB	Joel Barlow
JBP	Joel Barlow Papers, Houghton Library
JM	James Monroe
JMP	James Monroe Papers, Library of Congress
LC	Library of Congress
MHS	Massachusetts Historical Society
NYPL	New York Public Library
SSS	*The Papers of James Madison: Secretary of State Series.* 8 vols. to date. Ed. Robert J. Brugger et al. Charlottesville, 1985-.
TJ	Thomas Jefferson
TJP	*The Papers of Thomas Jefferson.* 35 vols. to date. Ed. Julian P. Boyd et al. Princeton, 1950-.
TJPLC	Thomas Jefferson Papers, Library of Congress
TP	Thomas Paine
WS	William Short
WSP	William Short Papers, Library of Congress

Introduction

1. The original arrest file is in F7/4774/61, AN. It includes the Committee of General Security's order for the arrest; the protocol of the arrest, signed by the arresting officers as well as by TP and JB; a note from the prison governor Benoit; the American petition for Paine's release, dated 8 Pluviôse II (28 Jan. 1794); a petition by Achille Audibert, a friend

and municipal officer from Calais, TP's constituency, dated 2 Fructidor II (19 Aug. 1794); an appeal by François Lanthenas, the translator of *Rights of Man,* dated 18 Thermidor II (5 Aug. 1794); and a letter from TP to the Committee of General Security, dated 19 Thermidor II (6 Aug. 1794).

2. *Archives parlementaires,* 83:724; *Gazette Nationale,* 10 Pluviôse II (29 Jan. 1794). See also Griffith, "Reminiscences," 51; GM to TJ, 21 Jan. 1794, GMP.

3. "TP, To the Citizens of the United States. Letter the Third," *National Intelligencer,* 29 Nov. 1802.

4. Scrivener, *Cosmopolitan Ideal;* Rapport, *Nationality and Citizenship;* Wahnich, *L'impossible Citoyen;* Brubaker, *Citizenship and Nationhood,* 43–48; Gauthier, *Triomphe et mort;* Guiraudon, "Cosmopolitanism and National Priority"; Schlereth, *Cosmopolitan Ideal in Enlightenment Thought;* Mathiez, *Révolution et les étrangers.*

5. Winik, *Great Upheaval;* Dunn, *Sister Revolutions;* Sa'adah, *Shaping of Liberal Politics;* Higonnet, *Sister Republics;* Nora and Clement, "L'Amérique et la France"; Arendt, *On Revolution.* Such contrasts between the two revolutions depend crucially on the erasure of violence from the history of the American Revolution. For critiques of this selective memory, see Andress, *Terror,* 2, 6–7; Kulikoff, "Revolutionary Violence"; Newman, "Writing the History," 30–31.

6. For French nation-building, see Bell, *Cult of the Nation;* Thiesse, *Création des identités nationales.*

7. TP, "The Rights of Man, Part II," in TP, *Complete Writings,* 1:360.

8. For American visions of a reformed international system, see Hendrickson, *Peace Pact;* Onuf and Onuf, *Federal Union, Modern World.* For foreign relations as an impetus for nation-building, see also Marks, *Independence on Trial.* For TP's contribution, see Fitzsimons, "Tom Paine's New World Order"; Whatmore, "'Gigantic manliness.'" For French theories of new international relations, see Belissa, *Fraternité universelle et intérêt national.* For French revolutionary diplomacy and warfare as challenges to traditional conceptions of international society, see Armstrong, *Revolution and World Order,* chap. 3. Conversely, T. C. W. Blanning emphasizes the conventionality of French revolutionary foreign policy in *Origins of the French Revolutionary Wars.*

9. For changing definitions of French citizenship, see Sahlins, *Unnaturally French,* esp. 224, 283–85, 288–89. For TP's explanation of his arrest, see TP to JM, 4 Oct. 1794, in TP, *Complete Writings,* 2:1355. For TP's involvement in the Deane affair, see Foner, *Tom Paine and Revolutionary America,* 160–61.

10. GM to John Thomas, 29 July 1793, GMP. See also R. M. Smith, "Constructing American National Identity," 31–35.

11. Sahlins, *Unnaturally French,* 289–90; Rapport, *Nationality and Citizenship,* 265–66; R. M. Smith, "Constructing American National Identity," 35–40.

12. For the interpretive insights of the exile perspective, see Kramer, *Threshold of a New World,* 1–11.

13. For the tension between universalism and difference in Enlightenment thought, see Crépon, *Géographies de l'esprit;* Todorov, *On Human Diversity;* Vyverberg, *Human Nature.* For the origins of cosmopolitanism, see Jacob, *Strangers Nowhere in the World.*

14. Recently, this idea has found new advocates among self-declared "cosmopolitan patriots." See Tan, *Justice without Borders;* Falk, *Great Terror War,* 145–46; Appiah, "Cosmopolitan Patriots."

15. For eighteenth-century conceptions of cosmopolitanism and patriotism, see D. Gordon, "Citizenship"; Rosenfeld, "Citizens of Nowhere in Particular"; Radcliffe, "Burke, Radical Cosmopolitanism"; Goodman, *Republic of Letters,* 2, 16, 20, 34–35, 45–52.

16. For American popular cosmopolitanism, see Loughran, *Republic in Print,* 74–78; Cotlar, "In Paine's Absence"; Bloch, *Visionary Republic,* 150–86.

17. Watson, *Men and Times of the Revolution,* 104. For eighteenth-century British patriotism and its cosmopolitan aspects, see Gould, *Persistence of Empire,* 30–31; H. Cunningham, "Language of Patriotism." For its relationship to Protestantism, see Colley, *Britons,* 18–55. For the American adaptations of British patriotism, see Cotlar, "In Paine's Absence," 31–34. For Americans' strong sense of attachment and identity as members of the British Empire, see also Greene, "Empire and Identity," 211–22. For French patriotism and Catholicism, see Bell, *Cult of the Nation,* 5–6, 8, 10, 15, 44–45, 47–48, 93–97.

18. For changing perceptions of the American Revolution in the wake of the French Revolution, see Appleby, "Radicalizing the War for Independence," 7. For American reception of the French Revolution generally, see Hale, "'Many Who Wandered in Darkness'"; Rossignol, *Nationalist Ferment,* 60–63, 99–105; Kelleter, *Amerikanische Aufklärung,* 548–612; Branson, *These Fiery Frenchified Dames,* 55–99; Waldstreicher, *In the Midst of Perpetual Fetes,* 112–40; Newman, *Parades, Festivals,* chap. 5; Kramer, "American Political Culture"; Davis, *Revolutions,* chap. 2; H. F. May, *Enlightenment in America,* 153–251; Nash, "American Clergy and the French Revolution"; Hyslop, "American Press Reports"; H. M. Jones, *America and French Culture.*

19. Hamilton to Lafayette, 6 Jan. 1799, in A. Hamilton, *Papers,* 22:404.

20. William L. Chew has attempted such a community study for the period from 1780 to 1815. See W. L. Chew, "Life before Fodor and Frommer"; idem, *Leben in Frankreich.* Anecdotal accounts of Americans in revolutionary France include Maurice, *Des Américains à Paris;* Levenstein, *Seductive Journeys;* Bizardel, *Américains à Paris pendant la Révolution;* Longstreet, *We All Went to Paris.*

21. Werner and Zimmermann, "Vergleich, Transfer, Verflechtung"; idem, "Beyond Comparison"; Gould, "Entangled Histories, Entangled Worlds."

22. Balibar, "Nation Form." For "Creole pioneers" see B. Anderson, *Imagined Communities,* chap. 4. For the Eurocentric argument, see Sewell, "French Revolution." For a case study of the process of comparative national self-definition, see Wolff, *Inventing Eastern Europe.* See also Sluga, "Nation and the Comparative Imagination."

23. For comparisons between the American and French revolutionary ideologies, see Hulliung, *Citizens and Citoyens;* Dunn, *Sister Revolutions;* Marienstras, *Amérique et la France;* Higonnet, *Sister Republics;* Arendt, *On Revolution.* For studies of national stereotypes and projections, see Vincent, "Américains à Paris sous la révolution"; W. L. Chew, *National Stereotypes in Perspective;* Echeverria, *Mirage in the West.* For the reception of Palmer, *Age of the Democratic Revolution,* and Godechot, *France and the Atlantic*

Revolution, see Bailyn, *Atlantic History,* 24–30; Bétourné and Hartig, *Penser l'histoire de la révolution,* 117–23. An earlier example of their approach is Faÿ, *L'esprit révolutionnaire.* For French historiography and its resistance to colonial and Atlantic history, see Vidal, "Reluctance of French Historians." On the reluctance of historians and the American public to view U.S. history as comparable to the history of other empires, see Colley, "Difficulties of Empire."

24. Armitage, "Three Concepts of Atlantic History," 20. For challenges to French and American exceptionalism, see, respectively, Jourdan, *La révolution;* F. Anderson and Cayton, *Dominion of War.*

25. Wood, *Radicalism,* 3, 231. For negative images of the French Revolution in high school and college textbooks, see Harison, "Teaching the French Revolution." For examples of twenty-first-century Francophobia, see Unger, *French War against America;* J. J. Miller and Molesky, *Our Oldest Enemy.*

26. François Furet has argued that interpretations of the French Revolution depend upon when and whether it is understood to have ended. The same could be said about the American case. In a critique of Furet, Isser Woloch points out that condemnations of the failures of the French Revolution—for example, in creating a viable constitution—often lack an accurate point of comparison. Even the much-vaunted U.S. Constitution and Bill of Rights did not protect African Americans from a reign of terror that long outlasted the abolition of slavery itself. See Furet, *Interpreting the French Revolution,* 1–79; Woloch, "On the Latent Illiberalism," 1460. See also Gould and Onuf, "Introduction," in *Empire and Nation,* 12–15. For the revolutions in a global context, see Osterhammel and Peterson, *Globalization,* chap. 4; Bayly, *Birth of the Modern World,* 89–95, 287.

27. For discussions of these differences, see Malia, *History's Locomotives,* 161–64; Rakove, "Why American Constitutionalism Worked"; Stourzh, "Declaration of Rights."

28. Sa'adah, *Shaping of Liberal Politics,* 5–6.

I. EXPORTING AMERICAN REVOLUTIONS

1. Entries of 7 and 8 Dec. 1791, in *Diary,* 2:321–23.

2. For GM in Paris, see Kirschke, *Gouverneur Morris,* 201–47; M. R. Miller, *Envoy to the Terror;* W. H. Adams, *Gouverneur Morris,* 171–250; Brookhiser, *Gentleman Revolutionary,* 97–155; Fiechter, *Diplomate américain sous la Terreur.* GM is also the hero of one French and one German historical novel, set in Paris: Moulin, *L'amant américain;* Heydenau, *Gouvero.* For accounts of TJ's tenure as minister to France, see W. H. Adams, *Paris Years;* O'Brien, *Long Affair,* 1–68; Fohlen, *Jefferson à Paris;* Rice, *Thomas Jefferson's Paris;* Kaplan, *Jefferson and France,* 18–36; Malone, *Jefferson and the Rights of Man,* 3–237; Kimball, *Jefferson on the Scene of Europe.* The Paris years also figure prominently in many general studies of Jefferson, particularly Halliday, *Understanding Thomas Jefferson,* 1–12, 56–69, 81–112; Ellis, *American Sphinx,* chap. 2; Burstein, *Inner Jefferson,* chap. 3.

3. For this nationalist paradox, see Bell, *Cult of the Nation,* esp. 5–6, 14; Dujardin, "Des États Généraux à l'Assemblée nationale," 258.

4. Entry of 11 Mar. 1789, in *Diary,* 1:10. GM began his diary on 1 Mar. 1789 and kept it almost every day until his death in 1816. He used the diary to record his daily routine, give some order to the overwhelming impressions and fast-moving events of Paris, vent his frustration with French businessmen and bureaucrats, and editorialize about politics. GM clearly did not intend the diaries to be read by anyone else, for they also contain detailed accounts of his affair with Adélaïde de Flahaut, many of which entries his widow painstakingly blotted out before handing the diaries over to GM's first biographer, Jared Sparks.

5. GM to George Washington, 12 Nov. 1788, in Washington, *Papers,* 1:103. On Robert Morris's monopoly on the Franco-American tobacco trade and its failure, see W. H. Adams, *Paris Years,* 186–87; M. R. Miller, "Gouverneur Morris and the French Revolution," 124–41. See also James Madison to TJ, 8 Dec. 1788, and TJ to WS, 9 Feb. 1789, both in *TJP,* 14:339, 530. GM's ambitious scheme to organize a private consortium for the purchase of the American debt to France is explained in great detail in M. R. Miller, "Gouverneur Morris and the French Revolution," 142–87.

6. TJ to JM, 18 Aug. 1785, in *TJP,* 8:43. For TJ's and GM's mutual esteem, see TJ to Maria Cosway, 25 July 1789, and TJ to Lord Wycombe, 25 July 1789, both in *TJP,* 15:305–6, 306–7; GM to Robert Morris, 21 July 1789, Gouverneur Morris Papers, Butler Library. Adams describes their relationship as one of "guarded formality," and "without any signs of intimacy or candor." However, given their widely differing temperaments, lifestyles, and politics, it seems remarkable how cordial their interactions remained while they were both in Paris (W. H. Adams, *Gouverneur Morris,* 179).

7. TJ to Anne Willing Bingham, 11 May 1788, in *TJP,* 13:151.

8. Chastellux, *Travels in North America,* 1:131, 294, 2:389–96. See also Mintz, *Gouverneur Morris,* 168.

9. On GM's reception in French salon society, see, e.g., entries of 1 and 25 Mar. 1789, in *Diary,* 1:1, 20. On the French fascination with America, see Echeverria, *Mirage in the West.*

10. For GM's initial reluctance to offer political opinions, see entry of 17 Mar. 1789, in *Diary,* 1:14. For GM's early reputation as an elitist, see *Diary,* 1:9. Madison is quoted in Farrand, *Records of the Federal Convention,* 3:534. For example, Adèle informed GM that Louis XVI was considering an escape to Spain, and at her request, he agreed to talk to Lafayette and urge measures in the National Assembly to dissuade the king and thereby prevent civil war (entry of 28 July 1789, in *Diary,* 1:164–65). The king's alleged escape plans never materialized until the failed flight to Varennes of June 1791. In addition to her role as a *salonnière,* her busy social calendar, and her multiple lovers, Adèle was also (without GM's knowledge) working on a semiautobiographical novel titled *Adèle de Sénage,* which was published to great acclaim in 1794. See Hesse, *Other Enlightenment,* 142–44. The novel is also discussed in Stewart, "Novelists and Their Fiction," 204–5, 209.

11. For American views of French gender roles and politics, see Steele, "Thomas Jefferson's Gender Frontier"; W. L. Chew, "'Straight' Sam meets 'Lewd' Louis"; J. Lewis, "'Those Scenes.'" For GM's and TJ's views, see entry of 14 Apr. 1789, in *Diary,* 1:39; TJ to George Washington, 4 Nov. 1788, in *TJP,* 14:330. These attitudes reflected longstanding British stereotypes of French women and feminized images of elite power and corruption; see Colley, *Britons,* 251–52.

12. For Adèle's salon, see Fassiotto, "La Comtesse de Flahaut." For the politics of salons before and during the revolution generally, see Kale, *French Salons;* Goodman, *Republic of Letters.*

13. TJ to Lafayette, 6 May 1789, in *TJP,* 15:97–98; GM to Lafayette, 16 Oct. 1789, in Sparks, *Life of Gouverneur Morris,* 1:330–31.

14. GM to the comte de Moustier, 23 Feb. 1789, in *Diary,* 1:xlii; TJ to James Madison, 12 Jan. 1789, in *TJP,* 14:437.

15. GM to George Washington, 29 Apr. 1789, in Washington, *Papers,* 2:147–48 (emphasis in the original). See also TJ to James Madison, 28 Aug. 1789, in *TJP,* 15:366–67.

16. GM quoted in Tansill, *Documents Illustrative of the Formation of the Union,* 742. For GM's political philosophy and his positions in the Constitutional Convention, see Nedelsky, *Private Property,* 67–95; Kaufman, "Constitutional Views of Gouverneur Morris."

17. TJ to John Adams, 13 Nov. 1787, TJ to Edward Carrington, 4 Aug. 1787, and TJ to Joseph Jones, 14 Aug. 1787, all in *TJP,* 12:351, 11:684, 12:34. For TJ's reactions to the new constitution, see Kaplan, "Jefferson and the Constitution"; Wood, "Origins of the American Bill of Rights," 41–42. For the French reception of the constitution, see also Echeverria, *Mirage in the West,* 162–63.

18. TJ to John Jay, 23 May 1788, and TJ to Francis Hopkinson, 13 Mar. 1789, both in *TJP,* 13:190, 14:650.

19. TJ to Richard Price, 8 Jan. 1789, and TJ to David Humphreys, 18 Mar. 1789, both in *TJP,* 14:423, 677; GM to Staats Long Morris, 11 Mar. 1789, in *Diary,* 1:xliv.

20. TJ to Eliza House Trist, 15 Dec. 1786, in *TJP,* 10:600. TJ could send a long list of the dangers of a European education to the son of his friend John Banister, but he also recommend to his future son-in-law, Thomas Mann Randolph Jr., that he should study politics, law, and history in France. TJ to John Banister Jr., 15 Oct. 1785, and TJ to Thomas Mann Randolph Jr., 6 July 1787, both in *TJP,* 8:635–37, 11:557.

21. GM to George Washington, 29 Apr. 1789, in Washington, *Papers,* 2:147–48; GM to William Carmichael, 4 July 1789, in *Diary,* 1:136. See also GM to John Jay, July 1, 1789, John Jay Papers, Butler Library.

22. GM to George Washington, 31 July 1789, in Washington, *Papers,* 2:361; GM to William Carmichael, 25 Feb. 1789, in *Diary,* 1:xl.

23. TJ to Lafayette, 28 Feb. 1787, and TJ to David Humphreys, 18 Mar. 1789, both in *TJP,* 11:186, 14:676–79. For the influence on Madison and TJ of French ideas about the power of public opinion and its relation to national morality, see Sheehan, "Madison and the French Enlightenment." For Condorcet and TJ, see also Albertone, "Condorcet, Jefferson et l'Amérique"; Sloan, *Principle and Interest,* 242–43.

24. Entry of 12 June 1789, in *Diary,* 1:113.

25. TJ to John Jay, 6 Aug. 1787, and TJ to Jean Paul Rabaut de St. Etienne, 3 June 1789, both in *TJP,* 11:696, 15:167. Rabaut was a Protestant pastor who was one of TJ's few acquaintances outside the nobility. He advocated a declaration of religious liberty in France along the lines of TJ's Statute.

26. For GM's membership in the Club Valois, see entry of 27 May 1789, in *Diary,* 1:94.

Louis Gottschalk argues that the club "reflected the prevalent accord among the social, intellectual, and economic elite in the early weeks of 1789" (Gottschalk and Maddox, *Lafayette in the French Revolution,* 18–19).

27. *Archives parlementaires,* 8:320. For the attitude of deputies in the National Assembly toward the American model, see generally C. B. Thompson, "American Founding"; Appleby, *Liberalism and Republicanism,* 232–52; Lemay, "Lafitau, Démeunier"; Raynaud, "American Revolution." For the influence of the Declaration of Independence and American bills of rights in particular, see Marienstras and Wulf, "French Translations"; Baker, "Idea of a Declaration of Rights," 158–60.

28. "Autobiography," in Jefferson, *Writings,* 85–86. See also W. H. Adams, *Paris Years,* 251–98; Malone, *Jefferson and the Rights of Man,* 264–300.

29. For the formation and influence of the *monarchiens,* see Tackett, *Becoming a Revolutionary,* 185–86; Griffiths, *Centre perdu;* Egret, *Révolution des notables.* For French Anglomania, see Grieder, *Anglomania in France.*

30. GM to George Washington, 3 Mar. 1789, in Washington, *Papers,* 1:359; entry of 4 July 1789, in *Diary,* 1:134. Lally-Tollendal, years earlier, had been an associate of John Adams, as the American affectionately remembered in his marginal notes to Mary Wollstonecraft's *Historical and Moral View of the Origin and Progress of the French Revolution* (1794): "Ah! Tollendal! . . . I have eaten and drunk in thine apartment. I am proud to say thou were my disciple and convert to the doctrine of branches" (quoted in Haraszti, *John Adams and the Prophets of Progress,* 204).

31. *Archives parlementaires,* 8:222; Mounier, *Motifs présentés,* 6–7; idem, *Considerations sur les gouvernemens,* 11.

32. Entries of 25 and 26 July 1789, in *Diary,* 1:161–62; GM, "Observations on Government, Applicable to the Political State of France," in Sparks, *Life of Gouverneur Morris,* 3:463–71.

33. GM, "Observations on Government." Note in particular the similarities between GM's "Observations on Government" and Mounier's *Nouvelles observations.* Both argued for national unity over corporate and local interests; a balance of powers in government, including a bicameral legislature and an absolute veto for the king; and the indispensable link between the establishment of liberty and security of property rights. They also shared an admiration for Montesquieu and a deep mistrust of the populace, or "multitude." For Mounier, see Doyle, *Officers, Nobles, and Revolutionaries,* 179–95.

34. Foulon and Bertier were both accused of involvement in grain-hoarding schemes. See entry of 22 July 1789, in *Diary,* 1:159; GM to Mrs. Robert Morris, 22 July 1789, Morris Papers, Butler Library.

35. TJ to John Jay, 23 July 1789, and TJ to TP, 23 July 1789, both in *TJP,* 15:302. For Shays's Rebellion, see TJ to Abigail Adams, 12 Feb 1787, in *TJP,* 11:174. On the impact of popular movements in the provinces on the deliberations on 4 Aug., see Fitzsimmons, *Night the Old Regime Ended,* chap. 4; Kessel, *Nuit du 4 Août 1789,* chaps. 6–10. TJ to Maria Cosway, 25 July 1789, in *TJP,* 15:305.

36. Clermont-Tonnerre and Barnave quoted in Tackett, *Becoming a Revolutionary,* 168–69.

37. Entry of June 23, 1789, in *Diary,* 1:121.

38. TJ to Jérôme-Marie Champion de Cicé, archbishop of Bordeaux, 22 July 1789, and Lafayette to TJ, 25 Aug. 1789, both in *TJP,* 15:298, 354. See also Gottschalk and Maddox, *Lafayette in the French Revolution,* 80–99, 220–26.

39. The suspensive veto entitled the king to temporarily block a new law until it was passed again at a later date. Some deputies understood the suspensive veto as leading to some kind of national referendum on any law that the king opposed, while others regarded it as a means of preserving the prerogatives of the king against the National Assembly. TJ's and Lafayette's declaration had included "le droit des générations qui se succèdent," the right of successive generations to revise the constitution at fixed intervals. However, the final version of the *Déclaration,* adopted on 26 Aug., ignored the issue of revision altogether.

40. "Autobiography," in Jefferson, *Writings,* 96. For a fuller account of the 26 Aug. meeting, see Gottschalk and Maddox, *Lafayette in the French Revolution,* 226–28.

41. For an analysis of Lafayette's various public personas, see Kramer, *Lafayette in Two Worlds.*

42. See TJ to John Jay, 19 Sept. 1789, in *TJP,* 15:458–59; Mounier, *Exposé de la conduite de M. Mounier,* 41; WS to TJ, 19 Nov. 1789, in *TJP,* 15:548.

43. *Archives parlementaires,* 8:515; TJ to James Madison, 6 Sept. 1789, in *TJP,* 15:392–97; Sloan, *Principle and Interest,* chap. 2. Sloan detects an "almost Burkean cast" in TJ's letter-essay (61). Two years later, Madison brought the passage on debts in Burke's *Reflections* to TJ's attention, noting "how your idea of limiting the right to bind posterity is germinating under the extravagant doctrines of Burke on that subject" (Madison to TJ, 1 May 1791, in *TJP,* 14:15).

44. For the American reception of Montesquieu's writings, see Lutz, "Relative Influence of European Thinkers"; Spurlin, *Montesquieu in America.* TJ's book was part of a well-established genre devoted to the comparative study of national character, which included Montesquieu's *De l'esprit des lois,* Voltaire's *Essai sur les mœurs,* Rousseau's *Considérations sur le gouvernement de Pologne,* and Chastellux's *Voyages de M. le marquis de Chastellux dans l'Amérique septentrionale* (see Bell, *Cult of the Nation,* 140–68; McCoy, *Elusive Republic,* 13–47).

45. GM to William Carmichael, 4 July 1789, in *Diary,* 1:136. See in particular Book 1, chap. 3, and Book 19, chap. 5, in Montesquieu, *Spirit of the Laws,* 8–9, 310. The comparison of the French Américanistes with the islanders of Laputa in Swift's *Travels into Several Remote Nations of the World* (1726), a.k.a. *Gulliver's Travels,* reflected GM's view of the French as hopelessly impractical and theoretical. As Gulliver described the people of Laputa: "Although they are dextrous enough upon a Piece of Paper in the management of the Rule, the Pencil and the Divider, yet in the common Actions and behaviors of Life, I have not seen a more clumsy, awkward, and unhandy People" (Swift, *Gulliver's Travels,* 137). Edmund Burke made the same comparison; see Burke, *Reflections,* 117.

46. On different definitions of "constitution" in late-eighteenth-century French thought, see Baker, *Inventing the French Revolution,* 252–57.

47. TJ to Thomas Mann Randolph, 30 May 1790, in *TJP,* 16:449. TJ's troubled

relationship with Montesquieu culminated in his translation of Destutt de Tracy's *Commentaire sur l'esprit des lois* in 1811. For TJ's changing view of Montesquieu, see Onuf and Onuf, *Nations, Markets, and War,* 225–39; D. N. Mayer, *Constitutional Thought of Thomas Jefferson,* 135–41. For the ambiguity of the American Revolution, see Zuckert, "Natural Rights in the American Revolution."

48. A. Young, *Travels in France,* 160.

49. Mounier quoted in Manin, "Montesquieu," 728; TJ to TP, 13 Sept. 1789, in *TJP,* 15:424.

50. Jean-Pierre-Louis de Luchet, *Les contemporains de 1789 et 1790, ou, Les opinions débattues pendant la première législature . . . ,* 3 vols. (Paris, 1790), 2:34–35, quoted in Aldridge, *Franklin and His French Contemporaries,* 92.

51. Sieyès quoted in Baker, "Idea of a Declaration of Rights," 159.

52. Entries of 11 and 18 Oct. 1789, in *Diary,* 1:255, 263.

53. TJ to Diodati, 3 Aug. 1789, TJ to David Humphreys, 18 Mar. 1789, and TJ to John Jay, 19 Sept. 1789, all in *TJP,* 15:326, 14:676–69, 15:458–60.

2. "WAS EVER SUCH A PRIZE WON WITH SO LITTLE INNOCENT BLOOD?"

1. WS to TJ, 26 Apr. 1791, and TJ to Jonathan B. Smith, 26 Apr. 1791, both in *TJP,* 20:266, 290. TJ did not to know either Jonathan Smith or his son Samuel and mistakenly assumed them to be brothers. See "Editorial Note: *Rights of Man:* The Contest of Burke and Paine . . . in America," in *TJP,* 20:268–90.

2. WS to TJ, 25 Apr. 1791, TJ to TP, 19 June 1792, TJ to TP, 29 July 1791, and WS to TJ, 17 July 1791, all in *TJP,* 20:257–60, 312, 308, 645.

3. WS to TJ, 28 Jan. 1790, in *TJP,* 16:133. See also WS to GM, 1 July 1790, WSP; WS to John Jay, 9 Mar. 1790, and WS to TJ, 6 June 1790, both in *TJP,* 16:219, 474.

4. For the politicization of salons, see Kale, *French Salons,* 47–51.

5. Sieyès, *Ébauche d'un nouveau Plan de Société Patriotique.* For Sieyès's concept of *l'art social,* see Forsyth, *Reason and Revolution,* 22–31. For the Société de 1789, see Tackett, *Becoming a Revolutionary,* 279–89; Olsen, "Failure of Enlightened Politics"; Baker, "Politics and Social Science."

6. Entry of 26 Jan. 1790, in *Diary,* 1:286; WS to TJ, 28 Jan. 1790, in *TJP,* 16:132.

7. A short history of the Société Gallo-Américaine can be found in Marcel Dorigny's preface to his modern edition of *De la France et des États-Unis:* "La *libre Amérique* selon Brissot et Clavière: Modèle politique, utopie libérale et réalisme économique" (7–29).

8. La Rochefoucauld, "Hommage rendu par le vœu unanime de la société de 1789 à Benjamin Franklyn, objet de l'admiration et des regrets des amis de la liberté," *Journal de la Société de 1789* 3 (19 June 1790): 43, 47. On the reactions to Franklin's death in France and America, see Julian P. Boyd, "Editorial Note: Death of Franklin: The Politics of Mourning in France and the United States," in *TJP,* 19:78–106.

9. Bizardel and Rice, "'Poor in Love Mr. Short.'"

10. Entry of 17 June 1789, in *Diary,* 1:116. For TJ's hopes for WS and reference to him as an "adoptive son," see TJ to James Madison, 20 Feb. 1784, and TJ to John Trumbull,

1 June 1789, both in *TJP,* 6:548–49, 15:164. On TJ's circle of younger friends, see Burstein, *Inner Jefferson,* 151–70. For WS's early years and his relationship with the La Rochefoucauld family, see Shackelford, *Jefferson's Adoptive Son,* 1–16, 20–21, 112–13. WS's correspondence with Rosalie is collected in Harsanyi, *Lettres de la duchesse de La Rochefoucauld.*

11. WS to GM, 12 Sept. 1790, WSP; WS to GM, 29 Nov. 1790, Morris Papers, Butler Library; entry of 26 Jan. 1790, in *Diary,* 1:286; WS to TJ, 23 Jan. 1790, in *TJP,* 16:122; WS to GM, 28 Mar. 1790, GM to WS, 31 Mar. 1790, GM to WS, 7 Apr. 1790, WS to GM, 11 Apr. 1790, GM to WS, 23 Apr. 1790, GM to WS, 10 Aug. 1790, WS to GM, 1 July 1790, and GM to WS, 20 July 1790, all in WSP.

12. Chenier, "Avis au Peuple François sur ses véritables ennemies," *Journal de la Société de 1789* 13 (28 Aug. 1790): 1–52; "Extrait du procès-verbal des séances de la Société de 1789, du vendredi 3 Septembre 1790," *Journal de la Société de 1789* 15 (15 Sept. 1790): 3–4; Olsen, "Enlightened Nationalism in the Early Revolution."

13. Sieyès, "What Is the Third Estate?" in Sieyès, *Political Writings,* 94.

14. WS to TJ, 5 Sept. 1790, in *TJP,* 17:489–91; Marat, "Infernal projet des ennemis de la Révolution," in Marat, *Oeuvres politiques,* 2:1055–57; *Révolutions de France et Brabant* 43 (1790): 187–89; *Révolutions de Paris* 53 (10–17 July 1790): 23.

15. For the flight to Varennes and its impact, see Tackett, *When the King Took Flight.*

16. WS to TJ, 29 June 1791, in *TJP,* 20:585.

17. TP, "The Rights of Man, Part I," in TJ, *Complete Writings,* 1:256; WS to TJ, 17 July 1791, in *TJP,* 20:645. For the influence of French republicanism on TP's thought, see Whatmore, "'Gigantic manliness,'" 149–55; Kates, "From Liberalism to Radicalism"; Baker, *Condorcet,* 303–6; "The Debate between Sieyès and Tom Paine," in Sieyès, *Political Writings,* 163–73.

18. TP, "Common Sense," in TP, *Complete Writings,* 1:3, 7; TP, "Rights of Man, Part I," 1:299–301; TP to George Washington, 21 July 1791, in Washington, *Papers,* 8:362. Enclosed with the letter to Washington were fifty copies of *Rights of Man, Part I.* Washington acknowledged receipt of the letter almost a year later, but never mentioned the dedication, which had become a political embarrassment (Washington to TP, 6 May 1792, in Washington, *Papers,* 10:357). TP had begun writing *Rights of Man* in Jan. 1790, before he became aware of Burke's hostility to the French Revolution. On 12 Jan., Lafayette proudly reported to Washington, "Common Sense is writing a Book for you–there you will See a part of My Adventures" (Lafayette to Washington, 12 Jan. 1790, in Washington, *Papers,* 4:567).

19. TJ to Edward Rutledge, 25 Aug. 1791, in *TJP,* 22:74–75.

20. WS to TJ, 20 June 1791, in *TJP,* 20:648–49; Rosalie to WS, 11 Nov. 1791, in Harsanyi, *Lettres de la duchesse de La Rochefoucauld,* 67; GM to George Washington, 30 Sept. 1791, in Washington, *Papers,* 9:32. For the Legislative Assembly, see L. Hunt, *Politics, Culture, and Class,* 149–79.

21. WS to TJ, 25 Mar. 1792, in *TJP,* 23:338, 340. For the pro-Americanism of the Girondins, see G. May, *Madame Roland,* 69–70, 165–66; Gidney, *Influence des États-Unis d'Amérique;* Echeverria, *Mirage in the West,* 144–47.

22. TJ to Madison, 29 June 1792, in *TJP,* 24:134.

23. *Gazette Nationale,* 4 Oct. 1791; WS to TJ, 6 Oct. 1791, in *TJP,* 22:193-95. For the Senate debate, see also George Washington to GM, 28 Jan. 1792, in Washington, *Papers,* 9:515-17; M. R. Miller, *Envoy to the Terror,* 93-95; WS to TJ, 15 May 1792, and WS to TJ, 26 July 1792, both in *TJP,* 23:506-7, 508-9, 24:252-54. WS's loyal supporters, the duchess d'Enville and Lafayette, complained to TJ and Washington about GM's appointment: Mme d'Enville to TJ, 13 Feb. 1792, in *TJP,* 23:112-13; Lafayette to GW, 15 Mar. 1792, in Washington, *Papers,* 10:116-17.

24. GM to TJ, 16 Aug. 1792, in *TJP,* 24:301-2. For the various plans for the king's escape, see M. R. Miller, *Envoy to the Terror,* 150, 153, 158-59; Fiechter, *Diplomate américain sous la Terreur,* chap. 9.

25. Entries of 13 and 14 Aug. 1792, in *Diary,* 2:490-91; Griffith, "Reminiscences," 30-31. Malouet, Monciel, and Adèle de Flahaut managed to escape to England.

26. GM to TJ, 22 Aug. 1792 (received 4 Dec. 1792), and TJ to GM, 7 Nov. 1792, both in *TJP,* 24:314, 593.

27. WS to TJ, 15 Aug 1792, in *TJP,* 24:298; WS to Alexander Hamilton, 25 Sept. 1792, GM to WS, 20 Sept. 1792, and enclosed in GM to Hamilton, 25 Sept. 1792, all in A. Hamilton, *Papers,* 12:472, 465, 425-69.

28. *Chronique de Paris* 259 (4 Sept. 1792): 990; A. J. Mayer, *Furies,* 177-84; Bluche, *Septembre 1792;* Dorigny, "Violence et révolution."

29. Alexandre de Liancourt to WS, 8 Sept. 1792, in Harsanyi, *Lettres de la duchesse de La Rochefoucauld,* 148-49; Rosalie to WS, 16 and 23 Sept., and 7 and 31 Oct. 1792, in ibid., 149-54; WS to GM, 10, 11, and 18 Sept., and 12 Oct 1792, and GM to WS, 6, 9, and 18 Sept. 1792, all in WSP. The duchess d'Enville blamed TJ for not having placed WS in Paris, where he would have been able to help the La Rochefoucauld family (Mme d'Enville to TJ, 30 Dec. 1792, in *TJP,* 24:798-99).

30. WS to TJ, 18 Sept. 1792, in *TJP,* 24:390-91.

31. GM to TJ, 10 Sept. 1792, in *TJP,* 24:364-65. GM's dispatch did not reach TJ until 10 Jan., after he had written the "Adam and Eve" letter to WS. For comments on the death of Lamballe by two other Americans in Paris, see a report to TJ by land salesman James Cole Mountflorence and the memoirs of Thomas Griffith: Mountflorence to TJ, 11 Nov. 1792, in *TJP,* 25:120-33; Griffith, "Reminiscences," 32-33.

32. For the symbolism of the Princess Lamballe's corpse, see Baecque, *Glory and Terror,* chap. 3, esp. 64-65, 68-70. On the place of Lamballe's death in the mythology of Marie-Antoinette, see Castle, "Marie-Antoinette Obsession," 218-19.

33. GM to Robert Morris, 28 Sept. 1792, GMP.

34. *National Gazette,* 7 Nov. 1792.

35. WS to TJ, 12 Oct. 1792, in *TJP,* 24:475.

36. TJ to WS, 3 Jan. 1793, in *TJP,* 25:14.

37. O'Brien, *Long Affair,* 150. Joseph J. Ellis comes to similar conclusions in his *American Sphinx* (127). For the defense of the letter as mere "rhetoric," see Halliday, *Understanding Thomas Jefferson,* 225; Appleby, *Thomas Jefferson,* 144; Malone, *Jefferson and the Ordeal of Liberty,* 46. The two best discussions of the letter are Kaplan, *Jefferson and France,* 48-51, and Onuf, *Jefferson's Empire,* 171-73.

38. WS to TJ, 19 Nov. 1789, WS to TJ, 25 Nov. 1789, WS to TJ, 30 Nov. 1789, and WS to TJ, 25 Mar. 1790, all in *TJP,* 15:550, 558–59, 564–65, 16:272–73; Lafayette to Washington, 23 Aug. 1790, and 6 June 1791, in Washington, *Papers,* 6:318, 8:240; Mme d'Enville to TJ, 27 July 1790, in *TJP,* 17:287.

39. TJ to WS, 24 Mar. 1789, in *TJP,* 14:695–6. For WS's future in America vs. Europe, see WS to TJ, 28 Oct. 1789, TJ to WS, 21 Nov. 1788, WS to TJ, 25 Feb. 1789, TJ to WS, 28 Feb. 1789, WS to TJ, 2 Mar. 1789, and WS to TJ, 3 Apr. 1789, all in *TJP,* 14:43, 276–77, 591, 597–98, 607–8, 27–29. For TJ's relationship with Sally Hemings as the solution of his "predicament" of finding long-term companionship without marriage, see Gordon-Reed, *Thomas Jefferson and Sally Hemings,* 118. For WS's possible knowledge of the TJ-Hemings relationship, see Gordon-Reed, *Hemingses of Monticello,* 274–75, 536–39.

40. TJ gave the same advice to his nephew Peter Carr (TJ to Carr, 10 Aug. 1787, in *TJP,* 12:17).

41. TJ to WS, 6 Apr. 1790, TJ to WS, 27 Apr. 1790, and TJ to WS, 30 Sept. 1790, all in *TJP,* 16:320, 388, 17:543–44.

42. WS to TJ, 23 and 29 Dec. 1790, and TJ to WS, 30 Sept. 1790, all in *TJP,* 18:356–57, 446, 17:543–44.

43. TJ to WS, 3 Jan. 1793, in *TJP,* 25:14–15. Similarly, when TJ urged WS in Mar. 1789 to pursue a political career in the United States, he did so "with a bleeding heart: for nothing can be more dreary than my situation will be when you and my daughters shall all have left me." But the new nation's need for virtuous and capable public servants was far more important than TJ's fears of loneliness in his old age. See TJ to WS, 24 Mar. 1789, in *TJP,* 14:696–97.

44. For TJ's moral thought, see Helo and Onuf, "Jefferson, Morality, and the Problem of Slavery," 584–86, 608–10. For the Amis, see Brissot to TJ, 10 Feb. 1788, and TJ to Brissot, 11 Feb. 1788, both in *TJP,* 12:577, 577–78; Geggus, "Racial Equality, Slavery, and Colonial Secession"; Davis, *Problem of Slavery,* 95–100.

45. TJ to WS, 3 Jan. 1793, in *TJP,* 25:14.

46. TJ to Dumas, 22 Sept. 1786, and TJ to WS, 3 Jan. 1793, both in *TJP,* 10:397, 25:14–15.

47. "Notes on a Conversation with George Washington," 27 Dec. 1792, and "Memoranda of Consultations with the President," 11 Mar.–9 Apr. 1792, both in *TJP,* 23:260.

48. See also TJ to Thomas Mann Randolph Jr., 2 June 1793, in *TJP,* 26:169.

49. French National Convention [Marguerite-Elie Guadet] to George Washington, 22 Dec. 1792, in Washington, *Papers,* 11:538–39. The letter was published in the *Gazette Nationale,* 23 Dec. 1792, and in the *National Gazette,* 2 Mar. 1793. For the "language of purgation," see Baecque, *Glory and Terror,* 66–71.

50. For the Catholic background of French nationalism, see Bell, *Cult of the Nation,* esp. 47–49. For the affinity between millennial Protestantism and radical Enlightenment thought, see Bloch, *Visionary Republic,* 200.

51. TJ to WS, 24 Mar. 1789, in *TJP,* 14:696.

52. TJ to WS, 3 Jan. 1793, in *TJP,* 25:15.

53. WS to TJ, 5 Apr. 1793, in *TJP,* 25:508–9.

54. TJ to WS, 23 Mar. 1793, in *TJP,* 25:436. In the end, Congress absolved Hamilton and neither WS nor GM was officially censured for his conduct.

55. TP, "Rights of Man, Part II," 1:347–48.

56. "French Translator's Preface," in TP, "Rights of Man, Part II," 1:347. For the French reception of *Rights of Man*, see Aldridge, *"Rights of Man* de Thomas Paine," 285–87.

57. Roland de La Platière, *Mémoires de Mme Roland,* 1:269–70.

3. Cosmopolitan Sensibilities and National Regeneration

1. The Society for Constitutional Information was a middle-class reform club that advocated broadening of the electoral franchise, annual elections to Parliament, and the abolition of the slave trade. Goodwin, *Friends of Liberty,* 252–5; E. P. Thompson, *Making of the English Working Class,* 86, 106, 121, 130–32, 137.

2. The text of the address was part of the evidence at Thomas Hardy's trial for high treason, and can be found in Howell and Howell, *Complete Collection of State Trials,* 24:527–30. It is also reprinted in *Archives parlementaires,* 53:636–37.

3. The best account of JB's eventful career is still Woodress, *Yankee's Odyssey.* For brief overviews, see Marienstras, "Joel Barlow"; Kramer, "Traveling through Revolutions." For JB's role in early American literature, see Dowling, *Poetry and Ideology in Revolutionary Connecticut;* Elliott, *Revolutionary Writers,* 92–127; Howard, *Connecticut Wits.*

4. JB, "An Oration Delivered at the Meeting . . . of the Cincinnati, July 4, 1787," in JB, *Works,* 1:13; Humphreys et al., *Anarchiad;* entry of 3 Oct. 1788, Diary, JBP. For JB's early years before his departure to France, see also Mulford, "Joel Barlow's Letters"; Zunder, *Early Days of Joel Barlow.*

5. JB, "Advice to the Privileged Orders, Part I," in JB, *Works,* 1:107; Godwin, "Autobiographical Fragments," in Godwin, *Collected Novels and Memoirs,* 1:49; P. H. Marshall, *William Godwin,* 86.

6. Henry May grouped JB with the "many other revolutionary characters in Europe and America [who were] always occupied with the task of making a fortune" (*Enlightenment in America,* 239). See also Woodress, *Yankee's Odyssey,* 118, 131; L. Gordon, *Vindication,* 165–66, 170–71; V. C. Miller, *Joel Barlow,* 7, 16.

7. JB, "Advice to the Privileged Orders, Part II" (1793), in JB, *Works,* 1:267–68.

8. For the etymology of "regeneration" and its significance in French revolutionary discourse, see Sepinwall, *Abbé Grégoire and the French Revolution,* 57–59; Baecque, *Body Politic,* 131–56; Ozouf, "Regeneration." For the absence of regeneration as a concept in the American Revolution, see Sepinwall, *Abbé Grégoire and the French Revolution,* 88.

9. Grégoire, *Essai sur la Régénération,* 141. For the problem of sameness, equality, and difference in the early American republic, see Carson, *Measure of Merit,* chap. 1; McMahon, "'Harmony of social life'"; Cott, *Public Vows,* 9–23; Kerber, *Women of the Republic.* For similar predicaments in the French Republic, see Sepinwall, *Abbé Grégoire and the French Revolution,* 97–102; Heuer, *Family and the Nation;* Desan, *Family on Trial;* L. Hunt, "Male Virtue and Republican Motherhood."

10. JB, "Letter to the National Convention," in JB, *Works,* 1:44, 78. For the ambiguity of regeneration, see Ozouf, *L'homme régénéré,* 116–57.

11. Howard, *Connecticut Wits,* 278–79. JB had first articulated the view that human

nature was malleable in his unpublished legal dissertation in 1786, in which he argued that human nature's capability for improvement was evidence of divine sanction for social and legal change ("Dissertation," JBP). See also Cantor, "Joel Barlow."

12. JB, "Advice, Part I," in JB, *Works,* 1:171.

13. Entry of 3 Oct. 1788, *Diary,* JBP.

14. JB, "Letter to the National Convention," in JB, *Works,* 1:39–40.

15. JB, "Advice, Part I," and "Advice, Part II," both in JB, *Works,* 1:114–16, 284–85.

16. JB, "Advice, Part I," in JB, *Works,* 1:170.

17. There is a vast and expanding literature on the cult of sensibility in America, France, and Britain. See, generally, Randall, "Feminizing the Enlightenment"; Mullan, *Sentiment and Sociability.* For American sensibility, see Bloch, *Gender and Morality in Anglo-American Culture,* 136–53; Knott, *Sensibility and the American Revolution;* Burstein, *Sentimental Democracy;* J. Lewis, *Pursuit of Happiness,* 216–29. For France, see Vila, *Enlightenment and Pathology;* Denby, *Sentimental Narrative;* Vincent-Buffault, *History of Tears.* For Britain, see Barker-Benfield, *Culture of Sensibility.*

18. JB, "Advice, Part II," in JB, *Works,* 1:222.

19. JB, "Advice, Part II," in JB, *Works,* 1:219–20. For the influence of moral philosophy on the debate about patriotism in the 1790s, see Radcliffe, "Revolutionary Writing, Moral Philosophy."

20. *Adresse des citoyens des Etats-unis de l'Amérique.* The text of the address is also printed in *Archives parlementaires,* 17:40–41, and in *Gazette of the United States,* 6 Oct. 1790. See also JB to Ruth Barlow, 11 July 1790, JBP. The address was delivered by William Henry Vernon and signed by JB, James Swan, Benjamin Jarvis, Thomas Appleton, John Paul Jones, Samuel Blackden, John Anderson, Alexander Contée[?], George Washington Greene, George Howell, John Lewis, and a man named Harrison. Though invited to participate, WS argued that his presence would have been "manifestly improper" (WS to TJ, 16 July 1790, in *TJP,* 17:213). For the decline of the British cult of sensibility in the second half of the 1780s, see Brewer, *Pleasures of the Imagination,* 121. On sensibility, the War of Independence, and French political culture, see Knott, "Sensibility and the American War for Independence," 38–40.

21. Williams, *Letters Written in France,* 13–14, 21.

22. JB, "Advice, Part I," 1:117–18. On the Jacobins' deep-seated fear of power, which ultimately subverted their own Revolutionary Government, see Sa'adah, *Shaping of Liberal Politics,* esp. 187–88.

23. Hamowy, *Scottish Enlightenment.*

24. JB, "Letter to the National Convention," in JB, *Works,* 1:75; JB, "Advice, Part I," in ibid., 1:184.

25. Grégoire quoted in Sepinwall, *Abbé Grégoire and the French Revolution,* 115.

26. JB, "The Conspiracy of Kings," in JB, *Works,* 2:71, 82. For a more detailed interpretation along similar lines, see Mulford, "Radicalism in Joel Barlow's *The Conspiracy of Kings.*"

27. Royster, *Revolutionary People at War,* 13–25, 152–61, 157 (quote). Ingersoll quoted in Watts, *Republic Reborn,* 100.

28. Grégoire, *Rapport sur la réunion de la Savoie à la France,* 6–7. On Grégoire's and JB's mission to Savoy, see Sepinwall, *Abbé Grégoire and the French Revolution,* 119–21; Durden, "Joel Barlow in the French Revolution," 341–48.

29. Henri Grégoire to JB, 16 Mar. 1793, JBP. See also JB to Ruth Barlow, 4 and 15 Dec. 1792, JBP.

30. JB, "Letter Addressed to the People of Piedmont, on the Advantages of the French Revolution, and the Necessity of Adopting Its Principles in Italy," in JB, *Works,* 1:339.

31. JB, *Works,* 1:334.

32. JB to TJ, 8 Mar. 1793, in *TJP,* 25:336; JB, "Letter Addressed to the People of Piedmont," in JB, *Works,* 1:315–16. There appears to be no extant copy of the Italian translation.

33. For American commercial relations with Britain and France, see Cheney, "False Dawn for Enlightenment Cosmopolitanism?"; Hill, "Suite imprévue de l'Alliance"; Fohlen, "Commercial Failure of France in America." For the debt to France, see Potofsky, "Political Economy of the French-American Debt Debate"; Sloan, *Principle and Interest,* 44–46, 148–49; Ferguson, *Power of the Purse,* 221, 234–38; W. G. Anderson, *Price of Liberty,* 56–59.

34. For the Scioto scheme, see Woodress, *Yankee's Odyssey,* chap. 4; R. F. Jones, *"King of the Alley,"* 121–23, 141–51; Belote, *Scioto Speculation.* For the fate of the French émigrés in America, see Clarke, *Émigrés in the Wilderness;* Childs, *French Refugee Life.*

35. *Gazette Nationale,* 6 Mar. 1790; *Chronique de Paris,* 5 Aug. 1790; Roux, *Nouveau Mississippi; Lettre écrite par un françois émigrant au Scioto;* D'Allemagne, *Nouvelles du Scioto;* Moustier, *Lettre de M. de Moustier.* For the theory of American degeneration and its longevity, see Roger, *American Enemy,* 1–29; Echeverria, *Mirage in the West,* 4–14, 138–39.

36. *Songe d'un habitant de Scioto; Parlement de Paris établi au Scioto; Départ du gaut clergé pour l'Isle du Scioto;* Andrieux, "François aux bords du Scioto."

37. Sheridan, "Recall of Edmond Charles Genet"; Sydenham, *Girondins,* 21–28.

38. "Séance du 16 Octobre 1793," in Robespierre, *Œuvres,* 10:155.

39. For the emergence of exclusive nationalism and xenophobia in 1793 as a result of the "state of siege" during the Terror, see Mathiez, *Révolution et les étrangers.* For the ideological contradiction between universal human rights and national sovereignty, see Wahnich, *L'impossible citoyen;* Furet, *Interpreting the French Revolution,* 62–64; Arendt, *Origins of Totalitarianism,* 230–31.

40. *Archives parlementaires,* 73:463. See also Sahlins, *Unnaturally French,* 283–84; Sewell, "French Revolution," 110–12.

41. "Séance du 27 Brumaire An II (17 Novembre 1793): Rapport sur la situation politique de la République," in Robespierre, *Œuvres,* 10:168.

42. Rapport, *Nationality and Citizenship;* M. R. Miller, *Envoy to the Terror,* 202–11.

43. For sensibility as a principle of social differentiation, see Knott, *Sensibility and the American Revolution,* 17–18. On the ideal of imminent virtue, see also L. Hunt, *Politics, Culture, and Class,* 45–49.

44. TP, "Rights of Man, Part I," 1:260.

45. Racine, *Francisco de Miranda*, 124.

46. JB to Oliver Wolcott, 6 Nov. 1794, Oliver Wolcott Papers, Connecticut Historical Society.

4. "Strange, that Monroe should warn us against Jacobins!"

1. For the full text of the address, see "Address to the National Convention," in JM, *Writings*, 2:13–15. Barney described JM's reception in a letter to his brother, quoted in Mayo, "Joshua Barney and the French Revolution," 359.

2. *Gazette Nationale*, 29 Thermidor II (16 Aug. 1794); *Archives parlementaires*, 95:120–22.

3. JM, *Autobiography*, 59–65; memoir on the reception of Monroe, Thermidor II (Aug. 1794), AAECPE-U. See also Elkins and McKitrick, *Age of Federalism*, 506–7. For the efforts to end the revolution after Thermidor, see H. G. Brown, *Ending the French Revolution*; Ozouf, *L'école de la France*, 91–108.

4. JM's diplomatic mission is discussed in detail in Elkins and McKitrick, *Age of Federalism*, 498–509; Scherr, "Limits of Republican Ideology"; Angel, "James Monroe's Mission to Paris"; Ammon, *James Monroe*, chaps. 7 and 8; Bowman, *Struggle for Neutrality*, chaps. 8 and 10; Clarfield, *Timothy Pickering*, 52–57; DeConde, *Entangling Alliances*, chap. 11; Bond, *Monroe Mission to France*.

5. On the reception of JM's speech in America, see JM to James Madison, 2 Sept. 1794, and Madison to JM, 4 Dec. 1794, both in Madison, *Papers*, 15:356, 405; Robert R. Livingston to JM, 18 Sept. 1794, and John Brown to JM, 5 Dec. 1794, both JMP.

6. For different periodizations of a Thermidorian phase in the American Revolution (immediately after the War of Independence, the Constitution of 1787, and TJ's election in 1800, respectively), see Zuckerman, "Thermidor in America"; Filimonova, "Eshche raz o thermidore v Amerike"; Newman, "American Political Culture," 78. Some historians of the French Revolution have reevaluated Thermidor as the salutary abandonment of the *idée fixe* of the totally regenerated nation and the return to the world of "*politique réelle*" with its half truths and compromises; see Gueniffey, *Politique de la Terreur*, 344–45; Livesey, *Making Democracy in the French Revolution*. By contrast, I argue that the enduring rejection of organized political opposition put severe limitations on any form of "real politics." For a historiographical overview of the Thermidorian period, see H. G. Brown and Miller, "New Paths from the Terror."

7. See, e.g., L. Hunt, Lansky, and Hanson, "Failure of the Liberal Republic in France"; Higonnet, *Goodness beyond Virtue*; Woloch, *New Regime*; Sa'adah, *Shaping of Liberal Politics*.

8. JM to Committee of Public Safety, 11 Brumaire III (1 Nov. 1794), James Monroe Papers, NYPL. For the dismantling of the Revolutionary Government, see Lefebvre, *Thermidorians and the Directory*, 10–25.

9. Barère quoted in Palmer, *Twelve Who Ruled*, 383. For the different interpretations of the Terror in its immediate aftermath, to which, according to Mona Ozouf, modern scholarship has had surprisingly little to add, see Ozouf, "Terror after the Terror." David

Waldstreicher has found similar strategies for dealing with the problem of the Terror (temporary delirium or conspiracy by a faction in the government) in American newspaper commentary and celebratory orations between 1794 and 1797. See Waldstreicher, *In the Midst of Perpetual Fetes,* 137 n46. For the debate about how to end and account for the Terror, see also Baczko, *Ending the Terror,* 33–135.

10. JM to Edmund Randolph, 15 Aug. 1794, in JM, *Writings,* 2:17–18. On the demonization of Robespierre, see also Baecque, *Glory and Terror,* 145–72; idem, "Robespierre"; D. P. Jordan, *Revolutionary Career of Maximilien Robespierre,* 14–20; TJ to JM, 26 May 1795, and TJ to Coxe, 1 June 1795, both in *TJP,* 28:360, 373.

11. JM to TJ, 7 Sept. 1794, in *TJP,* 28:145–46; JM to Randolph, 25 Aug. 1794, HSP; JM to James Madison, 2 Sept. 1794, in Madison, *Papers,* 15:354.

12. Felhémési, *Queue de Robespierre.* For the controversy about "la queue de Robespierre," see Baczko, *Ending the Terror,* 53–60; JM to TJ, 7 Sept. 1794, in *TJP,* 28:146; JM to Randolph, 15 Sept. 1794, HSP.

13. JM, *Autobiography,* 100. In his memoirs JM refers to himself in the third person. Thomas Perkins remembered that while in Paris, he dined "almost every Saturday with the minister of the United States, where I was in the habit of meeting distinguished men." Among these were Merlin, Thibaudeau, Tallien, Fréron, and other members of the Convention (*Memoirs,* 55, 76–77, 86). See also Griffith, "Reminiscences," 59–60.

14. JM to Randolph, 14 June 1795, JMP; JM to TJ, 27 June 1795, in *TJP,* 28:394. See also JM to Madison, 24 Oct. 1795, in Madison, *Papers,* 16:111; JM, *Autobiography,* 86, 97–8, 115. For Reubell, see also JM to Timothy Pickering, 5 Nov. 1795, HSP; Perkins, *Memoirs,* 73, 76–77, 85–86.

15. Kale, *French Salons,* 51, 59–61, 69–71; Bruson and Forray-Carlier, *Au temps des merveilleuses;* Spang, "Frivolous French," 110–25.

16. Journal of William S. Dallam, Evans Papers, University of Kentucky Library, quoted in Dietle, "William S. Dallam," 153–54; JM, *Autobiography,* 102–3; Griffith, "Reminiscences," 59.

17. Entry of 29 Ventôse III (19 Mar. 1795), in Perkins, *Memoirs,* 67. For conditions in Congress, see Freeman, *Affairs of Honor,* 25–27; J. S. Young, *Washington Community,* 94, 96–97.

18. JM to Randolph, 16 Oct. 1794, HSP.

19. JM to Madison, 18 Feb. 1795, in Madison, *Papers,* 15:476. For antiparty ideology in America and France, see Hofstadter, *Idea of a Party System;* L. Hunt, *Politics, Culture, and Class,* 43–45.

20. "Sixth Annual Address to Congress," 19 Nov. 1794, in Washington, *Writings* (ed. Rhodehamel), 888, 893; Madison to JM, 4 Dec. 1794, in Madison, *Papers,* 15:406.

21. JM to Madison, 18 Feb. 1795, in Madison, *Papers,* 15:475–76.

22. Randolph to JM, 8 Mar. 1795, HSP.

23. *Philadelphia Gazette,* 23 Feb. 1795; *Herald,* 28 Feb. 1795; *Daily Advertiser,* 27 Feb. and 3 Mar. 1795. The extracts were also reprinted in Randolph's anonymous "Germanicus" essays denouncing the Democratic-Republican Societies, first published in *Dunlap and Claypoole's American Daily Advertiser* between 19 Jan. and 1 Apr. 1795.

Ames to Christopher Gore, 24 Feb. 1795, in Ames, *Works*, 2:1104; Madison to JM, 11 Mar. 1795, in Madison, *Papers*, 15:487.

24. On Federalists' linking of Jacobins and Democratic-Republicans and calls for their suppression, see Cotlar, "Reading the Foreign News," 322–24; Koschnik, "Democratic Societies of Philadelphia," 631–33; Link, *Democratic-Republican Societies*, 201.

25. JM to Madison, 25 Feb. 1795, in Madison, *Papers*, 15:481. See also JM to Randolph, 6 Mar. 1795, in JM, *Writings*, 2:220–21.

26. Excerpts from Parkin's diary in S. C. Chew, "Diary of a Baltimorean," 365. Parkin died only eighteen months after his return from Europe, on 30 June 1797, at the age of twenty-four—possibly of the pneumonia he mentions contracting during his trip.

27. JM to Randolph, 1 Aug. 1795, in JM, *Writings*, 2:336–37. JM did not take the *jeunesse dorée* at all seriously, explaining their occasional "excesses" as due to the fact that the "relations of many of [them] had suffered under the reign of terror," and commending the Convention for treating their activities as "a frolic" and gently admonishing them. By contrast, Thomas Perkins reported battles between hundreds of Jeunesse and Jacobin supporters in the Palais d'Egalité (entry of 1 Germinal III [21 Mar. 1795], in Perkins, *Memoirs*, 70–71). For conditions in France in the winter of 1794–95, see Lyons, *France under the Directory*, 15–17; Lefebvre, *Thermidorians and the Directory*, 82–115.

28. JM to Randolph, 13 Jan. 1795, in JM, *Writings*, 2:167–79, quote at 172–73; JM to Randolph, 1 Feb. 1795, JMP.

29. Lyons, *France under the Directory*, 17; Woloch, *Jacobin Legacy*, 14–16; Cobb and Rudé, "Le dernier mouvement populaire de la Révolution."

30. JM to Randolph, 6 Mar. 1795, in JM, *Writings*, 2:224–25, 226, 223–24.

31. JM to Randolph, 14 Apr. 1795, in JM, *Writings*, 2:245–53. See the proclamations of the Convention on 12 Germinal in *Gazette Nationale*, 13 Germinal III (2 Apr. 1795). For a similar assessment, see entry of 13 Germinal III (2 Apr. 1795), in Perkins, *Memoirs*, 83.

32. JM to Randolph, 17 May 1795, in JM, *Writings*, 2:260–61.

33. On the uprisings of Germinal and Prairial, see Rudé, *Crowd in the French Revolution*, 142–59; Lefebvre, *Thermidorians and the Directory*, 116–34; Baczko, *Ending the Terror*, 231–42.

34. JM to Randolph, 14 June 1795, JMP. See also JM to Madison, 13 June 1795, in Madison, *Papers*, 16:18.

35. JM to TJ, 27 June 1795, in *TJP*, 28:390–97, quotes at 392–93, 397. The "Sketch" appeared in the *Aurora General Advertiser*, 31 Aug. 1795, as well as in the Republican *New York Journal*, 5 Sept. 1795. JM to George Logan, 24 June 1796, in JM, *Writings*, 3:6–7; Burr to JM, 11 Sept. 1795, in Burr, *Political Correspondence and Public Papers*, 1:227–28; Timothy Pickering to Washington, 2 July 1796, George Washington Papers, LC.

36. JM, *Autobiography*, 107–8. A draft of this "digest," emphasizing the importance of a bill of rights, is in James Monroe Papers, NYPL.

37. Lezay-Marnezia, *Qu'est-ce que la Constitution de 93?*, 27–34.

38. Scholarly assessments of the Constitution of 1795 vary widely, from branding it a betrayal of the revolution's democratic promise to declaring it a vindication of the

revolution's liberal ideals. For the former, see Jainchill, "Constitution of the Year III"; Lefebvre, *Thermidorians and the Directory,* 171–86; Woloch, *Jacobin Legacy,* 20; Brunel, *Thermidor,* 128; Lyons, *France under the Directory,* 18–19. For the latter, positive view, see Livesey, *Making Democracy in the French Revolution;* Conac and Machelon, *Constitution de l'an III;* Furet, *Interpreting the French Revolution,* 71–75; Palmer, *Age of the Democratic Revolution,* 2:131, 214–16.

39. "Farewell Address," 19 Sept. 1796, in Washington, *Writings* (ed. Rhodehamel), 968, 973. On Washington's role in redefining notions of political consent, see Furstenberg, *In the Name of the Father,* 10–11. On the exclusion of the people from governing as conducive to nation-building, see Loughran, *Republic in Print,* 211–12.

40. Boissy d'Anglas, *Projet de constitution,* 46, 74; JM to TJ (and others), 27 June 1795, in *TJP,* 28:394.

41. JM to Madison, 8 Sept. 1795, in Madison, *Papers,* 16:83; JM to Timothy Pickering, 10 Sept. 1795, James Monroe Papers, NYPL; Madison to TJ, 6 Dec. 1795, in *TJP,* 28:544.

42. For the Vendémiaire uprising, see Lyons, *France under the Directory,* 40–41; Godechot, *Counter-Revolution,* 260–62; Rudé, *Crowd in the French Revolution,* 160–77; Lefebvre, *Thermidorians and the Directory,* 187–212. For the role of the army in suppressing popular uprisings, see Bertaud, *Army of the French Revolution,* 269–312, esp. 301–12.

43. JM to Timothy Pickering, 20 Oct. 1795, HSP; Jainchill, "Constitution of the Year III," 432.

44. TJ to James Sullivan, 9 Feb. 1797 (emphasis in the original), and TJ to Elbridge Gerry, 13 May 1797, both in *TJP,* 29:289, 363.

45. TJ to Phillip Mazzei, 24 Apr. 1796, in *TJP,* 29:82. For the connection among Federalism, British capital, and foreign influence, as well as the specter of American corruptibility, see Onuf, *Jefferson's Empire,* 88–93. For the reversal of public opinion in favor of Jay's treaty, see Combs, *Jay Treaty,* 159–88.

46. JM to Timothy Pickering, 20 Oct. 1795, HSP. For the Reign of Terror, the uprisings during JM's tenure, and the "Conspiracy of Equals" as foreign plots, see above and JM to Pickering, 10 Mar. 1796, HSP (reporting that the Conspiracy of Equals was "put in motion by foreign influence; and, under the mask of patriotism, more effectually to promote the purpose of disorganization"); JM to TJ, 30 July 1796, in *TJP,* 29:163 (denouncing "Robespierre and his associates; men who were probably in the pay of foreign powers and employed to perpetrate those atrocities merely to make the revolution odious and thus oppose it").

47. For Jay's treaty as unmasking Federalist intentions, see JM to Madison, 8 Sept. 1795, in Madison, *Papers,* 16:81.

48. JM to Pickering, 5 Nov. 1795, HSP.

49. JM to Madison, 29 Oct. 1795, and JM to Madison, 12 Jan. 1796, both in Madison, *Papers,* 16:114, 185.

50. JM, *View of the Conduct of the Executive,* lxvi; JM, "Address of Mr. Monroe to the Directory on presenting his letter of recall," 30 Dec. 1796, in *American State Papers,* 1:747. For *View's* publication and reception, see Ammon, *James Monroe,* 165–67; Tagg, *Benjamin Franklin Bache,* 327–28.

51. "Answer of the President of the Directory," 30 Dec. 1796, in *American State Papers,* 1:747. Although the French foreign minister, Charles Delacroix, had assured JM that this would be a private audience, its proceedings were published two days later in the Directory's official paper, *Le Rédacteur* (12 Nivôse V [1 Jan. 1797]), further aggravating the Federalists. See Charles C. Pinckney to Timothy Pickering, 16 Jan. 1797, United States Department of State, Despatches from United States Ministers to France, 1789–1906 (microfilm); Timothy Pickering to Paine Wingate, 12 Apr. 1797, Timothy Pickering Papers, MHS; John Quincy Adams to John Adams, 14 Jan. 1797, in J. Q. Adams, *Writings,* 2:79–80.

52. William Tudor, John Buffington, Daniel Parker, Jesse Putnam, and John M. Forbes to JM, 8 Nov. 1796, JM to William Tudor, John Buffington, Daniel Parker, Jesse Putnam, and John M. Forbes, 9 Nov. 1796, and Samuel Broome et al. to JM, 6 Dec. 1796, all in JM, *View of the Conduct of the Executive,* 399, 399–400, 401; JM to Samuel Broome et al., Jan. 1797, JMP; JM to Madison, 5 July 1796, in Madison, *Papers,* 16:374–75; JM to John Dawson, 26 Mar. and 8 Apr. 1798, James Monroe Papers, NYPL; entry of 4 July 1796, in Diary of Thomas Hickling's Visit to France and England, 1796, MHS; Stephan Higginson to Timothy Pickering, 14 Oct. 1796, Timothy Pickering Papers, MHS. For the reactions of the French press, see Aulard, *Paris pendant la réaction Thermidorienne,* 3:299–300. For reactions in America, see *Herald,* 17 Sept. 1796.

5. The End of a Beautiful Friendship

1. Madison, "Political Reflections," in Madison, *Papers,* 17:237–43 (emphases in the original). It was first published in the *Aurora General Advertiser,* 23 Feb. 1799.

2. WS to John Cutting, 28 June 1791, WSP; JM, *Autobiography,* 102–3; Thomas Perkins Journal, 4 July 1795, Thomas H. Perkins Papers, MHS; Stinchcombe, *XYZ Affair,* 81.

3. The names of the French agents were withheld because the American envoys had promised never to make them public and to ensure the envoys' safety. There was a fourth French agent involved in the negotiations, Nicholas Hubbard ("W"); however, since he appeared only a few times in the printed accounts of the negotiations, the episode became known as the "XYZ Affair," the most complete account of which is Stinchcombe, *XYZ Affair.*

4. Elkins and McKitrick, *Age of Federalism,* 609–10; DeConde, *Quasi-War,* 157; Stinchcombe, *XYZ Affair,* chap. 5.

5. JB to James Cathalan, 14 June 1799, JBP; Skipwith to JM, 20 Oct. 1797, JMP. For Skipwith, see also Cox, *Parisian American,* 45–64.

6. For Mountflorence's contacts with the envoys, see John Marshall, "Paris Journal," 14 Oct., 6 and 7 Nov. 1797, in J. Marshall, *Papers,* 3:162, 185–86; Zahniser, *Charles Cotesworth Pinckney,* 155 n54, 211; Clarfield, *Timothy Pickering,* 112. Mountflorence's connection with Pinckney was well known among other Americans in Paris. TP warned Talleyrand that if Mountflorence should visit, "it will be best to keep him at a distance. He is the confidential intrigant of Pinckney" (TP to Talleyrand, 7 Vendémiaire VI [28 Sept. 1797], AAECPE-U).

7. Flavell, "American Patriots in London."

8. Nathaniel Cutting to Pierce Butler, 13 Mar. 1798, Nathaniel Cutting Papers, MHS (emphasis in the original); Trumbull, *Autobiography,* 220-23.

9. Pinckney to Rufus King, 14 Dec. 1797, Rufus King Papers, LC; Pinckney to Thomas Pinckney, 22 Feb. 1798, Pinckney Family Papers, LC; John Marshall, "Paris Journal," 11 Oct. 1797, in J. Marshall, *Papers,* 3:160 (emphasis in the original). Church had served as the American consul at Lisbon.

10. K. Hamilton and Langhorne, *Practice of Diplomacy,* 124-28.

11. For Franklin, see "'Lettre du Comte de Chanmburg [Schaumberg]': A Satire Attributed to Franklin" (before 13 Mar. 1777); duc de La Rochefoucauld to Franklin and Silas Deane, 20 Jan [1777], in Franklin, *Papers,* 23:214, 480-82. For TJ, see TJ to Charles F. Dumas, 31 July 1788, TJ to Dumas, 15 May 1788, TJ to Dumas, 30 July 1788, and JM to TJ, 27 June 1795, all in *TJP,* 13:438-49, 160, 436, 28:390-97; Timothy Pickering to Pinckney, 16 Jan. 1797, in *American State Papers,* 1:559-76. See also Zahniser, *Charles Coteworth Pinckney,* 156; Clarfield, *Timothy Pickering,* 112; Bowman, *Struggle for Neutrality,* 300-305.

12. JB to Abraham Baldwin, 4 Mar. 1798. The letter is reprinted in Dos Passos, *Ground We Stand On,* 346-58. JB to TJ, 12 Mar. 1798, in *TJP,* 30:174. On "public-minded" letters, see Freeman, *Affairs of Honor,* 114-15.

13. Skipwith to TJ, 17 Mar. 1798, in *TJP,* 30:184-85; Mary Pinckney to Margaret Manigault, 6 Dec. 1797, quoted in Stinchcombe, *XYZ Affair,* 80.

14. TP, *Letter to the People of France,* 17-18. For the grateful response of the Directory, see François de Neufchâteau to TP, 13 Nov. 1797, AF III/478/2955, AN.

15. Elkins and McKitrick, *Age of Federalism,* 550; Rossignol, *Nationalist Ferment,* 105. For the connection among the XYZ Affair, the Alien and Sedition Acts, and American nationalism, see Stine, *Perilous Times,* 16-78; Hale, "'Many Who Wandered in Darkness'"; Freeman, "Explaining the Unexplainable"; R. M. Smith, "Constructing American National Identity"; Sharp, *American Politics in the Early Republic,* 163-84; Ray, "'Not One Cent for Tribute'"; DeConde, *Quasi-War,* chap. 3; J. M. Smith, *Freedom's Fetters;* J. C. Miller, *Crisis in Freedom.*

16. Cotlar, "Federalists' Transatlantic Cultural Offensive," 274-99. For the lessons Federalists drew from the controversy around Jay's Treaty, see Waldstreicher, *In the Midst of Perpetual Fetes,* 160. See also Estes, "Shaping the Politics of Public Opinion."

17. Joseph Hopkinson to Oliver Wolcott, 17 May 1798, and George Cabot to Wolcott, 25 Oct. 1798, both in Gibbs, *Memoirs,* 2:49, 109. For Federalist electoral gains, see Sharp, *American Politics in the Early Republic,* 223; Kuehl, "Southern Reactions to the XYZ Affair." But see also J. C. Miller, *Federalist Era,* 255; N. E. Cunningham, *Jeffersonian Republicans,* 133-35.

18. Cotlar, "Federalists' Transatlantic Cultural Offensive," 276, 278, 281-82, 293-94; R. M. Smith, "Constructing American National Identity."

19. Talleyrand to American envoys, 18 Mar. 1798, and American envoys to Talleyrand, 3 Apr. 1798, both in J. Marshall, *Papers,* 3:413-22, 426-59; Stinchcombe, *XYZ Affair,* 111.

20. J. M. Smith, *Freedom's Fetters,* 194-200; Tagg, *Benjamin Franklin Bache,* 342-43,

378–88. Bache had probably received the letter from French minister Philippe de Létombe, who was under orders to give it the widest possible circulation in America.

21. [JB], *Copy of a Letter from an American Diplomatic Character;* Baldwin to JB, 14
Feb. and 30 Mar. 1799, Monroe Wakeman Holman Collection, Beinecke Library. For
Lyon, see Austin, *Matthew Lyon,* 109–10, 114; J. M. Smith, *Freedom's Fetters,* 226–27.

22. *Columbian Centinel,* 22 Dec. 1798. JB later claimed that the *Centinel* had "muti-
lated and distorted" his letter to Baldwin until there was "not a paragraph without some
omissions, additions or changes." At the same time, however, JB defiantly declared that
he found nothing in the allegedly mangled letter to retract or correct (*Joel Barlow to His
Fellow Citizens, of the United States of America. Letter I,* 2).

23. Alsop, *Political Green-House,* 13. A kind of capsule biography of JB, the poem
alludes to his various occupations as a chaplain in the Continental Army, a real estate
agent in France for the Scioto Company, and the author of *The Hasty Pudding* and a revised edition of Watts's Psalms.

24. Noah Webster to JB, 16 Nov. 1798, in Webster, *Letters,* 187–94. The letter also
appeared in the *Commercial Advertiser,* 16 Nov. 1798, merely signed "W."

25. Watson forwarded JB's letter and his response to Wolcott, adding, "Although there
are few men I have loved so much, there are few whose present conduct I detest more."
JB to Watson, 26 July 1798, Watson to JB, 26 Oct. 1798, and Watson to Wolcott, 25 Nov.
1798, all in Gibbs, *Memoirs,* 2:111–15.

26. *Philadelphia Gazette,* 6 July 1798; Watson to JB, 26 Oct. 1798, in Gibbs, *Memoirs,*
2:113; Mary Pinckney to Margaret Manigault, 6 Dec. 1797, quoted in Stinchcombe, *XYZ
Affair,* 80.

27. Tench Coxe to George Washington, 14 June 1796, enclosing a translation of a letter
from "Jean Baptiste Rochambeau Jr." [i.e., Donatien-Marie-Joseph de Rochambeau] to
Coxe, 18 Feb. 1796, Tench Coxe Papers, Historical Society of Pennsylvania.

28. The informers were often teachers, lawyers, journalists, and printers who reported
on the opinions of small property owners and wage earners. See the police reports collected in Aulard, *Paris pendant la réaction Thermidorienne,* 3:571; *L'observateur Démo-
crate, Sansculotte* (Paris), 13–18 Feb. 1796, quoted in Höfer, "Agiotage, Agioteur," 23.

29. Introduced in late 1789 as government bonds secured by nationalized Church
property, the assignats quickly became paper money with the face values of livres. As the
French state ran out of money, it began to print assignats in ever-increasing amounts in
Apr. 1790. The inevitable results were inflation and devaluation. On the assignats, see
Bosher, *French Finances,* 273–75, 309–10; Crouzet, *Grande Inflation.*

30. Bizardel, "French Estates, American Landlords," 112–13; Perkins, Journal, 1 and
4 Apr. 1795; Griffith, "Reminiscences," 67.

31. Mary Pinckney to Margaret Manigault, 23 Jan. 1798, quoted in Stinchcombe, *XYZ
Affair,* 90; Bizardel, "French Estates, American Landlords," 109–10; Stinchcombe, *XYZ
Affair,* 86.

32. Eustace, *Traité d'amitié;* Griffith, *L'indépendance absolue des Américains,* 16–29;
Griffith, "Reminiscences," 64, 66.

33. Marshall to Charles Lee, 3 Nov. 1797, in J. Marshall, *Papers,* 3:274. Jesse Putnam

was a merchant from Boston who acted as an agent for William Lee to collect claims against the French government. Skipwith and Lee unsuccessfully petitioned Talleyrand for Putnam's release (Griffith, "Reminiscences," 65). *Cartes de sûreté,* also known as *certificats d'autorisation de résidence,* were first introduced in Mar. 1792.

34. Cochon's report of 12 Prairial V (31 May 1797), AF III, dos. 167, 127, AN. See the reports on public opinion from Apr. and June 1797 in Aulard, *Paris pendant la réaction Thermidorienne,* 4:44, 57, 73, 84–85, 162; Rapport, *Nationality and Citizenship,* 269–71.

35. On Franklin's enduring popularity and the myth of "the good Quaker," see Leith, "Culte de Franklin"; McKee, "Popularity of the 'American'"; Philips, *Good Quaker in French Legend.* On French anti-Americanism, see Roger, *American Enemy;* Revel, *Obsession anti-américaine;* Echeverria, *Mirage in the West,* 140, 174.

36. Waldstreicher, *In the Midst of Perpetual Fetes,* 113–14; Estes, "Shaping the Politics of Public Opinion"; Noah Webster to Oliver Wolcott, 23 June 1800, quoted in Freeman, "Explaining the Unexplainable," 27–30. Jeffrey L. Pasley notes a similar irony in the Federalists' self-defeating persecution of Republican printers, for whom the "best and most devastating way to respond to a Federalist threat was to print it." But not only did the Federalists hand their opponents the weapons with which to fight back, but–in the case of the Americans in Paris–they also inadvertently provided them with a platform in the Federalist press (Pasley, *"Tyranny of Printers,"* 171–72 [quote], 189).

37. JB to George Washington, 2 Oct. 1798, in *Joel Barlow to His Fellow Citizens, of the United States of America. Letter I,* 41–49; Washington to John Adams, 1 Feb. 1799, in Washington, *Writings* (ed. Fitzpatrick), 37:119–20; Adams to Washington, 19 Feb. 1799, in J. Adams, *Works,* 8:624–26. In his first *Boston Patriot* letter (1809), Adams revised this harsh verdict: "I . . . considered General Washington's question, whether Mr. Barlow's [letter] was written with a very good or a very bad design; and as, with all my jealousy, I had not sagacity enough to discover the smallest room for suspicion of any ill design, I frankly concluded that it was written with a very good one" ("To the Printers of the Boston Patriot: Letter I," in J. Adams, *Works,* 9:242).

38. For Logan, see Tolles, *George Logan,* esp. 153–204. For his political economy, see McCoy, *Elusive Republic,* 223–24. For his involvement with the Philadelphia Democratic Society, see Ammon, *Genet Mission,* 79, 97, 106–7; Link, *Democratic-Republican Societies,* 10, 50.

39. *Philadelphia Gazette,* quoted in Logan, *Memoir of Dr. George Logan,* 59–60 (emphases in the original). See also *Porcupine's Gazette,* 18 June 1798; *Gazette of the United States,* 18 and 23 June 1798; *Debates and Proceedings in the Congress of the United States,* 5th Cong., 2nd sess. (1798), 8:1972 (hereafter *Annals of Congress*). See also J. M. Smith, *Freedom's Fetters,* 101–6. The correspondence in question was nothing more sinister than letters of introduction from Létombe, and certificates of citizenship from Thomas McKean, the chief justice of Pennsylvania, and TJ. The Federalists were eager to associate the vice-president with a Jacobin conspiracy, and TJ had to repeatedly protest his innocence (*Porcupine's Gazette,* 19 June and 21 July 1798; TJ to James Madison, 21 June 1798, TJ to Aaron Burr, 12 Nov. 1798, TJ to Elbridge Gerry, 26 Jan. 1799, and TJ to Edmund Pendleton, 29 Jan. 1799, all in *TJP,* 30:417, 576–77, 645–66, 662).

40. Mountflorence to Talleyrand, 22 Thermidor VI (9 Aug. 1798), vol. 50, 159, AAECPE-U.

41. Talleyrand, "Report to the Executive Directory," 12 Prairial VI (31 May 1798), vol. 49, 393–404, AAECPE-U, quoted in DeConde, *Quasi-War,* 145. Because of the public nature of this diplomatic crisis, Talleyrand also considered it necessary to issue a defense pamphlet, which was quickly translated into English under the title *Talleyrand's Defence.*

42. Codman described his meeting with Talleyrand in a letter to the Federalist congressman Harrison Gray Otis and advocated the appointment of a new commission. See Codman to Otis, 26 Aug. 1798, in Otis, *Life and Letters,* 1:168–70; Fulwar Skipwith to Elbridge Gerry, 6 Aug. 1798, Elbridge Gerry Papers, Pierpont Morgan Library.

43. Talleyrand to Louis-André Pichon, 29 Thermidor VI (16 Aug. 1798), vol. 50, 169, AAECPE-U. For Talleyrand's overtures to Murray, see Bowman, *Struggle for Neutrality,* 350–59; DeConde, *Quasi-War,* 147–54.

44. Logan, "To the Citizens of the United States," *Aurora General Advertiser,* 3 Jan. 1799; Murray to Pickering, 6 Sept. 1798, in Ford, "Letters of William Vans Murray," 466.

45. *Le Bien Informé,* 7 Fructidor VI (24 Aug. 1798); *Le Publiciste,* 8 Fructidor VI (25 Aug. 1798); *Nouvelles Politiques Publiées a Leyde* (Supp.), 31 Aug. 1798. It cited the *Publiciste* as its source.

46. This strategy was similar to that adopted by the North ministry at the beginning of the American Revolution. In late 1775, Lord North made himself more accessible to Americans in London in the hope of encouraging divisions within the Continental Congress between the moderate southern colonies and their more extreme northern neighbors (Flavell, "American Patriots in London," 357–59).

47. Adams to Pitcairn, 7 Sept. 1798, in T. B. Adams, "Letters," 20 (emphasis in the original).

48. Talleyrand to Pichon, 11 Fructidor VI (28 Aug. 1798), vol. 50, 202, AAECPE-U; Murray to Timothy Pickering, 31 Aug. 1798, in Ford, "Letters of William Vans Murray," 463; Murray to Timothy Pickering, 19 Sept. 1798, Timothy Pickering Papers, MHS; *Aurora General Advertiser,* 16, 22, and 30 Nov. 1798, 9 Jan. and 1 Feb. 1799; Nathaniel Cutting to TJ, 27 Aug. 1798, WS to TJ, 24 Aug. 1798, and TJ to John Wayles Eppes, 21 Jan. 1799, all in *TJP,* 30:499–500, 489–90, 631.

49. Logan, *Memoir of Dr. George Logan,* 86–87; "Memorandum of an Interview," 13 Nov. 1798, in Washington, *Writings* (ed. Fitzpatrick), 37:18–20; *Journal of the Senate,* 2:562–63.

50. *Annals of Congress,* 5th Cong., 3rd sess. (1798–99), 9:2493.

51. Ibid., 9:2619–26, 2637–45, 2694, 2703–4, 2708–9. The authorship of this letter is not entirely certain. Joseph Woodward brought an unsigned copy to the United States and, in a letter to Harrison Gray Otis, identified George Logan and JB as its authors (Woodward to Otis, 25 Jan. 1799, in Otis, *Life and Letters,* 1:170–71). Logan vehemently denied this and claimed to have been shown a draft by Richard Codman, who he said had asked him to present it to Talleyrand; Logan said that he had refused to do so because it would have had "too much the appearance of an official act" (*Aurora General Advertiser,* 14 and 15 Jan. 1799). There is no copy in the AAECPE-U, which suggests that it never

reached Talleyrand. Codman's praise for Logan in this 26 Aug. letter to Otis indicates that he approved of the content of the anonymous letter, whether or not he wrote it himself. Codman also argued that it was the display of American national unity that had convinced the Directory to revise its position, but he wrote that this new national spirit should not prevent the reconciliation between the two republics, "which ought to be desired by all true friends to both countries" (Codman to Otis, 26 Aug. 1798, in Otis, *Life and Letters,* 1:169).

52. *Annals of Congress,* 5th Cong., 3rd sess. (1798–99), 9:2618, 2629.

53. Ibid., 9:3795. The law is still in effect, although there has been only one indictment under it in two centuries. In 1803, Francis Flournoy was prosecuted for publishing a newspaper article advocating the secession of Kentucky and its annexation by France (Tolles, *George Logan,* 238–39). In 1947, the House Un-American Activities Committee considered using the law to prosecute Henry Wallace for criticizing American foreign policy toward the Soviet Union while traveling abroad (Culver and Hyde, *American Dreamer,* 441). See also Vagts, "Logan Act."

54. *Aurora General Advertiser,* 24 Dec. 1798 (emphasis in the original); JM to TJ, 26 Jan. 1799, in *TJP,* 30:658.

55. For the many considerations behind and long gestation of Adams's decision to send a new minister to France, see Elkins and McKitrick, *Age of Federalism,* 614–18; DeConde, *Quasi-War,* 112, 165–68, 172, 175.

56. Sedgwick to Alexander Hamilton, 17 Feb. 1799, in A. Hamilton, *Papers,* 22:488; Bradburn, "Clamor in the Public Mind," 565–600, esp. 586; Elkins and McKitrick, *Age of Federalism,* 618–19; Bowman, *Struggle for Neutrality,* 366–67.

57. *Joel Barlow to His Fellow Citizens, of the United States of America. Letter I,* 37–38, 39.

6. From Sister Republics to Republican Empires

1. "Discours du Général Bonaparte au Conseil des Anciens, dans la séance du 18 Brumaire," 18 Brumaire VIII (9 Nov. 1799), in Plon and Dumaine, *Correspondance de Napoléon Ier,* 6:1; TJ to Joseph Priestley, 21 Mar. 1801, in *TJP,* 33:394.

2. TJ to Elbridge Gerry, 21 June 1797, in *TJP,* 29:448.

3. Alexander Hamilton to Theodore Sedgwick, 22 Dec. 1800, in A. Hamilton, *Papers,* 25:270; "First Inaugural Address," 4 Mar. 1801, in *TJP,* 33:150.

4. Excerpts from Murray's diary are printed in Hoar, "Famous Fête," 253–54. According to a "tradition," Napoleon, upon meeting Ellsworth, was so struck with the chief justice's "grave, firm face" that he "said to some one, 'We must make a treaty with this man'" (W. G. Brown, *Life of Oliver Ellsworth,* 284). But Davie's secretary maintained that Napoleon appeared at times "to forget that Governor Davie was *second* in the commission, his attention being more particularly directed to him" (Robinson, *William R. Davie,* 354–55).

5. Fontanes, *Éloge funèbre de Washington,* 13–14. Extracts of the address were soon translated and reprinted in the *Washingtoniana* (210–16). For the commemoration of Washington's death in France, see also Echeverria, *Mirage in the West,* 253–35.

6. Letter dated 7 Apr. 1800, printed in *City Gazette and Daily Advertiser,* 23 May 1800. For an example of the view, widely held among Federalists, that the Consulate was the inevitable result of the "anarchy" of the French Revolution, see Tacitus, *Series of Letters to Thomas Jefferson,* 90–93.

7. *Aurora General Advertiser,* 22 Jan. 1800; *Philadelphia Gazette,* 21 Jan. 1800. TJ quipped that the British press, "after killing Buonaparte a thousand times," still had "a variety of parts to be acted by him" (TJ to Harry Innes, 23 Jan. 1800, TJ to John Breckinridge, 29 Jan. 1800, and TJ to Thomas Mann Randolph, 2 Feb. 1800, all in *TJP,* 31:336, 345, 358.

8. *Gazette Nationale,* 14 Vendémiaire IX (6 Oct 1800). A league of armed neutrality refers to an alliance of smaller European naval powers intended to protect their ships against the British Royal Navy's wartime policy of unlimited searches of neutral shipping for (French) contraband. During the previous century of Anglo-French wars, the French had repeatedly sponsored such alliances as a counterweight to Britain's sea power, most recently in 1780 during the American Revolution. See Richmond, "Napoleon and the Armed Neutrality of 1800."

9. JB to Abraham Baldwin, 1 Jan. 1800, JBP; Cutting to TJ, 3 Oct. 1800, in *TJP,* 32:194–95. For Cutting, see Newman, "American Political Culture"; John Vanderlyn to Peter Vanderlyn, 15 Nov. 1800, quoted in Oedel, "John Vanderlyn," 104–5.

10. This is a reference to Washington's much-publicized visit to Trenton in 1789 on the way to his inauguration in New York. See Skipwith to JM, 15 May 1797, JMP; TP, "On the Jacobinism of the English at Sea," in *Compact Maritime,* 15.

11. Lafayette to TJ, 10 Feb. 1800 (10 Jan. 1801?), in *TJP,* 32:428–29. For Crèvecoeur, see the preface, dated 17 Apr. 1800, to his *Voyage dans la haute Pensylvanie et dans l'état de New-York,* which extols Napoleon as "le Washington de la France" (1:viii–ix). For Cabanis, see Staum, *Cabanis,* 287–89. For Grégoire, see Sepinwall, *Abbé Grégoire and the French Revolution,* 160–61. For Volney, see Chinard, *Volney et l'Amérique,* 104–8. For Destutt de Tracy, see Kennedy, *Philosophe in the Age of the Revolution,* 79–80.

12. TP to TJ, 1 Oct. 1800, JB to TJ, 3 Oct. 1800, and Cutting to TJ, 3 Oct. 1800, all in *TJP,* 32:186, 193–94, 194–95.

13. Cutting to TJ, 3 Oct. 1800, in *TJP,* 32:194–95. TP's first three enclosures were the untitled manuscript described below, "On the Jacobinism of the English at Sea," and "Compact Maritime." On 6 and 16 Oct., TP sent "Dissertation on the Law of Nations" and "Observations on some passages in the Discourse of Sir William Scott" (TP to TJ, 6 Oct. 1800, TP to TJ, 24 Vendémiaire IX [16 Oct. 1800], and WS to TJ, 9 Dec. 1800, all in *TJP,* 32:204, 222–23, 293–94).

14. Not surprisingly, TP argued that, on the contrary, Britain should be isolated from Austria, its last ally on the continent, and instead of making peace, France should take advantage of the British government's weakened state and attack England's North Sea coast from Belgium and Holland with a large flotilla of gunboats (TP to TJ, 1 Oct. 1800, in *TJP,* 32:191n, 188; *Gazette nationale,* 18–22 Fructidor IX [5–9 Sept. 1800]). There appears to be no extant copy of TP's *Du Jacobinisme des Anglais.*

15. *Joel Barlow to his Fellow Citizens of the United States. Letter II,* 58; JB to TJ, 3 Oct. 1800, in *TJP,* 32:193–94.

16. *Joel Barlow to his Fellow Citizens of the United States. Letter II,* 67; TP, "Compact Maritime," in *Compact Maritime,* 16; JB, *Letter Addressed to the People of Piedmont,* 41. TP invoked the Armed Neutrality Act of 1780 as "the only thing that has any pretension of right to be called and considered as a law of nations," because it was "signed and ratified by a large majority of the maritime commercial nations of Europe" (TP, "Dissertation on the Law of Nations," 3–4). While rejecting the old law of nations, JB still cited existing treaties and philosopher Christian Wolff in support of neutral rights and the principle of "free ships, free goods" (*Joel Barlow to his Fellow Citizens of the United States. Letter II,* 84–87, 91). For JB's and TP's interpretation of the law of nations, see also Onuf and Onuf, *Federal Union, Modern World,* 139–44, 202–6.

17. TP, "Dissertation on the Law of Nations," 6–7; TP, "On the Jacobinism of the English at Sea," 12; TP, "Compact Maritime," 17, 19, 20; *Joel Barlow to his Fellow Citizens of the United States. Letter II,* 60–67, 69–70, 74–75, 99.

18. *Joel Barlow to his Fellow Citizens of the United States. Letter II,* 11–14, 15.

19. DeConde, *Quasi-War,* 308; Kaplan, *Entangling Alliances with None,* 103. JB first made the case for a complete U.S. embargo against Britain, including the confiscation of all debts owed to British companies and subjects, in an undated manuscript titled "On the prospect of a war with England," most likely written in 1793 (JBP). In a letter to Director Merlin of 12 Feb. 1799, coauthored with Fulwar Shipwith, JB called for "a new system of international intercourse, or Law of nations." This letter is reprinted in the American edition of *Joel Barlow to his Fellow Citizens of the United States. Letter II,* 67–70. TP first criticized the failure of the United States to enter into an alliance with other neutral powers in a letter to TJ of 1 Apr. 1797 (*TJP,* 29:344). He outlined the principle of his *Pacte maritime* in the conclusion to *Letter to the People of France* and in a letter to Talleyrand of 9 Vendémiaire VI (30 Sept. 1797) (vol. 48, 273, AAECPE-U). He enclosed this letter in a message of 11 Oct. 1797 to the American envoys Pinckney, Marshall, and Gerry (J. Marshall, *Papers,* 3:243–45; Livingston to James Madison, 1 July 1801, in Madison, *Papers* [SSS], 1:367–68; Barton, *Dissertation on the Freedom of Navigation*).

20. Hauterive, *De l'etat de la France.* For Hauterive, see Rothschild, "Language and Empire," 208–29; Stinchcombe, *XYZ Affair,* 35; Forsyth, "Old European State-System," 521–38. Among its most careful and critical American readers were John Adams and John Quincy Adams. John wrote a running commentary in the margins of his copy, while John Quincy, who had received the book from Friedrich von Gentz, published a scathing review in the magazine *Portfolio* in 1801 (Haraszti, *John Adams and the Prophets of Progress,* 259–79; Hase, "John Quincy Adams als Kritiker von Hauterive und Gentz," 33–48; Gentz, *Von dem Politischen Zustande von Europa,* 2:310).

21. *Joel Barlow to his Fellow Citizens of the United States. Letter II,* 89–90; TP, "On the Jacobinism of the English at Sea," 11–12, 13–14.

22. On slaveholders' views of the French Revolution, see Newman, "American Political Culture"; Fox-Genovese and Genovese, "Political Virtue and the Lessons of the French

Revolution," 202–17; Fox-Genovese and Genovese, *Mind of the Master Class,* 11–40; Egerton, *Gabriel's Rebellion,* 41–48.

23. On the Jeffersonians' rejection of "many of the key elements of the radical, trans-atlantic, Painite political ideology that emerged in the early 1790s," see Cotlar, "Joseph Gales." On officially decreed reconciliation in France, see Woloch, "Napoleonic Regime and French Society," 60–63; Woloch, *Napoleon and His Collaborators,* 55–59.

24. TJ to TP, 18 Mar. 1801, "Jefferson's Reports of Balloting in the House of Representatives," 12 Feb. 1801, TJ to Archibald Stuart, 13 Feb. 1799, TP to TJ, 4 Oct. 1800, and "Appendix I: Lists of Appointments and Removals," all in *TJP,* 33:358–59, 32:578–79, 35, 195 33:665. TJ conveyed TP's manuscripts, with the exception of the first, untitled piece, to printer Samuel Harrison Smith, who published them in Feb. as a pamphlet under the title *Compact Maritime.* The pamphlet has never been reprinted in any collection of TP's works, and his biographers have paid only scant attention to it.

25. TP to JB, 14 Mar. 1801, in *TJP,* 33:274. William Duane published the first American edition of *Joel Barlow to his Fellow Citizens of the United States. Letter II* in Jan. 1801.

26. TP to WS, 17 Mar. 1801, and TP to WS, 3 Oct. 1801, both in *TJP,* 33:338, 35:382. There appears to be no extant reply from TJ to Cutting.

27. JB to TJ, 26 Oct. 1801, TP to TJ, 9 June 1801, and TP to TJ, [Aug. 1801], all in *TJP,* 35:509, 34:281, 35:191–92. In 1797–98, TP had produced a series of articles for *Le Bien Informé,* and memoirs to the French government, advocating the "liberation" of England and Ireland. According to TP's recollections, when the Directory appointed Napoleon as commander of the Army of England in 1798, he asked TP to accompany the expeditionary forces (TP to TJ, 30 Jan. 1806, TJPLC). This appears extremely unlikely if for no other reason than Napoleon's firm conviction that a successful invasion of Britain was impossible. For JB's and Fulton's efforts to interest the Directory, Napoleon, and TJ in the submarine as a weapon to destroy the British Navy and to liberate maritime commerce, see JB to TJ, 15 Sept. 1800, in *TJP,* 32:143; Philip, *Robert Fulton,* 72–84, 94–101, 109–18.

28. AF 194, 41–42, AN; *Le Bien Informé,* 1 Sans-culottide VI (17 Sept. 1798); TP to Directory, [1798], AF/III/544/3620/8–10, AN; *Le Bien Informé,* 19 Brumaire VIII (10 Nov. 1799); Kates, *Cercle Social,* 274–75.

29. TJ to TP, 18 Mar. 1801, in *TJP,* 33:359; *Gazette of the United States,* 21 July and 13 Aug. 1801. TP had asked TJ to allow him to return on an American frigate, due to his fear of getting caught at sea and being deported to England for trial (TP to TJ, 1 Oct. 1800, in TJP, 32:191). The *National Intelligencer* first reported on 15 July 1801 that John Dawson had delivered to TP "a very affectionate letter" from TJ inviting him to travel home on a government ship.

30. Cheetham, *Life of Thomas Paine,* 227. For the reactions to TP's return to the United States, see Knudson, *Jefferson and the Press,* 68–86; Cotlar, "In Paine's Absence," 1–3, 257.

31. Lyon, *Louisiana in French Diplomacy,* 101–26.

32. Madison to Charles Pinckney, 9 June 1801, Madison to Livingston, 28 Sept. 1801, and Livingston to James Madison, 10 Dec. 1801, all in Madison, *Papers* (SSS), 1:275–76, 144–45, 2:305 n1; J. E. Lewis, *American Union and the Problem of Neighborhood,* 24–27.

The right of deposit, established in the Treaty of San Lorenzo in 1795, entitled Americans to bring their produce down the Mississippi into Spanish territory, to unload it to New Orleans's docks and warehouses, and to reload it from there onto oceangoing vessels.

33. Livingston to James Madison, 10 and 31 Dec. 1801, in Madison, *Papers* (SSS), 2:303, 359; *Décade Philosophique,* 10 Floréal IX (30 Apr. 1801). JB likewise predicted that the address would have "a good effect" in France, and helped distribute it in a "tetraglotte" translation, to be "distributed to all the ambassadors & other persons from foreign countries," and another in English, "printed for the use of the Americans here" (JB to TJ, 4 Oct. 1801, in *TJP,* 35:385). The octavo edition, with text in English, French, Italian, and German of *The Speech of Thomas Jefferson, President of the United States, Delivered At His Installment, March 4, 1801, At the City of Washington,* was issued by the English Press of JB's friend and collaborator John Hurford Stone (Stern, *Studies in the Franco-American Booktrade,* 125).

34. TJ to Du Pont, 25 Apr. 1802, TJPLC. Du Pont probably did not communicate to the French government the contents of the 18 Apr. letter, which he thought would only serve to antagonize Napoleon. But he did play an important role in the negotiations leading up to the Louisiana Purchase; see Saricks, *Pierre Samuel Du Pont de Nemours,* 293–300.

35. All quotations from TJ to Livingston, 18 Apr. 1802, are from Jefferson, *Writings,* 1105–7.

36. Here I follow the interpretation in J. E. Lewis, *Louisiana Purchase,* 36–37.

37. TJ to Volney, 20 Apr. 1802, TJPLC.

38. TJ to Du Pont de Nemours, 18 Jan. 1802, TJPLC. Montesquieu established the distinction between the nature of the government–its structure, "that which makes it what it is"–and its principles–"that which makes it act"–in Book 3, chap. 1, in Montesquieu, *Spirit of the Laws,* 21.

39. TJ to Spencer Roane, 6 Sept. 1819, and TJ to Du Pont de Nemours, 18 Jan. 1802, both TJPLC.

40. Livingston to James Madison, 13 Jan. 1802, in Madison, *Papers* (SSS), 2:391; Livingston to GM, 14 Jan. and 22 May 1802, Robert R. Livingston Papers, New-York Historical Society; Livingston to Rufus King, 25 Jan. 1802, in Livingston, *Letters,* 25.

41. JB to Ruth Barlow, 1 Fructidor and 27 Thermidor X (19 and 15 Aug. 1802), JBP.

42. William Plumer to Daniel Plumer, 15 Jan. 1803, William Plumer Papers, LC. Livingston expressed the same concern and regarded JM's mission as undermining his own efforts and his ability to take full credit for a successful outcome of the negotiations (Livingston to James Madison, 3 Mar. 1803, in Madison, *Papers* [SSS], 4:385; JM, *Autobiography,* 161–62). The two consuls did recommend JM to Napoleon as a "personal friend & the friend of France" (JM to Madison, 14 May 1803, in Madison, *Papers* [SSS], 4:613).

43. There continues to be debate about whether Napoleon reluctantly gave up Louisiana because of the imminence of war with Britain or, conversely, whether, confronted with the choice of building an empire in the western hemisphere or an empire in Europe and the East, he chose to go to war in pursuit of the latter. For the second position, see Lyon, *Louisiana in French Diplomacy,* 195–96; Tucker and Hendrickson, *Empire of Liberty,* 130–31.

44. *Joel Barlow to his Fellow Citizens of the United States. Letter II,* 48, 51, 54–55, 52, 55; JM to unknown recipient, 12 Feb. 1801, JMP.

45. Livingston and JM to Madison, 13 May 1803, and JM to Madison, 31 Aug. 1803, both in Madison, *Papers* (SSS), 4:602–3, 5:366.

46. For JB's outraged reaction, see JB to Ruth Barlow, 30 Floréal–1 Prairial X (20–21 May 1802), JBP.

47. TJ to JM, 24 Nov. 1801, in *TJP,* 35:719–20. For colonization plans involving the Louisiana territory, see W. D. Jordan, *White over Black,* 564–65.

48. JB to Wolcott, 28 July 1803, JBP.

49. Two examples of the celebration of the Purchase by prominent Republicans are Camillus, *Mississippi Question,* 39, and Magruder, *Political, Commercial and Moral Reflections.* Breckinridge quoted in Horsman, "Dimensions of an 'Empire for Liberty,'" 7.

50. "Second Inaugural Address," 4 Mar. 1805, in Jefferson, *Writings,* 519. For Federalist Western policies, see Cayton, "Radicals in the 'Western World.'"

51. TJ to Destutt de Tracy, 26 Jan. 1811, in Jefferson, *Papers,* 3:337–38; TJ to Cabanis, 13 July 1803, TJPLC.

52. "Treaty for the Cession of Louisiana, signed at Paris April 30, 1803," in United States, *Treaties,* 2:501; TJ to Dewitt Clinton, 2 Dec. 1803, in Jefferson, *Works,* 10:55; Fisher Ames to Thomas Dwight, 31 Oct. 1803, in Ames, *Works,* 2:1468–69. For the congressional debates surrounding the incorporation of the Louisiana Territory into the union, see Kastor, *Nation's Crucible,* 45–52.

53. TJ to Albert Gallatin, 9 Nov. 1803, TJPLC. For the genesis of the law, see Scanlon, "Sudden Conceit."

54. TJ to Breckinridge, 24 Nov. 1803, TJPLC. Its name was changed to "Legislative Council" in the final version of the Governance Act (TJ to George Washington, 14 Aug. 1787, and TJ to John Adams, 13 Nov. 1787, both in *TJP,* 12:36, 350).

55. *Annals of Congress,* 8th Cong., 1st sess. (1803–4), 13:480; entry of 26 Oct. 1803, in Plumer, *William Plumer's Memorandum,* 27; GM to Roger Griswold, 25 Nov. 1803, in Sparks, *Life of Gouverneur Morris,* 3:184.

56. TP to TJ, 2 Aug. 1803, TJPLC; TP to Breckinridge, 2 Aug. 1803, in Paine, *Complete Writings,* 2:1445. For the politics of language in France, see Bell, *Cult of the Nation,* chap. 6; Rosenfeld, *Revolution in Language.*

57. Common Sense, "To the French Inhabitants of Louisiana," *National Intelligencer,* 28 Sept. 1804. Terrified that Louisianans might realize their threats of disunion, and aware that the U.S. citizens most likely to settle in the territory were slaveholders, Congress did not renew the bulk of the restrictions in 1805. For the debate about slavery in the Louisiana Purchase, see Hammond, *Slavery, Freedom, and Expansion,* 30–54.

58. TP to TJ, 25 Jan. 1805, TJPLC. TP's animosity toward the French inhabitants of Louisiana was widely shared among Republicans. See Hammond, *Slavery, Freedom, and Expansion,* 49. William H. Sewell Jr. has pointed out the conceptual similarities between the Northwest Ordinance of 1787 and the Constituent Assembly's creation of *départments* in 1790, both of which envisioned the national territory as neatly divided into perfect squares ("French Revolution," 105).

59. Furstenberg, *In the Name of the Father,* 206–19.

60. Common Sense, "To the French Inhabitants of Louisiana."

61. Randolph to Albert Gallatin, 14 Oct. 1804, Albert Gallatin Papers, New-York Historical Society. For the Jeffersonian state's spheres of operation, see Saler, "Empire for Liberty," 361-62, 373–74, 376, 378.

Epilogue

1. For the eighteenth-century origins of the *mission civilisatrice,* see Pitts, *Turn to Empire,* 166; Bell, *Cult of the Nation,* 96; Woolf, *Napoleon's Integration of Europe,* 8–13. For the broad ideological consensus behind France's imperial expansion under Napoleon, see Dwyer, "Napoleon and the Drive for Glory," 125–26.

2. Adams to Gentz, 16 June 1800, in J. Q. Adams, *Writings,* 2:463; Gentz, "Ursprung und die Grundsätze der Amerikanischen Revolution." The translation by an "American Gentleman," none other than Adams himself, was published as *Origins and Principles of the American Revolution.* For a discussion of Gentz in the context of German comparisons of the two revolutions, see Dippel, *Germany and the American Revolution,* 295–99. On Federalists' use of British conservative literature, see Cotlar, "Federalists' Transatlantic Cultural Offensive," 286–90.

3. Gentz, *Origins and Principles of the American Revolution,* 56, 61.

4. JB, "Outline of projected history of the French Revolution," JBP.

5. For the consensus view of the American Revolution, see Purcell, *Sealed with Blood,* esp. 3, 15–16; Kammen, *Season of Youth,* 39–40, 73. For American reactions to foreign revolutions, see Roberts, "'Revolutions Have Become the Bloody Toy of the Multitude'"; Davis, *Revolutions,* 59-60, 73-74; M. Hunt, *Ideology and U.S. Foreign Policy,* chap. 4.

6. TJ to John Adams, 22 Jan. 1821, in Cappon, *Adams-Jefferson Letters,* 2:570.

Bibliography

MANUSCRIPT COLLECTIONS

Archives des Affaires Etrangères, Paris
  Correspondance Politique, États-Unis
Archives Nationales, Paris
  Series AF III
  Series F/7
Beinecke Library, Yale University,
    New Haven
  Monroe Wakeman Holman Collection
Butler Library, Columbia University,
    New York
  John Jay Papers
  Gouverneur Morris Papers
Connecticut Historical Society, Hartford
  Oliver Wolcott Papers
Historical Society of Pennsylvania,
    Philadelphia
  Tench Coxe Papers
  Simon Gratz Collection
Houghton Library, Harvard University,
    Cambridge
  Joel Barlow Papers

Library of Congress, Washington, DC
  Thomas Jefferson Papers
  Rufus King Papers
  James Monroe Papers
  Gouverneur Morris Papers
  Pinckney Family Papers
  William Plumer Papers
  William Short Papers
  George Washington Papers
Massachusetts Historical Society, Boston
  Nathaniel Cutting Papers
  Thomas Hickling's Diary
  Timothy Pickering Papers
New-York Historical Society, New York
  Albert Gallatin Papers
  Robert R. Livingston Papers
New York Public Library, New York
  James Monroe Papers
Pierpont Morgan Library, New York
  Elbridge Gerry Papers

NEWSPAPERS

Aurora General Advertiser (Philadelphia)
Le Bien Informé (Paris)
Chronique de Paris (Paris)
City Gazette and Daily Advertiser
    (Charleston)
Columbian Centinel (Boston)
Commercial Advertiser (New York)

Daily Advertiser (New York)
Décade Philosophique (Paris)
*Dunlap and Claypoole's American Daily
    Advertiser* (Philadelphia)
Gazette de Leyde (Leiden)
Gazette Nationale ou le Moniteur Universel
    (Paris)

Gazette of the United States (Philadelphia)

Herald (New York)

Journal de la Société de 1789 (Paris)

National Gazette (Philadelphia)

National Intelligencer (Washington)

New York Journal (New York)

Philadelphia Gazette (Philadelphia)

Porcupine's Gazette (Philadelphia)

Le Publiciste (Paris)

Le Rédacteur (Paris)

Révolutions de France et Brabant (Paris)

Révolutions de Paris (Paris)

Other Sources

Adams, John. *The Works of John Adams.* Edited by Charles Francis Adams. 10 vols. Boston, 1856.

Adams, John Quincy. *Writings of John Quincy Adams.* Edited by Washington C. Ford. 7 vols. New York, 1913–17.

Adams, Thomas Boylston. "Letters of Thomas Boylston Adams to Joseph Pitcairn." *Quarterly Publication of the Historical and Philosophical Society of Ohio* 12, no. 1 (1917): 7–48.

Adams, William Howard. *Gouverneur Morris: An Independent Life.* New Haven, 2003.

———. *The Paris Years of Thomas Jefferson.* New Haven, 1997.

Adresse des Citoyens des Etats-Unis de l'Amérique, prononcé devant l'Assemblée nationale, par M. William Henry Vernon, dans la Séance de Samedi au soir, le 10 Juillet 1790. Paris, 1790.

Albertone, Manuela. "Condorcet, Jefferson et l'Amérique." In *Condorcet: Homme des Lumières et de la Révolution,* edited by Anne-Marie Chouillet and Pierre Crépel, 187–99. Paris, 1997.

Aldridge, Alfred Owen. *Franklin and His French Contemporaries.* Washington Square, 1957.

———. *"The Rights of Man* de Thomas Paine: Symbole du siècle des Lumières et leur influence en France." In *Utopie et institutions au XVIIIe siècle: Le pragmatisme des Lumières,* edited by Pierre Francastel, 277–87. Paris, 1963.

D'Allemagne. *Nouvelles du Scioto, ou Relation fidèle du voyage et des infortunes d'un Parisien qui arrive de ce pays-là, où il étoit allé pour s'établir.* Paris, 1790.

Alsop, Richard. *The Political Green-House, for the Year 1798, Addressed to the Readers of the Connecticut Courant, January 1st. 1799.* Hartford, [1799].

American State Papers: Foreign Relations. Selected and edited, under the authority of Congress, by Walter Lowrie and Matthew St. Clair Clarke. 38 vols. Washington, DC, 1832–61.

Ames, Fisher. *Works of Fisher Ames.* Edited by Seth Ames and W. B. Allen. 2 vols. Indianapolis, 1983.

Ammon, Harry. *The Genet Mission.* New York, 1973.

———. *James Monroe: The Quest for National Identity.* New York, 1971.

Anderson, Benedict. *Imagined Communities: Reflections on the Origins and Spread of Nationalism.* Rev. ed. London, 1991.

Anderson, Fred, and Andrew Cayton. *The Dominion of War: Empire and Liberty in North America, 1500–2000.* New York, 2005.

Bibliography

Anderson, William G. *The Price of Liberty: The Public Debt of the American Revolution.* Charlottesville, 1983.

Andress, David. *The Terror: The Merciless War for Freedom in Revolutionary France.* New York, 2006.

Andrieux, François. "Le François aux Bords du Scioto, epître a un émigrant pour Kentuky." In *Almanach des Muses,* 224-30. Paris, 1790.

Angel, Edward. "James Monroe's Mission to Paris, 1794-1796." PhD diss., George Washington University, 1979.

Appiah, Kwame Anthony. "Cosmopolitan Patriots." In *Cosmopolitics: Thinking and Feeling Beyond the Nation,* edited by Pheng Cheah and Bruce Robbins, 91-116. Minneapolis, 1998.

Appleby, Joyce. *Liberalism and Republicanism in the Historical Imagination.* Cambridge, MA, 1992.

——."Radicalizing the War for Independence: American Responses to the French Revolution." *Amerikastudien/American Studies* 41, no. 1 (1996): 7-16.

——. *Thomas Jefferson.* New York, 2003.

Archives parlementaires de 1787 à 1860, première série. Paris, 1862-.

Arendt, Hannah. *On Revolution.* New York, 1965.

——. *The Origins of Totalitarianism.* New York, 1958.

Armitage, David. "Three Concepts of Atlantic History." In *The British Atlantic World, 1500-1800,* edited by David Armitage and Michael J. Braddick, 11-27. Houndsmills, Basingstoke, UK; New York, 2002.

Armstrong, James D. *Revolution and World Order: The Revolutionary State in International Society.* New York, 1993.

Aulard, François V. A., ed. *Paris pendant la réaction Thermidorienne et sous le Directoire: Recueil de documents pour l'histoire d'esprit public à Paris.* 5 vols. Paris, 1898-1902.

Austin, Aleine. *Matthew Lyon, "New Man" of the Democratic Revolution, 1749-1822.* University Park, PA, 1981.

Baczko, Bronislaw. *Ending the Terror: The French Revolution after Robespierre.* Translated by Michel Petheram. Cambridge, UK, 1994.

Baecque, Antoine de. *The Body Politic: Corporeal Metaphor in Revolutionary France, 1770-1800.* Translated by Charlotte Mandell. Stanford, 1997.

——. *Glory and Terror: Seven Deaths under the French Revolution.* Translated by Charlotte Mandell. London, 2001.

——. "Robespierre: Monstre-cadavre du discours thermidorien." *Eighteenth-Century Life* 21, no. 2 (1997): 203-21.

Bailyn, Bernard. *Atlantic History: Concept and Contours.* Cambridge, MA, 2005.

Baker, Keith Michael. *Condorcet: From Natural Philosophy to Social Mathematics.* Chicago, 1975.

——. "The Idea of a Declaration of Rights." In *The French Idea of Freedom: The Old Regime and the Declaration of Rights of 1789,* edited by Dale Van Kley, 154-96. Stanford, 1994.

——. *Inventing the French Revolution: Essays on French Political Culture in the Eighteenth Century.* Cambridge, UK, 1990.

———. "Politics and Social Science in Eighteenth-Century France: The *Société de 1789.*" In *French Government and Society, 1500–1850: Essays in Memory of Alfred Cobban,* edited by J. F. Bosher, 208–50. London, 1973.

Balibar, Etienne. "The Nation Form: History and Ideology." In *Becoming National: A Reader,* edited by Geoff Eley and Ronald Grigor Suny, 132–50. New York, 1996.

Barker-Benfield, G. J. *The Culture of Sensibility: Sex and Society in Eighteenth-Century Britain.* Chicago, 1992.

[Barlow, Joel.] *Copy of a Letter from an American Diplomatic Character in France to a Member of Congress in Philadelphia.* [Fairhaven, VT?, 1798].

———. *Joel Barlow to His Fellow Citizens, of the United States of America. Letter I. On the System of Policy hitherto pursued by their Government. Paris. 4 March 1799.* [Paris, 1799].

———. *Joel Barlow to his Fellow Citizens of the United States. Letter II. On certain political Measures proposed to their Consideration.* [Paris, 1800].

———. *A Letter Addressed to the People of Piedmont.* New York, 1795.

———. *The Works of Joel Barlow.* Edited by William K. Bottorff and Arthur L. Ford. 2 vols. Gainesville, FL, 1970.

Barton, William. *A Dissertation on the Freedom of Navigation and Maritime Commerce, and Such Rights of States, Relative Thereto, as Are Founded on the Law of Nations.* Philadelphia, 1802.

Bayly, C. A. *The Birth of the Modern World, 1780–1914.* Oxford, UK, 2004.

Belissa, Marc. *Fraternité universelle et intérêt national (1713–1795): Les cosmopolitiques de droit des gens.* Paris, 1998.

Bell, David A. *The Cult of the Nation in France: Inventing Nationalism, 1680–1800.* Cambridge, MA, 2001.

Belote, Theodore T. *The Scioto Speculation and the French Settlement at Gallipolis.* Cincinnati, 1907.

Bertaud, Jean-Paul. *The Army of the French Revolution: From Citizen-Soldiers to the Instrument of Power.* Translated by Robert R. Palmer. Princeton, 1988.

Bétourné, Olivier, and Aglaia I. Hartig, eds. *Penser l'histoire de la Révolution: Deux siècles de passion française.* Paris, 1989.

Bizardel, Yvon. *Les Américains à Paris pendant la Révolution.* Paris, 1972.

———. "French Estates, American Landlords." *Apollo* 101, no. 2 (1975): 108–15.

Bizardel, Yvon, and Howard C. Rice Jr. "'Poor in Love Mr. Short.'" *William and Mary Quarterly* 21, no. 4 (1964): 516–33.

Blanning, T. C. W. *The Origins of the French Revolutionary Wars.* London, 1986.

Bloch, Ruth H. *Gender and Morality in Anglo-American Culture, 1650–1800.* Berkeley, 2003.

———. *Visionary Republic: Millennial Themes in American Thought, 1756–1800.* Cambridge, UK, 1985.

Bluche, Frédéric. *Septembre 1792: Logiques d'un massacre.* Paris, 1986.

Boissy d'Anglas, François-Antoine. *Projet de constitution pour la République française et discours préliminaire prononcé par Boissy d'Anglas, au nom de la commission des Onze.* Paris, [1795].

Bibliography

Bond, Beverly W., Jr. *The Monroe Mission to France, 1794–1795.* Baltimore, 1907.

Bosher, J. F. *French Finances, 1770–1795: From Business to Bureaucracy.* Cambridge, UK, 1970.

Bowman, Albert H. *The Struggle for Neutrality: Franco-American Diplomacy during the Federalist Era.* Knoxville, TN, 1974.

Bradburn, Douglas. "A Clamor in the Public Mind: Opposition to the Alien and Sedition Acts." *William and Mary Quarterly* 65, no. 3 (2008): 565–600.

Branson, Susan. *These Fiery Frenchified Dames: Women and Political Culture in Early National Philadelphia.* Philadelphia, 2001.

Brewer, John. *The Pleasures of the Imagination: English Culture in the Eighteenth Century.* London, 1997.

Brissot, Jacques-Pierre, and Etienne Clavière. *De la France et des États-Unis.* Edited by Marcel Dorigny. Paris, 1996.

Brookhiser, Richard. *Gentleman Revolutionary: Gouverneur Morris, the Rake Who Wrote the Constitution.* New York, 2003.

Brown, Howard G. *Ending the French Revolution: Violence, Justice, and Repression from the Terror to Napoleon.* Charlottesville, 2006.

Brown, Howard G., and Judith A. Miller. "New Paths from the Terror to the Empire: An Historiographical Introduction." In *Taking Liberties: Problems of a New Order from the French Revolution to Napoleon,* edited by Howard G. Brown and Judith A. Miller, 1–19. Manchester, 2002.

Brown, William G. *The Life of Oliver Ellsworth.* New York, 1905.

Brubaker, Rogers. *Citizenship and Nationhood in France and Germany.* Cambridge, MA, 1992.

Brunel, Françoise. *Thermidor: La chute de Robespierre.* Bruxelles, 1989.

Bruson, Jean-Marie, and Anne Forray-Carlier. *Au temps des merveilleuses: La Société parisienne sous le Directoire et le Consulat: Musée carnavalet, histoire de Paris, 9 mars– 12 juin 2005.* Paris, 2005.

Burke, Edmund. *Reflections on the Revolution in France.* Edited by J. G. A. Pocock. Indianapolis, 1987.

Burr, Aaron. *Political Correspondence and Public Papers of Aaron Burr.* Edited by Mary-Jo Kline. 2 vols. Princeton, 1983.

Burstein, Andrew. *The Inner Jefferson: Portrait of a Grieving Optimist.* Charlottesville, 1995.

———. *Sentimental Democracy: The Evolution of America's Romantic Self-Image.* New York, 1999.

Camillus [William Duane]. *The Mississippi Question Fairly Stated, and the Views and Arguments of Those Who Clamor for War, Examined.* Philadelphia, 1803.

Cantor, Milton. "Joel Barlow: Lawyer and Legal Philosopher." *American Quarterly* 10, no. 2 (1958): 165–74.

Cappon, Lester J., ed. *The Adams-Jefferson Letters: The Complete Correspondence between Thomas Jefferson and Abigail and John Adams.* 2 vols. Chapel Hill, 1959.

Carson, John. *The Measure of Merit: Talents, Intelligence, and Inequality in the French and American Republics, 1750–1940.* Princeton, 2007.

Castle, Terry. "Marie-Antoinette Obsession." In *Marie-Antoinette: Writings on the Body of a Queen,* edited by Dena Goodman, 199–238. London, 2003.

Cayton, Andrew R. L. "Radicals in the 'Western World': The Federalist Conquest of Trans-Appalachian North America." In *Federalists Reconsidered,* edited by Doron Ben-Atar and Barbara B. Oberg, 77–96. Charlottesville, 1998.

Chastellux, François-Jean, marquis de. *Travels in North America in the Years 1780, 1781 and 1782.* Translated and edited by Howard C. Rice Jr. 2 vols. Chapel Hill, 1963.

Cheetham, James. *The Life of Thomas Paine, Author of Common Sense, The Crisis, Rights of Man, &c., &c. &c.* New York, 1809.

Cheney, Paul. "A False Dawn for Enlightenment Cosmopolitanism? Franco-American Trade during the American War of Independence." *William and Mary Quarterly* 63, no. 3 (2006): 463–88.

Chew, Samuel C. "A Diary of a Baltimorean of the Eighteenth Century." *Maryland Historical Magazine* 7, no. 4 (1912): 356–74.

Chew, William L. *Das Leben in Frankreich zwischen 1780 und 1815 im Zeugnis Amerikanischer Reisender.* Tübingen, 1986.

——. "Life before Fodor and Frommer: Americans in Paris from Thomas Jefferson to John Quincy Adams." *French History* 18, no. 1 (2004): 25–49.

——, ed. *National Stereotypes in Perspective: Americans in France, Frenchmen in America.* Amsterdam and Atlanta, 2001.

——. "'Straight' Sam meets 'Lewd' Louis: American Perceptions of French Sexuality, 1775–1815." In *Revolutions and Watersheds: Transatlantic Dialogues, 1775–1815,* edited by W. M. Verhoeven and Beth Dolan Kautz, 61–86. Amsterdam, 1999.

Childs, F. S. *French Refugee Life in the United States, 1790–1800.* Baltimore, 1940.

Chinard, Gilbert, ed. *The Letters of Lafayette and Jefferson.* Baltimore and Paris, 1929.

——, ed. *Trois amitiés françaises de Jefferson, d'après sa correspondance inédite avec Madame de Bréhan, Madame de Tessé et Madame de Corny.* Paris, 1927.

——. *Volney et l'Amérique d'après des documents inédits et sa correspondance avec Jefferson.* Baltimore and Paris, 1923.

Clarfield, Gerard H. *Timothy Pickering and American Diplomacy, 1795–1800.* Columbia, MO, 1969.

Clarke, T. W. *Émigrés in the Wilderness.* New York, 1941.

Cobb, Richard, and George Rudé. "Le dernier mouvement populaire de la Révolution à Paris: Les journées de Germinal et de Prairial an III." *Revue Historique* 214, no. 2 (1955): 250–81.

Colley, Linda. *Britons: Forging the Nation, 1707–1837.* New Haven, 1992.

——. "The Difficulties of Empire: Present, Past, and Future." *Historical Research* 79, no. 205 (2006): 367–74.

Combs, Jerald A. *The Jay Treaty: Political Battleground of the Founding Fathers.* Berkeley, 1970.

Conac, Gérard, and Jean-Pierre Machelon, eds. *Constitution de l'An III: Boissy d'Anglas et la naissance du libéralisme constitutionnel.* Paris, 1999.

Cotlar, Seth. "The Federalists' Transatlantic Cultural Offensive of 1798 and the

Moderation of American Democratic Discourse." In *Beyond the Founders: New Approaches to the Political History of the Early American Republic,* edited by Jeffrey L. Pasley, Andrew W. Robertson, and David Waldstreicher, 274–99. Chapel Hill, 2004.

———. "In Paine's Absence: The Trans-Atlantic Dynamics of American Popular Political Thought, 1789–1804." PhD diss., Northwestern University, 2000.

———. "Joseph Gales and the Making of the Jeffersonian Middle Class." In *The Revolution of 1800: Democracy, Race, and the New Republic,* edited by James Horn, Jan Ellen Lewis, and Peter S. Onuf, 331–59. Charlottesville, 2002.

———. "Reading the Foreign News, Imagining an American Public Sphere: Radical and Conservative Visions of 'the Public' in Mid-1790s Newspapers." In *Periodical Literature in Eighteenth-Century America,* edited by Mark L. Kamrath and Sharon M. Harris, 307–38. Knoxville, TN, 2005.

Cott, Nancy F. *Public Vows: A History of Marriage and the Nation.* Cambridge, MA, 2000.

Cox, Henry B. *The Parisian American: Fulwar Skipwith of Virginia.* Washington, DC, 1964.

Crépon, Marc. *Les géographies de l'esprit: Enquête sur la caractérisation des peuples de Leibniz à Hegel.* Paris, 1996.

Crèvecoeur, Michel-Guillaume St. Jean de. *Voyage dans la haute Pensylvanie et dans l'état de New-York, par un membre adoptif de la Nation Onéida.* 3 vols. Paris, An XI [1801].

Crouzet, François. *La grande inflation: La monnaie en France de Louis XVI à Napoléon.* Paris, 1983.

Culver, John C., and John Hyde. *American Dreamer: The Life and Times of Henry A. Wallace.* New York, 2000.

Cunningham, Hugh. "The Language of Patriotism." In *Patriotism: The Making and Unmaking of British National Identity,* edited by Raphael Samuel, 57–89. London, 1989.

Cunningham, Noble E., Jr. *The Jeffersonian Republicans: The Formation of Party Organization, 1789–1801.* Chapel Hill, 1957.

Davis, David Brion. *The Problem of Slavery in the Age of Revolution, 1770–1823.* New York, 1999 [1975].

———. *Revolutions: Reflections on American Equality and Foreign Liberations.* Cambridge, MA, 1990.

DeConde, Alexander. *Entangling Alliances: Politics and Diplomacy under George Washington.* Durham, 1958.

———. *The Quasi-War: The Politics and Diplomacy of the Undeclared War with France, 1797–1801.* New York, 1966.

Denby, David. *Sentimental Narrative and the Social Order in France, 1760–1820.* Cambridge, UK, 1994.

Départ du haut clergé pour l'isle du Scioto. Et ses adieux à l'Assemblée nationale. [Paris], 1791.

Desan, Suzanne. *The Family on Trial in Revolutionary France.* Berkeley, 2004.

Dickinson, John. *The Political Writings of John Dickinson.* Wilmington, DE, 1801.

Dietle, Robert L. "William S. Dallam: An American Tourist in Revolutionary Paris." *Filson Club History Quarterly* 73, no. 2 (1999): 139–65.

Dippel, Horst. *Germany and the American Revolution, 1770–1800: A Sociohistorical Investigation of Late Eighteenth-Century Political Thinking.* Translated by Bernhard A. Uhlendorf. Chapel Hill, 1977.

Dorigny, Marcel. "Violence et révolution: Les Girondins et les Massacres de Septembre." In *Girondins et Montagnards,* edited by Albert Soboul, 103–20. Paris, 1980.

Dos Passos, John. *The Ground We Stand On.* New York, 1941.

Dowling, William C. *Poetry and Ideology in Revolutionary Connecticut.* Athens, GA, 1990.

Doyle, William. *Officers, Nobles, and Revolutionaries: Essays on Eighteenth-Century France.* London, 1995.

———. *The Oxford History of the French Revolution.* Oxford, UK, 1989.

Dujardin, Philippe. "Des États Généraux à l'Assemblée nationale: Figures et formules de l'universalité de Mai à Juin 1789." In *Les mots de la nation,* edited by Sylvianne Rémi-Giraud and Pierre Rétat, 245–59. Lyon, 1996.

Dunn, Susan. *Sister Revolutions: French Lightning, American Light.* New York, 1999.

Durden, Robert F. "Joel Barlow in the French Revolution." *William and Mary Quarterly* 8, no. 3 (1951): 327–54.

Dwyer, Philip G. "Napoleon and the Drive for Glory: Reflections on the Making of French Foreign Policy." In *Napoleon and Europe,* edited by Philip G. Dwyer, 118–35. Harlow and New York, 2001.

Echeverria, Durand. *Mirage in the West: A History of the French Image of American Society to 1815.* Princeton, 1957.

Egerton, Douglas R. *Gabriel's Rebellion: The Virginia Slave Conspiracies of 1800 and 1802.* Chapel Hill, 1993.

Egret, Jean. *La révolution des notables: Mounier et les Monarchiens.* Paris, 1950.

Elkins, Stanley, and Eric McKitrick. *The Age of Federalism.* New York, 1993.

Elliott, Emory. *Revolutionary Writers: Literature and Authority, 1725–1810.* New York, 1982.

Ellis, Joseph J. *American Sphinx: The Character of Thomas Jefferson.* New York, 1997.

Estes, Todd. "Shaping the Politics of Public Opinion: Federalists and the Jay Treaty Debate." *Journal of the Early Republic* 20, no. 3 (2000): 393–422.

Eustace, John Skey. *Traité d'amitié, de commerce et de navigation entre S. M. Britannique et les Etats-Unis d'Amérique.* Paris, An IV [1796].

Falk, Richard A. *The Great Terror War.* New York, 2003.

Farrand, Max, ed. *Records of the Federal Convention.* 4 vols. New Haven, 1937.

Fassiotto, Marie-José. "La Comtesse de Flahaut et son cercle: Un exemple du salon politique sous le Révolution." *Studies on Voltaire and the Eighteenth Century* 303 (1992): 344–48.

Faÿ, Bernard. *L'esprit révolutionnaire en France et aux États-Unis à la fin du XVIIIe siècle.* Paris, 1925.

Felhémési [Jean-Claude Méhée]. *La queue de Robespierre ou les dangers de la liberté de la presse.* Paris, [1795].

Ferguson, E. James. *The Power of the Purse: A History of American Public Finance, 1776–1790.* Chapel Hill, 1961.

Bibliography

Fiechter, Jean-Jacques. *Un diplomate américain sous la Terreur: Les années européennes de Gouverneur Morris, 1789–1798.* Paris, 1983.

Filimonova, M. A. "Eshche raz o thermidore v Amerike." *Amerikanskii ezhegodnik* (1999): 72–83.

Fitzsimmons, Michael P. *The Night the Old Regime Ended: August 4, 1789, and the French Revolution.* University Park, PA, 2003.

Fitzsimons, David M. "Tom Paine's New World Order: Idealistic Internationalism in the Ideology of Early American Foreign Relations." *Diplomatic History* 19, no. 4 (1995): 569–82.

Flavell, Julie M. "American Patriots in London and the Quest for Talks, 1774–1775." *Journal of Imperial and Commonwealth History* 20, no. 3 (1992): 335–69.

Fohlen, Claude. "The Commercial Failure of France in America." In *Two Hundred Years of Franco-American Relations,* edited by Nancy L. Roelker and Charles K. Warner, 93–119. [Raleigh, NC,] 1978.

———. *Jefferson à Paris.* Paris, 1995.

Foner, Eric. *Tom Paine and Revolutionary America.* New York, 1976.

Fontanes, Jean-Pierre Louis, marquis de. *Éloge funèbre de Washington.* [Paris], [1800].

Ford, Washington C., ed. "Letters of William Vans Murray." *Annual Report of the American Historical Association* (1912): 341–708.

Forsyth, Murray. "The Old European State-System: Gentz versus Hauterive." *Historical Journal* 23, no. 3 (1980): 521–38.

———. *Reason and Revolution: The Political Thought of the Abbé Sieyès.* New York, 1987.

Fox-Genovese, Elizabeth, and Eugene D. Genovese. *The Mind of the Master Class: History and Faith in the Southern Slaveholders' Worldview.* Cambridge, UK, 2005.

———. "Political Virtue and the Lessons of the French Revolution: The View from the Slaveholding South." In *Virtue, Corruption, and Self-Interest: Political Values in the 18th Century,* edited by Richard K. Matthews, 202–17. Bethlehem, PA, 1994.

Franklin, Benjamin. *The Papers of Benjamin Franklin.* Edited by Leonard W. Labaree et al. 39 vols. to date. New Haven, 1959–.

Freeman, Joanne B. *Affairs of Honor: National Politics in the New Republic.* New Haven, 2001.

———. "Explaining the Unexplainable: The Cultural Context of the Sedition Act." In *The Democratic Experiment: New Directions in American Political History,* edited by Meg Jacobs, William J. Novak, and Julian E. Zelizer, 20–49. Princeton, 2003.

Furet, François. *Interpreting the French Revolution.* Translated by Elborg Forster. Cambridge, UK, 1981.

Furstenberg, François. *In the Name of the Father: Washington's Legacy, Slavery, and the Making of a Nation.* New York, 2006.

Gauthier, Florence. *Triomphe et mort du droit naturel en révolution, 1789–1795–1802.* Paris, 1992.

Geggus, David P. "Racial Equality, Slavery, and Colonial Secession during the Constituent Assembly." *American Historical Review* 94, no. 5 (1989): 1290–1308.

Gentz, Friedrich von. "Der Ursprung und die Grundsätze der Amerikanischen

Revolution, verglichen mit dem Ursprung und den Grundsätzen der Französischen." *Historisches Journal* 2, no. 2 (1800): 3–140.

——. *The Origins and Principles of the American Revolution, Compared with the Origins and Principles of the French Revolution.* Translated by John Quincy Adams. Philadelphia, 1800.

——. *Von dem Politischen Zustande von Europa vor und nach der Französischen Revoluzion: Eine Prüfung des Buches De l'état de la France à la fin de l'an VIII.* 2 vols. Berlin, 1801.

Gibbs, George, ed. *Memoirs of the Administrations of Washington and John Adams, Edited from the Papers of Oliver Wolcott.* 2 vols. New York, 1846.

Gidney, Lucy M. *L'influence des États-Unis d'Amérique sur Brissot, Condorcet et Mme Roland.* Paris, 1930.

Godechot, Jacques. *The Counter-Revolution: Doctrine and Action, 1789–1804.* Translated by Salvator Attanasio. New York, 1971.

——. *France and the Atlantic Revolution of the Eighteenth Century, 1770–1799.* Translated by Herbert H. Rowen. New York, 1965.

Godwin, William. *Collected Novels and Memoirs of William Godwin.* Edited by Mark Philp. 8 vols. London, 1992.

Goodman, Dena. *The Republic of Letters: A Cultural History of the French Enlightenment.* Ithaca, NY, 1994.

Goodwin, Albert. *The Friends of Liberty: The English Democratic Movement in the Age of the French Revolution.* London, 1979.

Gordon, Daniel. "Citizenship." In *Encyclopedia of the Enlightenment,* edited by Alan Charles Kors, 241–47. Oxford, UK, 2002.

Gordon, Lyndall. *Vindication: A Life of Mary Wollstonecraft.* New York, 2005.

Gordon-Reed, Annette. *The Hemingses of Monticello: An American Family.* New York, 2008.

——. *Thomas Jefferson and Sally Hemings: An American Controversy.* Charlottesville, 1997.

Gottschalk, Louis, ed. *Letters of Lafayette to Washington, 1777–1799.* New York, 1944.

Gottschalk, Louis, and Margaret Maddox. *Lafayette in the French Revolution through the October Days.* Chicago, 1969.

Gould, Eliga H. "Entangled Histories, Entangled Worlds: The English-Speaking Atlantic as a Spanish Periphery." *American Historical Review* 112, no. 3 (2007): 764–86.

——. *The Persistence of Empire: British Political Culture in the Age of the American Revolution.* Chapel Hill, 2000.

Gould, Eliga H., and Peter S. Onuf, eds. *Empire and Nation: The American Revolution in the Atlantic World.* Baltimore, 2005.

Greene, Jack P. "Empire and Identity from the Glorious Revolution to the American Revolution." In *The Oxford History of the British Empire: The Eighteenth Century,* edited by P. J. Marshall, 208–30. Oxford, UK, and New York, 1998.

Grégoire, Henri. *Essai sur la régénération physique, morale et politique des juifs.* Edited by Rita Hermon-Belot. Paris, 1988.

Bibliography

——. *Rapport sur la réunion de la Savoie à la France: Fait au nom des Comités diplomatique et de Constitution.* Paris, 1792.

Grieder, Josephine. *Anglomania in France, 1740–1789: Fact, Fiction, and Political Discourse.* Geneva, 1985.

Griffith, Thomas W. *L'indépendance absolue des Américains des Etats-Unis prouvée par l'état actuel de leur commerce avec les nations européennes.* Paris, An VI/1798.

——. "Reminiscences of an American Gentleman Resident in Paris from 1791 to 1799." In *My Scrap-Book of the French Revolution,* edited by Elizabeth W. Latimer, 9–69. Chicago, 1898.

Griffiths, Robert. *Le centre perdu: Malouet et les "Monarchiens" dans la Révolution française.* Grenoble, 1988.

Gueniffey, Patrice. *La politique de la Terreur: Essai sur la violence révolutionnaire, 1789–1794.* Paris, 2000.

Guiraudon, Virginie. "Cosmopolitanism and National Priority: Attitudes towards Foreigners in France between 1789 and 1794." *History of European Ideas* 13, no. 5 (1991): 591–604.

Hale, Matthew Rainbow. "'Many Who Wandered in Darkness': The Contest over American National Identity, 1795–1798." *Early American Studies* 1, no. 1 (2003): 127–75.

Halliday, E. M. *Understanding Thomas Jefferson.* New York, 2001.

Hamilton, Alexander. *The Papers of Alexander Hamilton.* Edited by Harold C. Syrett. 27 vols. New York, 1961–87.

Hamilton, Keith, and Richard Langhorne. *The Practice of Diplomacy: Its Evolution, Theory and Administration.* London, 1995.

Hammond, John Craig. *Slavery, Freedom, and Expansion in the Early American West.* Charlottesville, 2007.

Hamowy, Ronald. *The Scottish Enlightenment and the Theory of Spontaneous Order.* Carbondale, IL, 1987.

Haraszti, Zoltán. *John Adams and the Prophets of Progress.* Cambridge, MA, 1952.

Harison, Casey. "Teaching the French Revolution: Lessons and Imagery from Nineteenth and Twentieth Century Textbooks." *History Teacher* 35, no. 2 (2002): 137–62.

Harsanyi, Doina Pasca, ed. *Lettres de la duchesse de La Rochefoucauld à William Short.* Paris, 2001.

Hase, Alexander von. "John Quincy Adams als Kritiker von Hauterive und Gentz (1801): Ein amerikanischer Beitrag zu einem europäischen Gespräch." *Historische Zeitschrift* 215 (1972): 33–48.

Hauterive, Alexandre-Maurice Blanc de Lanautte, comte d'. *De l'etat de la France à la fin de l'An VIII.* Paris, An 9 [1800].

Helo, Ari, and Peter Onuf. "Jefferson, Morality, and the Problem of Slavery." *William and Mary Quarterly* 60, no. 3 (2003): 583–614.

Hendrickson, David C. *Peace Pact: The Lost World of the American Founding.* Lawrence, KS, 2003.

Hesse, Carla. *The Other Enlightenment: How French Women Became Modern.* Princeton, 2001.

Bibliography

Heuer, Jennifer N. *The Family and the Nation: Gender and Citizenship in Revolutionary France, 1789–1830.* Ithaca, NY, 2005.

Heydenau, Friedrich. *Gouvero.* Berchtesgaden, 1953.

Higonnet, Patrice. *Goodness beyond Virtue: Jacobins during the French Revolution.* Cambridge, MA, 1998.

———. *Sister Republics: The Origins of French and American Republicanism.* Cambridge, MA, 1988.

Hill, Peter P. "La suite imprévue de l'Alliance: L'ingratitude américaine, 1783–1798." In *La Révolution américaine et l'Europe,* edited by Claude Fohlen and Jacques Godechot, 385–98. Paris, 1979.

Hoar, George F., ed. "A Famous Fête." *Proceedings of the American Antiquarian Society* 12 (April 1898): 240–59.

Höfer, Annete. "Agiotage, Agioteur." In *Handbuch politisch-sozialer Grundbegriffe in Frankreich, 1680–1820,* edited by Rolf Reichardt and Eberhard Schmitt, 12: 7–30. Munich, 1985–96.

Hofstadter, Richard. *The Idea of a Party System: The Rise of Legitimate Opposition in the United States, 1780–1840.* Berkeley, 1969.

Horn, James, Jan Ellen Lewis, and Peter S. Onuf, eds. *The Revolution of 1800: Democracy, Race, and the New Republic.* Charlottesville, 2002.

Horsman, Reginald. "The Dimensions of an 'Empire for Liberty': Expansion and Republicanism, 1775–1825." *Journal of the Early Republic* 9, no. 1 (1989): 1–20.

Howard, Leon. *The Connecticut Wits.* Chicago, 1943.

Howell, T. B., and Thomas Jones Howell, eds. *A Complete Collection of State Trials, and Proceedings, for High Treason, and Other Crimes and Misdemeanors.* 33 vols. London, 1816–26.

Hulliung, Mark. *Citizens and Citoyens: Republicans and Liberals in America and France.* Cambridge, MA, 2002.

Humphreys, David, et al. *The Anarchiad: A New England Poem, 1786–1787.* Edited by Luther G. Riggs. Gainesville, FL, 1967.

Hunt, Lynn. "Male Virtue and Republican Motherhood." In *The French Revolution and the Creation of Modern Political Culture,* edited by Keith Michael Baker, 4: 195–209. Oxford, UK, 1987–94.

———. *Politics, Culture, and Class in the French Revolution.* Berkeley, 1984.

Hunt, Lynn, David Lansky, and Paul Hanson. "The Failure of the Liberal Republic in France, 1795–1799: The Road to Brumaire." *Journal of Modern History* 51, no. 4 (1979): 734–59.

Hunt, Michael. *Ideology and U.S. Foreign Policy.* New Haven, 1987.

Hyslop, Beatrice F. "American Press Reports of the French Revolution, 1789–1794." *New-York Historical Society Quarterly* 42, no. 4 (1958): 329–48.

Jacob, Margaret C. *Strangers Nowhere in the World: The Rise of Cosmopolitanism in Early Modern Europe.* Philadelphia, 2006.

Jainchill, Andrew. "The Constitution of the Year III and the Persistence of Classical Republicanism." *French Historical Studies* 26, no. 3 (2003): 399–435.

Bibliography

Jefferson, Thomas. *The Papers of Thomas Jefferson, Retirement Series.* Edited by J. Jefferson Looney. 5 vols. to date. Princeton, 2004-.

——. *Thomas Jefferson: Writings.* Edited by Merrill Peterson. New York, 1984.

——. *The Works of Thomas Jefferson.* Edited by Paul Leicester Ford. 12 vols. New York, 1904-5.

Jones, Howard M. *America and French Culture, 1750-1848.* Chapel Hill, 1927.

Jones, Robert F. *"The King of the Alley": William Duer: Politician, Entrepreneur, and Speculator, 1768-1799.* Philadelphia, 1992.

Jordan, David P. *The Revolutionary Career of Maximilien Robespierre.* New York, 1985.

Jordan, Winthrop D. *White over Black: American Attitudes toward the Negro, 1550-1812.* Chapel Hill, 1968.

Jourdan, Annie. *La révolution, une exception française?* Paris, 2004.

Kale, Steven. *French Salons: High Society and Political Sociability from the Old Regime to the Revolution of 1848.* Baltimore, 2004.

Kammen, Michael. *A Season of Youth: The American Revolution and the Historical Imagination.* Ithaca, NY, 1978.

Kaplan, Lawrence S. *Entangling Alliances with None: American Foreign Policy in the Age of Jefferson.* Kent, OH, 1987.

——. *Jefferson and France: An Essay on Politics and Political Ideas.* New Haven, 1967.

——. "Jefferson and the Constitution: The View from Paris, 1786-1789." *Diplomatic History* 11, no. 4 (1987): 321-335.

Kastor, Peter J. *The Nation's Crucible: The Louisiana Purchase and the Creation of America.* New Haven, 2004.

Kates, Gary. *The Cercle Social, the Girondins, and the French Revolution.* Princeton, 1985.

——. "From Liberalism to Radicalism: Tom Paine's *Rights of Man.*" *Journal of the History of Ideas* 50, no. 4 (1989): 569-87.

Kaufman, Arthur P. "The Constitutional Views of Gouverneur Morris." PhD diss., Georgetown University, 1992.

Kelleter, Frank. *Amerikanische Aufklärung: Sprachen der Rationalität im Zeitalter der Revolution.* Paderborn, 2002.

Kennedy, Emmet. *A Philosophe in the Age of the Revolution: Destutt de Tracy and the Origins of "Ideology."* Philadelphia, 1978.

Kerber, Linda K. *Women of the Republic: Intellect and Ideology in Revolutionary America.* Chapel Hill, 1980.

Kessel, Patrick. *La nuit du 4 Août 1789.* Paris, 1969.

Kimball, Marie. *Jefferson on the Scene of Europe, 1784 to 1789.* New York, 1950.

Kirschke, James J. *Gouverneur Morris: Author, Statesman, and Man of the World.* New York, 2005.

Knott, Sarah. *Sensibility and the American Revolution.* Chapel Hill, 2009.

——. "Sensibility and the American War for Independence." *American Historical Review* 109, no. 1 (2004): 19-40.

Knudson, Jerry W. *Jefferson and the Press: Crucible of Liberty.* Columbia, SC, 2006.

Koschnik, Albrecht. "The Democratic Societies of Philadelphia and the Limits of the

American Public Sphere, circa 1793–1795." *William and Mary Quarterly* 58, no. 3 (2001): 615–36.

Kramer, Lloyd S. "American Political Culture." In *The Global Ramifications of the French Revolution,* edited by Joseph Klaits and Michael H. Haltzel, 26–54. Cambridge, UK, 1994.

——. *Lafayette in Two Worlds: Public Cultures and Personal Identities in an Age of Revolution.* Chapel Hill, 1996.

——. *Threshold of a New World: Intellectuals and the Exile Experience, 1830–1848.* Ithaca, NY, 1988.

——. "Traveling through Revolutions: Chastellux, Barlow, and Transatlantic Political Culture." In *Revolutionary Histories: Transatlantic Cultural Nationalism, 1775–1815,* edited by W. M. Verhoeven, 10–25. Houndmills, Basingstoke, and New York, 2002.

Kuehl, John W. "Southern Reactions to the XYZ Affair: An Incident in the Emergence of American Nationalism." *Kentucky State Historical Society Register* 70 (January 1972): 21–49.

Kulikoff, Allan. "Revolutionary Violence and the Origins of American Democracy." *Journal of the Historical Society* 2, no. 2 (2002): 229–60.

Lefebvre, Georges. *The Thermidorians and the Directory: Two Phases of the French Revolution.* Translated by Robert Baldick. New York, 1964.

Leith, James A. "Le culte de Franklin avant et pendant la Révolution française." *Annales historique de la Révolution française* 48, no. 4 (1976): 543–71.

Lemay, Edna Hindie. "Lafitau, Démeunier, and the Rejection of the American Model at the French National Assembly, 1789–1791." In *Images of America in Revolutionary France,* edited by Michèle R. Morris, 171–84. Washington, DC, 1990.

Lettre écrite par un françois émigrant au Scioto. New York [Paris?], 1790.

Levenstein, Harvey. *Seductive Journeys: American Tourists in France from Jefferson to the Jazz Age.* Chicago, 1986.

Lewis, James E., Jr. *The American Union and the Problem of Neighborhood: The United States and the Collapse of the Spanish Empire, 1783–1829.* Chapel Hill, 1998.

——. *The Louisiana Purchase: Jefferson's Noble Bargain?* Charlottesville and Chapel Hill, 2003.

Lewis, Jan. *The Pursuit of Happiness: Family and Values in Jefferson's Virginia.* New York, 1983.

——. "'Those Scenes for Which Alone My Heart Was Made': Affection and Politics in the Age of Jefferson and Hamilton." In *An Emotional History of the United States,* edited by Peter N. Stearns and Jan Lewis, 52–65. New York, 1998.

Lezay-Marnezia, Adrien de. *Qu'est-ce que la Constitution de 93?* Paris, An III [1795].

Link, Eugene P. *Democratic-Republican Societies, 1790–1800.* Morningside Heights, NY, 1942.

Livesey, James. *Making Democracy in the French Revolution.* Cambridge, MA, 2001.

Livingston, Robert. *The Original Letters of Robert R. Livingston, 1801–1803.* Edited by Edward A. Parsons. New Orleans, 1953.

Logan, Deborah N. *Memoir of Dr. George Logan of Stenton.* Edited by Frances A. Logan. Philadelphia, 1899.

Longstreet, Stephen. *We All Went To Paris: Americans in the City of Lights, 1776–1971.* New York, 1972.

Loughran, Trish. *The Republic in Print: Print Culture in the Age of U.S. Nation Building, 1770–1870.* New York, 2007.

Lutz, Donald S. "The Relative Influence of European Thinkers on Late Eighteenth-Century American Political Thought." *American Political Science Review* 78, no. 1 (1984): 189–97.

Lyon, E. Wilson. *Louisiana in French Diplomacy, 1759–1804.* Norman, 1934.

Lyons, Martyn. *France under the Directory.* Cambridge, UK, 1975.

Madison, James. *The Papers of James Madison.* Edited by William T. Hutchinson et al. 17 vols. Chicago and Charlottesville, 1962–91.

Magruder, Allan Bowie. *Political, Commercial and Moral Reflections, on the Late Cession of Louisiana, to the United States.* Lexington, KY, 1803.

Malia, Martin. *History's Locomotives: Revolutions and the Making of the Modern World.* Edited by Terence Emmons. New Haven, 2006.

Malone, Dumas. *Jefferson and the Ordeal of Liberty.* Boston, 1946.

——. *Jefferson and the Rights of Man.* Boston, 1951.

Manin, Bernard. "Montesquieu." In *A Critical Dictionary of the French Revolution,* edited by François Furet and Mona Ozouf, translated by Arthur Goldhammer, 728–41. Cambridge, MA, 1989.

Marat, Jean-Paul. *Oeuvres politiques, 1789–1793.* Edited by Jacques de Cock and Charlotte Goëtz. 10 vols. Bruxelles, 1989–95.

Marienstras, Elise, ed. *L'Amérique et la France: Deux révolutions.* Paris, 1990.

——. "Joel Barlow, de Redding (1754) à Zarnowiec (1812): Rêves cosmopolitiques et cauchemars tyranniques d'un Américain de bonne volonté." *Revue Française d'Etudes Américaines* 92 (May 2002): 68–85.

Marienstras, Elise, and Naomi Wulf. "French Translations and Reception of the Declaration of Independence." *Journal of American History* 85, no. 4 (1999): 1299–1315.

Marks, Frederick. *Independence on Trial: Foreign Affairs and the Making of the Constitution.* Baton Rouge, 1973.

Marshall, John. *The Papers of John Marshall.* Edited by Herbert A. Johnson et al. 12 vols. Chapel Hill, 1974–2006.

Marshall, Peter H. *William Godwin.* New Haven, 1984.

Mathiez, Albert. *The French Revolution.* Translated by Catherine Alison Phillips. New York, 1962.

——. *La Révolution et les étrangers: Cosmopolitisme et défense nationale.* Paris, 1918.

Maurice, René. *Des Américains à Paris: De Benjamin Franklin à Ernest Hemingway.* Paris, 2004.

May, Gita. *Madame Roland and the Age of Revolution.* New York, 1970.

May, Henry F. *The Enlightenment in America.* New York, 1976.

Mayer, Arno J. *The Furies: Violence and Terror in the French and Russian Revolutions.* Princeton, 2000.

Mayer, David N. *The Constitutional Thought of Thomas Jefferson.* Charlottesville, 1994.

Mayo, Bernard. "Joshua Barney and the French Revolution." *Maryland Historical Magazine* 36, no. 4 (1941): 357–62.

McCoy, Drew R. *The Elusive Republic: Political Economy in Jeffersonian America.* Chapel Hill, 1980.

McKee, Kenneth N. "The Popularity of the 'American' on the French Stage during the Revolution." *Proceedings of the American Philosophical Society* 83 (September 1940): 479–91.

McMahon, Lucia F. "'The harmony of social life': Gender, Education, and Society in the Early Republic." PhD diss., Rutgers The State University of New Jersey–New Brunswick, 2004.

Miller, John C. *Crisis in Freedom: The Alien and Sedition Acts.* Boston, 1951.

——. *The Federalist Era, 1789–1801.* New York, 1963.

Miller, John J., and Mark Molesky. *Our Oldest Enemy: A History of America's Disastrous Relationship with France.* New York, 2004.

Miller, Melanie R. *Envoy to the Terror: Gouverneur Morris and the French Revolution.* Dulles, VA, 2005.

——. "Gouverneur Morris and the French Revolution, 1789–1794." PhD diss., George Washington University, 2000.

Miller, Victor C. *Joel Barlow: Revolutionist, London 1791–2.* Hamburg, 1932.

Mintz, Max M. *Gouverneur Morris and the American Revolution.* Norman, 1970.

Monroe, James. *The Autobiography of James Monroe.* Edited by Stuart Gerry Brown. Syracuse, NY, 1959.

——. *A View of the Conduct of the Executive, in the Foreign Affairs of the United States Connected with the Mission to the French Republic During the Years 1794, 5 & 6.* Philadelphia, 1797.

——. *The Writings of James Monroe.* Edited by Stanislaus Hamilton. 7 vols. New York, 1898–1903.

Montesquieu, Charles-Louis de Secondat, baron de. *The Spirit of the Laws.* Translated and edited by Anne M. Cohler et al. Cambridge, UK, 1989.

Moulin, Jean-Pierre. *L'amant américain: Roman.* Paris, 1992.

Mounier, Jean-Joseph. *Considerations sur les gouvernemens, et principalement sur celui qui convient a la France.* Paris, 1789.

——. *Exposé de la conduite dans l'Assemblée nationale; et motifs de mon retour en Dauphiné.* Paris, 1789.

——. *Motifs présentés dans la séance de l'Assemblée nationale du 4 Septembre 1789, au nom du Comité de Constitution.* Versailles, [1789].

——. *Nouvelles observations sur les Etats-généraux de France.* [Paris], 1789.

Moustier, Elénore-François-Elie, comte de. *Lettre de M. de Moustier, Ministre de Roi auprès des Etats-Unis, à l'Assemblée nationale: Séance de 2 Août 1790.* Paris, 1790.

Bibliography

Mulford, Carla J. "Joel Barlow's Letters, 1775–1788." PhD diss., University of Delaware, 1983.

——. "Radicalism in Joel Barlow's The Conspiracy of Kings (1792)." In *Deism, Masonry, and the Enlightenment,* edited by J. A. Leo Lemay, 137–57. Newark, 1987.

Mullan, John. *Sentiment and Sociability: The Language of Feeling in the Eighteenth Century.* Oxford, UK, 1988.

Nash, Gary B. "The American Clergy and the French Revolution." *William and Mary Quarterly* 22, no. 3 (1965): 392–412.

Nedelsky, Jennifer. *Private Property and the Limits of American Constitutionalism.* Chicago, 1990.

Newman, Simon P. "American Political Culture and the French and Haitian Revolutions: Nathaniel Cutting and the Jefferson Republicans." In *The Impact of the Haitian Revolution in the Atlantic World,* edited by David P. Geggus, 72–89. Columbia, SC, 2001.

——. *Parades, Festivals, and the Politics of the Street: Popular Political Culture in the Early American Republic.* Philadelphia, 1997.

——. "Writing the History of the American Revolution." In *The State of U.S. History,* edited by Melvyn Stokes, 23–44. Oxford, UK, and New York, 2002.

Nora, Pierre, and Alain Clement. "L'Amérique et la France: Deux révolutions et deux mondes." In *La Révolution américaine et l'Europe,* edited by Claude Fohlen and Jacques Godechot, 329–40. Paris, 1979.

O'Brien, Conor Cruise. *The Long Affair: Thomas Jefferson and the French Revolution, 1785–1800.* Chicago, 1996.

Oedel, William T. "John Vanderlyn: French Neoclassicism and the Search for an American Art." PhD diss., University of Delaware, 1981.

Olsen, Mark. "Enlightened Nationalism in the Early Revolution: The Nation in the Language of the Société de 1789." *Canadian Journal of History* 29, no. 1 (1994): 23–50.

——. "A Failure of Enlightened Politics in the French Revolution: The Société de 1789." *French History* 6, no. 3 (1992): 303–34.

Onuf, Peter S. *Jefferson's Empire: The Language of American Nationhood.* Charlottesville, 2000.

Onuf, Peter, and Nicholas Onuf. *Federal Union, Modern World: The Law of Nations in an Age of Revolution, 1776–1814.* Madison, 1993.

——. *Nations, Markets, and War: Modern History and the American Civil War.* Charlottesville, 2006.

Osterhammel, Jürgen, and Niels P. Peterson. *Globalization: A Short History.* Translated by Dona Geyer. Princeton, 2005.

Otis, Harrison Gray. *The Life and Letters of Harrison Gray Otis.* Edited by Samuel E. Morrison. 2 vols. Boston, 1913.

Ozouf, Mona. *L'école de la France: Essais sur la Révolution, l'utopie et l'enseignement.* Paris, 1984.

——. *L'homme régénéré: Essais sur la Révolution française.* Paris, 1989.

——. "Regeneration." In *A Critical Dictionary of the French Revolution,* edited by

François Furet and Mona Ozouf, translated by Arthur Goldhammer, 781-91. Cambridge, MA, 1989.

———. "The Terror after the Terror: An Immediate History." In *The French Revolution and the Creation of Modern Political Culture,* edited by Keith Michael Baker, 4: 3-18. Oxford, UK, 1987-94.

Paine, Thomas. *Compact Maritime.* Washington, DC, 1801.

———. *The Complete Writings of Thomas Paine.* Edited by Philip S. Foner. 2 vols. New York, 1945.

———. *Letter to the People of France, and the French Armies, on the Event of the 18th Fructi-dor—Sep. 4—and its Consequences.* New York, 1798.

Palmer, Robert R. *The Age of the Democratic Revolution.* 2 vols. Princeton, 1959-64.

———. *Twelve Who Ruled: The Year of the Terror in the French Revolution.* Princeton, NJ, 1989 [1941].

Le Parlement de Paris établi au Scioto. Paris, 1790.

Pasley, Jeffrey L. *"The Tyranny of Printers": Newspaper Politics in the Early American Republic.* Charlottesville, 2001.

Perkins, Thomas H. *Memoirs of Thomas Handasyd Perkins.* Edited by Thomas G. Cary. Boston, 1856.

Philip, Cynthia Owen. *Robert Fulton: A Biography.* New York, 1985.

Philips, Edith. *The Good Quaker in French Legend.* Philadelphia, 1932.

Pitts, Jennifer. *A Turn to Empire: The Rise of Imperial Liberalism in Britain and France.* Princeton, 2005.

Plon, Henri, and J. Dumaine, eds. *Correspondance de Napoléon Ier.* 32 vols. Paris, 1858-70.

Plumer, William. *William Plumer's Memorandum of Proceedings in the United States Senate, 1803-1807.* Edited by Everett Somerville Brown. New York, 1923.

Potofsky, Allan. "The Political Economy of the French-American Debt Debate: The Ideological Uses of Atlantic Commerce, 1787 to 1800." *William and Mary Quarterly* 63, no. 3 (2006): 489-516.

Purcell, Sarah J. *Sealed with Blood: War, Sacrifice, and Memory in Revolutionary America.* Philadelphia, 2002.

Racine, Karen. *Francisco de Miranda: A Transatlantic Life in the Age of Revolution.* Wilmington, DE, 2002.

Radcliffe, Evan. "Burke, Radical Cosmopolitanism, and the Debate on Patriotism in the 1790s." *Studies in Eighteenth-Century Culture* 28 (1999): 311-39.

———. "Revolutionary Writing, Moral Philosophy, and Universal Benevolence in the Eighteenth Century." *Journal of the History of Ideas* 54, no. 2 (1993): 221-40.

Rakove, Jack N. "Why American Constitutionalism Worked." In *Reflections on the Revolution in France,* edited by Frank M. Turner, 248-67. New Haven, 2003.

Randall, Jane. "Feminizing the Enlightenment: The Problem of Sensibility." In *The Enlightenment World,* edited by Martin Fitzpatrick et al., 253-71. London, 2004.

Rapport, Michael. *Nationality and Citizenship in Revolutionary France: The Treatment of Foreigners, 1789-1799.* Oxford, UK, 2000.

Ray, Thomas M. "'Not One Cent for Tribute': The Public Addresses and American

Popular Reaction to the XYZ Affair, 1798–1799." *Journal of the Early Republic* 3, no. 4 (1983): 389–412.

Raynaud, Philippe. "The American Revolution." In *A Critical Dictionary of the French Revolution,* edited by François Furet and Mona Ozouf, translated by Arthur Goldhammer, 593–603. Cambridge, MA, 1989.

Règlements de la Société de 1789 et Liste de ses Membres. Paris, 1790.

Revel, Jean-François. *L'obsession anti-américaine.* Paris, 2002.

Rice, Howard C., Jr. *Thomas Jefferson's Paris.* Princeton, 1976.

Richmond, Arthur A. "Napoleon and the Armed Neutrality of 1800: A Diplomatic Challenge to British Sea Power." *Journal of the Royal United Service Institution* 104 (May 1959): 186–94.

Roberts, Timothy M. "'Revolutions Have Become the Bloody Toy of the Multitude': European Revolutions, the South, and the Crisis of 1850." *Journal of the Early Republic* 25, no. 2 (2005): 259–83.

Robespierre, Maximilien. *Œuvres de Maximilien Robespierre.* Edited by Marc Bouloiseau and Albert Soboul. 10 vols. Paris, 1958–67.

Robinson, Blackwell P. *William R. Davie.* Chapel Hill, 1957.

Roger, Philippe. *The American Enemy: A Story of French Anti-Americanism.* Translated by Sharon Bowman. Chicago, 2005.

Roland de La Platière, Manon-Jeanne Philipon. *Mémoires de Mme Roland.* Edited by Claude Perroud. Paris, 1905.

Rosenfeld, Sophia. "Citizens of Nowhere in Particular: Cosmopolitanism, Writing, and Political Engagement in Eighteenth-Century Europe." *National Identities* 4, no. 1 (2002): 25–43.

———. *A Revolution in Language: The Problem of Signs in Late Eighteenth-Century France.* Stanford, 2001.

Rossignol, Marie-Jeanne. *The Nationalist Ferment: The Origins of U.S. Foreign Policy, 1789–1812.* Translated by Lillian A. Parrott. Columbus, OH, 2004.

Rothschild, Emma. "Language and Empire, c. 1800." *Historical Research* 78, no. 200 (2005): 208–29.

Roux. *Le nouveau Mississippi, ou les Dangers d'habiter les bords du Scioto, par un patriote voyageur.* Paris, 1790.

Royster, Charles. *A Revolutionary People at War: The Continental Army and American Character, 1775–1783.* Chapel Hill, 1979.

Rudé, George. *The Crowd in the French Revolution.* Oxford, UK, 1959.

Sa'adah, Anne. *The Shaping of Liberal Politics in Revolutionary France: A Comparative Perspective.* Princeton, 1990.

Sahlins, Peter. *Unnaturally French: Foreign Citizens in the Old Regime and After.* Ithaca, NY, 2004.

Saler, Bethel. "An Empire for Liberty, a State for Empire: The U.S. National State before and after the Revolution of 1800." In *The Revolution of 1800: Democracy, Race, and the New Republic,* edited by James Horn, Jan Ellen Lewis, and Peter S. Onuf, 360–82. Charlottesville, 2002.

Bibliography

Saricks, Ambrose. *Pierre Samuel Du Pont de Nemours.* Lawrence, KS, 1965.

Scanlon, James E. "A Sudden Conceit: Jefferson and the Louisiana Government Bill of 1804." *Louisiana History* 9, no. 2 (1968): 139-62.

Scherr, Arthur. "The Limits of Republican Ideology: James Monroe in Thermidorian Paris, 1794-1796." *Mid-America* 79, no. 1 (1997): 5-45.

Schlereth, Thomas J. *The Cosmopolitan Ideal in Enlightenment Thought.* Notre Dame, IN, 1977.

Scrivener, Michael. *The Cosmopolitan Ideal in the Age of Revolution and Reaction, 1776-1832.* London, 2007.

Sepinwall, Alyssa Goldstein. *The Abbé Grégoire and the French Revolution: The Making of Modern Universalism.* Berkeley, 2005.

Sewell, William H., Jr. "The French Revolution and the Emergence of the Nation Form." In *Revolutionary Currents: Nation Building in the Transatlantic World,* edited by Michael A. Morrison and Melinda Zook, 91-125. Lanham, MD, 2004.

Shackelford, George Green. *Jefferson's Adoptive Son: The Life of William Short, 1759-1848.* Lexington, KY, 1993.

Sharp, James Roger. *American Politics in the Early Republic: The New Nation in Crisis.* New Haven, 1993.

Sheehan, Colleen A. "Madison and the French Enlightenment: The Authority of Public Opinion." *William and Mary Quarterly* 59, no. 4 (2002): 925-57.

Sheridan, Eugene R. "The Recall of Edmond Charles Genet: A Study in Transatlantic Politics and Diplomacy." *Diplomatic History* 18, no. 4 (1994): 463-88.

Sieyès, Emmanuel-Joseph. *Ébauche d'un nouveau plan de Société patriotique, adopté par le Club de Mil-sept-cent-quatre-vingt-neuf.* Paris, [1789].

——. *Emmanuel Joseph Sieyès: Political Writings.* Edited by Michael Sonenscher. Indianapolis, 2003.

Sloan, Herbert E. *Principle and Interest: Thomas Jefferson and the Problem of Debt.* New York, 1995.

Sluga, Glenda. "The Nation and the Comparative Imagination." In *Comparison and History: Europe in Cross-National Perspective,* edited by Deborah Cohen and Maura O'Connor, 103-14. New York, 2004.

Smith, James Morton. *Freedom's Fetters: The Alien and Sedition Laws and American Civil Liberties.* Ithaca, NY, 1956.

Smith, Rogers M. "Constructing American National Identity: Strategies of the Federalists." In *Federalists Reconsidered,* edited by Doron Ben-Atar and Barbara B. Oberg, 19-40. Charlottesville, 1998.

Songe d'un habitant du Scioto, publié par lui-même. Paris, 1790.

Spang, Rebecca L. "The Frivolous French: 'Liberty of Pleasure' and the End of Luxury." In *Taking Liberties: Problems of a New Order from the French Revolution to Napoleon,* edited by Howard G. Brown and Judith A. Miller, 110-25. Manchester, 2002.

Sparks, Jared, ed. *The Life of Gouverneur Morris with Selections from his Correspondence and Miscellaneous Papers.* 3 vols. Boston, 1832.

Spurlin, Paul M. *Montesquieu in America, 1760-1801.* Baton Rouge, 1940.

Staum, Martin S. *Cabanis: Enlightenment and Medical Philosophy in the French Revolution.* Princeton, 1980.

Steele, Brian. "Thomas Jefferson's Gender Frontier." *Journal of American History* 95, no. 1 (2008): 17–42.

Stern, Madeleine. *Studies in the Franco-American Booktrade during the Late 18th and Early 19th Centuries.* London, 1994.

Stewart, Joan Hinde. "The Novelists and Their Fiction." In *French Women and the Age of Enlightenment,* edited by Samia I. Spencer, 197–211. Bloomington, IN, 1984.

Stinchcombe, William C. *The XYZ Affair.* Westport, CT, 1980.

Stine, Geoffrey R. *Perilous Times: Free Speech in Wartime from the Sedition Act of 1798 to the War on Terrorism.* New York, 2004.

Stourzh, Gerald. "The Declaration of Rights: Popular Sovereignty and the Supremacy of the Constitution. Divergences between the American and the French Revolutions." In *La Révolution américaine et l'Europe,* edited by Claude Fohlen and Jacques Godechot, 347–67. Paris, 1979.

Swift, Jonathan. *Gulliver's Travels.* Edited by Albert J. Rivero. New York, 2002.

Sydenham, M. J. *The Girondins.* London, 1961.

Tacitus [Thomas Evans]. *A Series of Letters to Thomas Jefferson, Esq., President of the United States, concerning His Official Conduct and Principles.* Philadelphia, 1802.

Tackett, Timothy. *Becoming a Revolutionary: The Deputies of the French National Assembly and the Emergence of a Revolutionary Culture (1789–1790).* Princeton, 1996.

———. *When the King Took Flight.* Cambridge, MA, 2003.

Tagg, James. *Benjamin Franklin Bache and the Philadelphia* Aurora. Philadelphia, 1991.

Talleyrand-Périgord, Charles-Maurice de. *Talleyrand's Defence. Strictures on the American State Papers Delivered by the President of the United States, to the American Congress, on April 5 1798.* London, 1798.

Tan, Kok-Chor. *Justice without Borders: Cosmopolitanism, Nationalism, and Patriotism.* Cambridge, UK, 2004.

Tansill, Charles C., ed. *Documents Illustrative of the Formation of the Union of the American States.* Washington, DC, 1927.

Thiesse, Anne-Marie. *La création des identités nationales: Europe XVIIIe–XXe siècle.* Paris, 1999.

Thompson, C. Bradley. "The American Founding and the French Revolution." In *The Legacy of the French Revolution,* edited by Ralph C. Hancock and L. Gary Lambert, 109–50. Lanham, MD, 1996.

Thompson, E. P. *The Making of the English Working Class.* London, 1963.

Todorov, Tzvetan. *On Human Diversity: Nationalism, Racism, and Exoticism in French Thought.* Translated by Catherine Porter. Cambridge, MA, 1993.

Tolles, Frederick B. *George Logan of Philadelphia.* New York, 1953.

Trumbull, John. *The Autobiography of Colonel John Trumbull, Patriot-Artist, 1756–1843.* Edited by Theodore Sizer. New Haven, 1953.

Tucker, Robert W., and David C. Hendrickson. *Empire of Liberty: The Statecraft of Thomas Jefferson.* New York, 1990.

Unger, Harlow G. *The French War against America: How a Trusted Ally Betrayed Washington and the Founding Fathers.* Hoboken, NJ, 2005.

United States. *Treaties and Other International Acts of the United States of America.* Edited by Hunter Miller. 8 vols. Washington, DC, 1931–48.

United States. Congress. *Debates and Proceedings in the Congress of the United States.* 42 vols. Washington, DC, 1834–56.

——. *Journal of the Senate of the United States.* 5 vols. Washington, DC, 1820–21.

United States. Department of State. Despatches from United States Ministers to France, 1789–1906 (microfilm).

Vagts, Detlev F. "The Logan Act: Paper Tiger or Sleeping Giant?" *American Journal of International Law* 60, no. 2 (1966): 268–302.

Vidal, Cécile. "The Reluctance of French Historians to Address Atlantic History." *Southern Quarterly* 43, no. 4 (2006): 153–89.

Vila, Anne C. *Enlightenment and Pathology: Sensibility in the Literature and Medicine of Eighteenth-Century France.* Baltimore, 1999.

Vincent, Bernard. "Les Américains à Paris sous la Révolution: Mythes et réalités." In *Thomas Paine ou la république sans frontières,* edited by Bernard Vincent, 87–103. Nancy and Paris, 1993.

Vincent-Buffault, Anne. *The History of Tears: Sensibility and Sentimentality in France.* Translated by Teresa Bridgeman. London, 1991.

Vyverberg, Henry. *Human Nature, Cultural Diversity, and the French Enlightenment.* New York, 1989.

Wahnich, Sophie. *L'impossible citoyen: L'étranger dans le discours de la Révolution française.* Paris, 1997.

Waldstreicher, David, *In the Midst of Perpetual Fetes: The Making of American Nationalism, 1776–1820.* Chapel Hill, 1997.

Washington, George. *George Washington: Writings.* Edited by John Rhodehamel. New York, 1997.

——. *The Papers of George Washington: Presidential Series.* Edited by Dorothy Twohig et al. 14 vols. to date. Charlottesville, 1987–.

——. *The Writings of George Washington.* Edited by John C. Fitzpatrick. 39 vols. Washington, DC, 1931–44.

The Washingtoniana: Containing a Biographical Sketch of the Late Gen. George Washington, with various Outlines of his Character, from the Pens of different eminent Writers, both in Europe and America. Baltimore, 1800.

Watson, Elkanah. *Men and Times of the Revolution; or, Memoirs of Elkanah Watson.* Edited by Winslow C. Watson. New York, 1856.

Watts, Steven. *The Republic Reborn: War and the Making of Liberal America, 1790–1820.* Baltimore, 1987.

Webster, Noah. *Letters of Noah Webster.* Edited by Harry Warfel. New York, 1953.

Werner, Michael, and Bénédicte Zimmermann. "Beyond Comparison: *Histoire Croisée* and the Challenge of Reflexivity." *History and Theory* 45, no. 1 (2006): 30–50.

——. "Vergleich, Transfer, Verflechtung. Der Ansatz der Histoire croisée und die Herausforderung des Transnationalen." *Geschichte und Gesellschaft* 28, no. 4 (2002): 607-36.

Whatmore, Richard. "'A gigantic manliness': Paine's Republicanism in the 1790s." In *Economy, Polity, and Society,* edited by Stefan Collini et al., 135-57. Cambridge, UK, 2000.

Williams, Helen Maria. *Letters Written in France in the Summer of 1790.* London, 1790.

Winik, Jay. *The Great Upheaval: America and the Birth of the Modern World, 1788-1800.* New York, 2007.

Wolff, Larry. *Inventing Eastern Europe: The Map of Civilization on the Mind of the Enlightenment.* Stanford, 1994.

Woloch, Isser. *Jacobin Legacy: The Democratic Movement under the Directory.* Princeton, 1970.

——. *Napoleon and His Collaborators: The Making of a Dictatorship.* New York, 2001.

——. "The Napoleonic Regime and French Society." In *Napoleon and Europe,* edited by Philip G. Dwyer, 60-78. Harlow and New York, 2001.

——. *The New Regime: Transformations of the French Civic Order, 1789-1820s.* New York, 1994.

——. "On the Latent Illiberalism of the French Revolution." *American Historical Review* 95, no. 5 (1990): 1452-70.

Wood, Gordon S. "The Origins of the American Bill of Rights." *La Revue Tocqueville/ The Tocqueville Review* 14, no. 1 (1993): 33-47.

——. *The Radicalism of the American Revolution.* New York, 1991.

Woodress, James L. *A Yankee's Odyssey: The Life of Joel Barlow.* Philadelphia, 1958.

Woolf, Stuart. *Napoleon's Integration of Europe.* London and New York, 1991.

Young, Arthur. *Travels in France during 1787, 1788 & 1789.* Edited by Constantia Maxwell. Cambridge, UK, 1929.

Young, James Sterling. *The Washington Community, 1800-1828.* New York, 1966.

Zahniser, Marvin R. *Charles Cotesworth Pinckney: Founding Father.* Chapel Hill, 1967.

Zuckerman, Michael. "Thermidor in America: The Aftermath of Independence in the South." *Prospects* 8 (1983): 349-68.

Zuckert, Michael. "Natural Rights in the American Revolution: The American Amalgam." In *Human Rights and Revolutions,* edited by Jeffrey N. Wasserstrom et al., 59-76. Lanham, MD, 2000.

Zunder, Theodore A. *The Early Days of Joel Barlow, a Connecticut Wit.* New Haven, 1934.

Index

nation, the: definitions of, 4–5, 10–11,
12, 41; as embodiment of universal
principles, 60, 167; political opponents
defined as alien to, 41, 45, 59–60,
163–64; religious quality of, 60; will of,
as unanimous, 45–46, 51, 57, 91
National Assembly (France), 19, 24,
29–30, 40, 44, 47, 48, 49, 75; address
by Americans in Paris to, 74; divisions within, 17, 26, 31, 32, 37, 41–42,
45–46; and French Constitution (1791),
28, 31, 34, 36
national character: American, 7, 16,
57, 61, 72, 153–54, 155; believed to
circumscribe political reform, 7, 12,
16–17, 23–25, 33–34, 35, 153–54, 160,
166, 170; British, 7; French, 7, 16–17,
23–25, 28, 29, 30, 52, 61, 102, 153–54,
160; and Montesquieu, 16–17, 25,
33–34
National Convention (France), 1, 4, 54,
60, 84, 95; anti-Jacobin campaign of,
100, 101–2, 107; Barlow's address to,
64–66, 78, 79, 85, 88; compared to U.S.
Congress, 96; declares wars of liberation, 65, 77; ends Terror, 92; estab-
lishes Revolutionary Government, 81;
foreigners expelled from, 83; Girondins
purged from, 82; Monroe's address to,
88–89, 110; partisan conflict in, 96;
uprisings against, 101–4, 106–7
National Intelligencer, 149, 162
nationalism: and cosmopolitanism, 2–4,
60–61, 120–21, 165, 166–67; and patriotism, 2–3; and religion, 7; and territorial expansion, 163–64, 166–67; and
transformation of America, after XYZ
Affair, 120–21
nation-building: and American and French
revolutions, 2–3; constitutions as tools
of, 16–17; by example vs. by export,
156–57; and foreign policy, 4, 165;
France as model of, 5, 159; in Louisi-

ana, 159–62, 163–64; origins of, 10–11;
similarities of, in American and French
republics, 5, 11, 12; and territorial
expansion, 167; United States as model
of, 3, 5, 12, 16, 156–57; and violence, 8,
58, 77, 89, 166
Naturalization and Alien Acts (1798), 120
neutrality, U.S., in French revolutionary
wars, 82, 84, 90, 130
New York Herald, 99
Northwest Ordinance (1787), 160, 200n58
Notes on the State of Virginia (Jefferson), 33
Nouveau Mississippi . . . , Le (Anonymous),
82

O'Brien, Conor Cruise, on "Adam and
Eve" letter, 55, 58
October Days, 16, 36, 37, 48, 53
Orateur du Peuple, L', 100
Orléans, Louise-Marie-Adélaïde de Bour-
bon-Penthièvre, duchesse d', 19
Orléans, Louis-Philippe-Joseph, duc de, 26
Osmond, Antoine-Eustace, baron d', 115

Paine, Thomas, 168; Adams on, 128;
advocates free trade, 3; advocates
French republic, 47–48; application for
diplomatic post in France, 147; arrest
of, 1–2, 4, 83–84, 86, 92, 171n1; and
Barlow, 1, 68, 86, 118; and Bonneville,
47, 131, 142, 148; and Burke, 47–48,
85; caricature of, 8, *9;* citizenship
of, 1–4; and Consulate, 142, 144–45,
148–49; on Convention of 1800, 141;
and Directory, 119, 148; and Girondins,
41, 62–63, 104; and Jefferson, 39–40,
47, 61–62, 141–43, 147, 148–49, 152,
161, 162–63; and Lafayette, 48, 62–63,
180n18; on law of nations, 143; on
league of neutral nations, 143–45; and
Logan, 131; and Napoleon, 141, 142,
144, 198n27; as nation-builder, 2–3;
and nation-building in Louisiana,

Index